One of the best leadership books I' ... ˙ I
know. In *All Change*, Rich Robinson h ... ꓕ
transformation.
CHRISTINE CAINE, founder, A21 and Pro

All Change overflows. It is that rare kind of wri ...ꓕt is both practical and inspiring. If
you are sensing, experiencing, or dreaming of change, this book is for you.
BRIAN SANDERS, founder, Underground Network; author, *Microchurches*

We are in the middle of seismic shifts: technological developments, mental health
crises, social upheaval, and political polarization, all threatening to drastically change
life as we know it. Yet, in *All Change*, author Rich Robinson challenges us to lean into
the change by reminding us that God has most often moved in such times. Robinson
brilliantly provides a roadmap for this journey into the unknown by showing leaders
how to dream big, lead consistently, adapt, and ultimately make the most of these
moments pregnant with the possibility of movement. If you want to navigate through
change, you want this book!
DAVE FERGUSON, author, *Hero Maker* and *B.L.E.S.S.*

This book is right on time! Infused with entrepreneurial impulse, spiritual insights, and
practical guidance, Rich Robinson helps us do what we were made to do: re-create. Let
us begin together!
DANIELLE STRICKLAND, entrepreneur, advocate, author

In *All Change*, Rich Robinson pours out a lifetime of experience, moving us away from
the curse of competence to flexibly embrace the constant change that characterizes our
lives. With clear and compelling direction, this book is a masterclass for leaders who
want to dream again, innovators dissatisfied with the status quo, and all who want to see
kingdom transformation.
ONEYA OKUWOBI, assistant professor of Sociology, University of Cincinnati; author,
Multiethnic Conversations and *Multiethnic Conversations for Kids*

The only constant is change. There are no maps for this holy disruptive moment. But
Rich Robinson gives us a compass guiding us to the North Star while encouraging us
not to fall into the temptation of building our own kingdoms. Grab this book if you and
your fellow pioneers want to collaboratively develop Spirit-formed dreams and discover

many simple, sticky, and scalable tools to guide you to experientially innovate. Robinson inspires us to imagine, develop fresh prototypes, build pilots, generate strategic frames, and take risks for the kingdom!

JR WOODWARD, PhD, national director, V3 Movement; author, *The Scandal of Leadership* and *Creating a Missional Culture*; coauthor, *The Church as Movement*

I often see leaders either underestimate the challenge of leading change and are surprised to receive backlash, or they overestimate the difficulty and become paralyzed. Rich Robinson does a fantastic job of threading the needle to provide hope for leaders who want to see kingdom-focused change in their church and gives the needed principles and tools to make this change possible. You will be inspired by an initial read-through of the book and will continue to refer back to it as you engage in the difficult but important work of leading change.

REV. DR. DANA ALLIN, synod executive, ECO

Rich Robinson's book is a game-changer, blending inspiration with practicality to create a masterful blueprint for navigating both the spiritual and strategic dimensions of change. In a world where adaptive challenges are the norm, leaders need tools that make a real difference. This book is that tool. It's an invaluable guide, offering clear strategies and profound insights for maximizing kingdom impact. If you're serious about leading in today's world, this book is essential reading.

LISA RODRIGUEZ-WATSON, national director, Missio Alliance; contributing author, *Voices of Lament*, *Red Skies*, and *Least of These*

Rich Robinson's *All Change* will compel you to want to change—missionally, organizationally, and personally. It combines necessary elements of change management rarely seen together, and in fact sometimes seen as mutually exclusive—personal and organizational, internal and external, conceptual and instinctual, dreams and reality, micro and exponential, management science and scriptural spark. Whether or not you are in a change process now, soon you will be, because change is a guaranteed constant. Robinson's book will give you a journey and a map but leave you free to innovate. It is at once intellectually informing, communally inspiring, and spiritually galvanizing. You will glean concepts, knowledge, behaviors, and next steps. But most of all, you will experience that the "prophetic powerful pause" may be the most transformative learning of all.

MISSY WALLACE, founder, 90Seventeen; former managing director, Redeemer City to City and Global Faith and Work Initiative

Movement means change, and good change needs a guide. Rich Robinson has been just such a trusty guide and mentor to countless teams. Let him take you through the downs and ups of managing that change journey, reflectively and creatively. You will be better and stronger and healthier as a result.

RIC THORPE, Bishop of Islington, serving in the Church of England nationally as "Bishop of Church Planting"

Rich Robinson provides leaders with a roadmap on how to courageously lead organizations in a chaotic world of change and volatility. What a need there is for deep gospel change in large swaths of the Western evangelical church, where many have grown institutional, slow, fearful, and inward-looking. *All Change* provides a paradigm, rooted in the gospel, that will reawaken the hearts and minds of leaders; it will exhort them to "think again," as Adam Grant would say, and potentially change the landscape of the church in the West.

STEVE SHACKLEFORD, CEO, Redeemer City to City

If you are stuck, frustrated, or out of hope with your God-given mission, Rich Robinson can help. Why? Robinson has had to climb the same mountain. *All Change* distills his experience in a framework—Dream, Discover, Design, Deploy—that gives dissatisfied leaders who dare to believe in something better, the key ingredient they lack: a track to run on that will get them where they want to go. Robinson's experience can be your Sherpa to get you to the top of the mountain!

HARRY BROWN, president, New Generations

Rich Robinson is one of the wisest and most catalytic leaders I know. I have watched with a sense of awe as he has guided the Movement Leaders Collective (MLC) from an idea to a dynamic collective of organizations and emerging movements that are now learning from one another and increasing their impact as potential movements in the West. Robinson does this all while deeply embodying the character and ways of Jesus. The Kansas City Underground has become a covenant partner with MLC, and they are guiding and equipping us at a pivotal moment in our story. That's the best recommendation I could give. This book is a necessary read for any organizational leader who is called to be a part of what Jesus is doing to shift the tracks of history. If you are leading or are part of an organization that wants to see the transformative energy and catalytic impact of the church as a movement rediscovered and unleashed through Spirit-led strategic change, this is the book for you. I recommend you read it NOW!

ROB WEGNER, codirector and cofounder, KC Underground; North American director, NewThing; coauthor, *The Starfish and the Spirit* and *Find Your Place*

This is a treasure trove of a book. With clarity and dexterity, Rich Robinson provides leaders with a roadmap of how to initiate, deliver, and sustain change. This well-written book contains all the principles needed to create the higher-level thinking that must first occur before change takes place and then provides a field guide of tools and exercises that turn that thinking into practice. I enjoyed the carefully chosen and compelling stories, the pithy quotes, and the illuminating diagrams that all added to the genuinely excellent content. This book is a gift for those who are called to bring about change and want to do it well.

NESS WILSON, leader, Pioneer UK

All Change provides an invaluable theoretical framework and a practical guide for leaders aspiring to effect significant change. Rich Robinson challenges readers to reexamine their role as leaders, urging them to become proactive agents of change rather than managers of the status quo. If you desire to transform your organization, you need this book.

BRAD BRISCO, author, *Missional Essentials* and *Covocational Church Planting*

The essence of leadership is the ability to create vision, inspiration, and momentum in a group of people. It starts by being able to picture and imagine a future with greater possibilities and then clearly passing on and communicating the same to those you lead. Vision allows a leader to clearly paint a picture of the future that inspires people and emboldens them to rise above fear, cynicism, and doubt. Rich Robinson shares priceless thoughts that guide every leader on how to shift the culture in the room and mobilize people toward a clear vision.

OSCAR AMISI, senior associate pastor, Deliverance Church Umoja, Nairobi, Kenya; lead trainer, SeeditOut

This book resonates on so many levels! Rich Robinson has captured the Holy Spirit's heart for leaders struggling to reimagine the future of their churches and Christian organizations. Far from telling us what to think, Robinson carefully guides us on a journey of how to think, while coming alongside and cheering us on (loudly!). This book is a timely roadmap, written with urgency, clarity, and humor. If you're already on the road or thinking of embarking, take this along, and don't put it down until you get there!

REV. DR. KATE COLEMAN, founding director, Next Leadership; author, *7 Deadly Sins of Women in Leadership*

Pastoral renewal, church revival, revitalization, parish renewal ... whatever you call it, it's about change; Spirit-inspired and empowered change! The church of Jesus Christ stands at the most important threshold since Peter crossed into the home of Cornelius. St. Augustine once said, "Without God, we cannot; without us, God will not." The change that God is calling the church to will not happen without us; it must be led. While recognizing that without God we can do nothing, Rich Robinson leverages his years of experience working with movement leaders around the world and presents us with a manual for organizational transformation. *All Change* will challenge, inspire, and motivate you to push against the gravitational pull of the status quo and midwife new models of church life that will bring forth much fruit for the kingdom.

FATHER JAMES MALLON, founder, Divine Renovation Ministry; pastor, Our Lady of Guadalupe Parish; author, *Divine Renovation, Divine Renovation Guidebook, Unlocking Your Parish, Beyond the Parish*, and *Thriving Faith*

In *All Change*, Rich Robinson masterfully distills two decades of leadership training into a vital resource for today's missional pioneers. Whether you're leading a church, nonprofit, or business, this book offers an innovative, four-phase framework to rethink traditional approaches and confidently lead others into a better future. Robinson's approach encourages a communal, experimental learning process, allowing leaders and their teams to uncover and pursue a clear, shared vision effectively. A must-read for any leader seeking transformative insights and practical strategies in an ever-evolving landscape.

ERIC SWANSON, cofounder, City Leaders Collective; coauthor, *The Externally Focused Church*

Rich Robinson is a change agent. I am a witness and beneficiary of his capacity to coach and catalyze, design and develop, mentor and release. No doubt, his book is perfectly titled *All Change*. This book is a valuable treasure for those who desire and imagine God-envisioned changes in lives, ministries, and communities. The content of the book is refreshing, and anyone who immerses themselves in it and applies its wisdom will develop the potential to be a model leader, disciple maker, catalyst, and movement leader.

SAMIT MISHRA, founder and leader, HI72

Invitation, learn, grow, encounter God—unique words for a book on change, yet it is in this refreshing tone and with these ideas that Rich Robinson has written this much-needed work. Enter in with anticipation of a holy mindset change!

DR. TAMMY DUNAHOO, executive dean, Portland Seminary of George Fox University; co-creator, Reimagine by WomenCo

Rich Robinson's nearly twenty-five-year journey, spanning the globe from Great Britain to Asia, equips you with the field-tested knowledge needed to navigate every stage of your venture. This powerful guide is detailed, systematic, and clear, making it an invaluable resource for anyone ready to make a lasting impact. In *All Change*, Robinson reminds us that disciples of Christ are part of the most significant movement for change in human history—a movement embodying the holy disruption God desires for our world. Now is the time to fully embrace our roles in this call for "all change." Together, we can indeed answer the call!

OLADELE JOHN OKUWOBI, founder, Wonder Association

All Change is a much-needed tool kit for leaders navigating the complexities of twenty-first-century churches and organizations. Rich Robinson accompanies you on a journey of transformation (if you dare to join him!), as he shares his wisdom and insight through the lens of lived experience, thought leadership, strategy, and coaching, in easily accessible and practical ways.

REV. CHAM KAUR-MANN, codirector, Next Leadership

Rich Robinson is an exceptional leader, whose wisdom and humility have impressed me for years. Now finally he has put his knowledge and experience to print. *All Change* does not disappoint. It is packed full of hard-won insights on creating kingdom transformation projects. But what impressed me most was that although *All Change* is packed with deep insight, it always pushes the reader to return to an ultimate reliance on Jesus and the need to journey as a community rather than a lone ranger. I will be using it with my people.

JUSTIN DUCKWORTH, Anglican Bishop of Wellington, New Zealand; cofounder, Urban Vision movement; coauthor, *Against the Tide, Towards the Kingdom* and *In-tension-al* (forthcoming)

Rich Robinson has been a close friend for the last fifteen years. I've been blessed and impressed to see him operate as a servant pioneer, pioneering not to build his own thing but to help others build and, even more, to catalyze the dreams and vision God has put in other's hearts. This work is a blend of wide knowledge, real experience, and deep spirituality. I highly recommend it!

EGIL ELLING ELLINGSON, pastor, IMI-kirken

This book will equip a generation of change makers. Rich Robinson draws on years of both strategic and thought leadership to lay a way forward full of practical tools and training that will equip followers of Jesus to unlock kingdom potential in their context. Amid a period of significant cultural change, this book will enable you to uncover the current flawed paradigms in our churches and ministries and help follow Jesus' lead to bring transformational change, firstly in yourself and then in those you lead. It will be a resource you will continually revisit in your life and ministry!

BREE MILLS, disciple maker; Canon for Church Planting, Anglican Diocese of Melbourne

In *All Change*, you will find insightful ideas and concrete practical steps to take, to bring about change—a "holy disruption" as Rich Robinson calls it. Readers will be challenged and encouraged to communally embrace the "kairos moment" in which change takes place and will receive the tools needed to do it. In the process, they will catalyze kingdom change and unlock kingdom potential. This is a book worth reading thoughtfully and applying thoroughly; change will surely come.

JAVIER G VELÁSQUEZ, associate dean, Partnerships and Hispanic Initiatives, Antioch School; global resource team leader, La Gran Estrategia

All Change is a much-needed breath from the Holy Spirit in leadership dynamics for the global church. Rich Robinson gives us practical and profound insights, hard-won from decades of grassroots leadership within Jesus movements. Robinson gives us solid foundations to lead with God by letting God lead, learning with God's people in authentic reciprocity, and living into our true potential. I long for our church in its rich variety to live into this fullness.

ELEANOR SANDERSON, Bishop of Hull

Rich Robinson is one of a small number of leaders I know who has genuinely learned to see kingdom dreams turn into movements. It is surprising how difficult this can be to achieve. In this remarkable book, Robinson sets out a simple but profound process for identifying the dreams God had put in your heart and developing them to the point that they become multiplying movements. Full of both foundational principles and practical steps, *All Change* is essential reading if God has called you to unlock kingdom change in the lives of others.

PAUL MACONOCHIE, director, Uptick; executive leadership team, Baptist General Association of Virginia; midwest network leader, 3DMovements

I have seen Rich Robinson up close lead one of the most significant convening organizations of global church leaders that I know—Movement Leaders Collective. *All Change* isn't just about a theory, framework, or change process. It is the journey,

and current culmination, of how Robinson leads in obedience to the Spirit and in communion with Jesus and his church. Through this book, you will catch a vision for how to lead change in your movement with greater impact, and maybe more importantly, with friends on mission reflecting the great diversity of kingdom leadership.
DANIEL YANG, national director, Churches of Welcome at World Relief

Rich Robinson has delivered both a masterclass and a tour de force for effectively stewarding change in churches and faith-based organizations. Midway through the book and onward, I frequently imagined Indiana Jones quickly packing his shoulder bag with the minimum essentials for his journey, and this book was one of those must-have items. Like Indy, I'll be keeping a copy at hand as a field guide for change.
LANCE FORD, author, *The Atlas Factor*; coauthor, *The Starfish and the Spirit*

It has been said, "There are two things everyone hates: 1) The way things are and 2) Change." Leadership is what stands in the tension between these two things, and it is why being a leader is so difficult. Rich Robinson embodies the art of standing in this tension and leading the way. In this breakout and breakthrough book, Robinson now passes on to others what I have seen demonstrated in his life and leadership for many years. *All Change* is a must-read for anyone who is a leader or wants to be a leader that creates lasting change.
DAVE RHODES, cofounder, Clarity House

All Change is a book that every Christian movement leader with a vision from God in this changing world must read. Rich Robinson encourages us not only to face the need for cultural, social, and spiritual transformation but also to recognize that our movement vision is conditioned by constant cultural change. *All Change* challenges us to cultivate movements of the gospel characterized by authentic contextualization that bear lasting fruit through the leading of the Holy Spirit. I appreciate Robinson and his mind for addressing this difficult topic through a simple process: Dream, Discover, Design, and Deploy. Fabulous!
ANDRÉS GARZA AYALA, city planner and pastor, Monterrey, Mexico; director, City to City, Latin America

In a world of accelerated disruption, how do we obtain a clear line of sight in a sea of moving targets? In *All Change*, Rich Robinson does a masterful job in offering us a simple and scalable framework to help us actualize our God dreams. This much-needed book invites us into a proven journey to help us move from the ordinary to the extraordinary. If you are a leader who is saying yes to a bigger kingdom vision and wondering how in the world to get there, this is the book for you to read!
WILL PLITT, executive director, Christ Together

All Change is a game-changing roadmap for leaders navigating today's rapidly evolving landscape. With real-life examples and actionable strategies, Rich Robinson will inspire you to rethink traditional paradigms and help you unlock kingdom potential, catalyze kingdom change, and pursue kingdom transformation. Don't go on this journey alone; read this book with your team, and be prepared to dream, discover, develop, and deploy your God-given mission in innovative ways.

MAC LAKE, founder and CEO, Multiply Group

In a time of great change and uncertainty for the church, Rich Robinson offers a compelling vision for the future. A timely and important resource for the church, *All Change* is a must-read for anyone who wants to be part of shaping the church's future.

PATRICK O'CONNELL, global director, NewThing

ALL CHANGE

ALL CHANGE

Rich
Robinson

UNLOCKING *KINGDOM*
Potential IN A WORLD
We W~~er~~e Weren't
Prepared For

100 MOVEMENTS
PUBLISHING

Library of Congress Control Number: 2024936420

ISBN 978-1-955142-53-3 (print)
ISBN 978-1-955142-54-0 (ebook)

Cover design: Jude May
Interior Design: Revo Creative

100 Movements Publishing
An imprint of Movement Leaders Collective
Richmond, Virginia
www.movementleaderscollective.com

For Anna, Josiah, Esther, and Samuel.
And for the pioneers, dreamers, and innovators in the global community of
Movement Leaders Collective, Creo, and Catalyse Change.

CONTENTS

Foreword by Alan Hirsch   xix

1 THE ALL-CHANGE JOURNEY: An Invitation   1
2 THE ONLY WAY UP IS DOWN: A Briefing for the Journey   17

PHASE 1: DREAM   34
How to move from human management to kingdom imagination.

3 THE BIGGER STORY: Created to Dream   37
4 SQUARE PEGS IN ROUND HOLES: Learning to Dream   51
5 IMAGINEERING TOGETHER: Equipping Others to Dream   67
DREAM 101   83

PHASE 2: DISCOVER   86
How to move from conceptual theory to experiential learning.

6 BUT BECAUSE YOU SAY SO: Created to Discover   89
7 FACTORY OR FIELD?: Learning to Discover   99
8 PROTOTYPING YOUR WAY FORWARD: Equipping Others to Discover   119
DISCOVER 101   140

PHASE 3: DESIGN   142
How to move from one-size-fits-all to Spirit-led,
contextualized core principles.

9 BEAUTY AND BLUEPRINTS: Created to Design   145
10 THREE IS A MAGIC NUMBER: Learning to Design   161
11 FRAMING THE FUTURE: Equipping Others to Design   181
DESIGN 101   199

PHASE 4: DEPLOY   202

*How to move from a centrally driven institution
to a generative people movement.*

12 **A PEOPLE MOVEMENT AND A MOVING PEOPLE:** Created to Deploy   205

13 **MASTERING THE RUBIK'S CUBE:** Learning to Deploy   223

14 **TO INFINITY AND BEYOND:** Equipping Others to Deploy   239

DEPLOY 101   261

15 **THE WAY OF THE WISE WINDS UPWARD:** Final Words   263

Acknowledgments   271

*Appendix One: Awareness and Application:
The Journey to Maturity*   273

*Appendix Two: mDNA:
The Six Essential Elements of a Jesus Movement*   281

FOREWORD

ALAN HIRSCH

It's a genuine privilege to introduce the debut book by my dear friend and comrade, Rich Robinson. Our shared commitment, forged over years of partnering in mission and leadership, has nurtured a profound bond. We often express our mutual respect and appreciation, a connection akin to the undeniable pairing of fish and chips or eggs and bacon—complementary and inseparable. Our paths were destined to converge, leading us to cofound Movement Leaders Collective (MLC) in 2017.

Having collaborated closely with Rich, I have seen his exceptional leadership qualities. His unwavering integrity is matched by a rare blend of strategic vision and practical know-how, all underpinned by a deep commitment to building meaningful mentoring relationships with the numerous people he works with. What is more, he has significant experience in diverse global contexts, including his native Great Britain but also across Western Europe, North America, Oceania, Africa, and Asia. Not bad for a man in his mid-forties! As the reader will no doubt experience, Rich brings a wealth of practical insights to the table.

Given the book's close ties to Rich's work within MLC, it might be useful to shed light on this somewhat unique organization. MLC seeks to help the church reimagine itself as a movement. We work with leaders and organizations who see the church's role in our contemporary world through the distinctive lens of apostolic movements that are centered squarely on Jesus, and which prioritize adventurous discipleship, incarnational mission, APEST typology, and build scalability into the very foundation of the organization.

We believe that this shift to understanding the church as an apostolic movement is critical for the viability of Christianity in the contexts where most readers of this book now find themselves. Alarming statistics across Europe, Australia, and Canada paint a picture of diminishing biblical Christianity, with similar trends emerging in the United States. However, this dire picture of the Western church is juxtaposed by the remarkable rise of movemental Christianity in regions in the Majority World, where the gospel thrives even amidst the most challenging environments, including among Muslim and other unreached communities.

As the reader of this book will no doubt be aware, the current landscape presents a formidable challenge that demands a critical reevaluation of traditional "legacy church" structures, which were established in Christendom—a vastly different era to the one in which we now live. The outdated models that comprise the operating systems of the majority of churches in the West have proven themselves inherently unable to adapt to the rapidly evolving cultural and societal landscape. The future is reasonably bleak if we refuse to change … if we fail to undergo metanoia (repentance leading to a change of mindset). We cannot retain our old ways of thinking and expect new results. We need not only a paradigm shift in the way we think but also an accompanying all-change strategy if we are to faithfully respond to this unavoidable challenge.

This book doesn't merely highlight the problem; it offers a credible and practical path forward—one that has been developed in coaching leaders over many years and has been honed amid the white-hot experiences of some of the high-caliber leaders and movements involved in the various learning cohorts of MLC. It follows the path of Jesus, the archetypal movement maker and change agent, and delves into what organizational theorists and practitioners call a "redesign process." By guiding Christian leaders through a transformative change process that addresses the root cause—primarily its flawed paradigms—*All Change* equips you to navigate the inevitable adaptive challenges you face and to build a platform and initiate practices that will transform you and your leadership context.

In the four phases outlined in these pages, Rich brings together his strategic insight and thought leadership, grounded in practical tools and training processes, creating a roadmap that will help leaders unlock kingdom potential and go on a communal journey of kingdom transformation.

If this is his debut book, it is a pretty awesome start. It's a really *good* book! Rich quickly establishes himself as a thought leader and skilled writer, readily sharing his hard-earned wisdom with readers ready to embrace the challenge of radical transformation. *All Change* is a guide for the future paths we must explore.

Buckle up, and prepare to be changed.

THE ALL-CHANGE JOURNEY

AN INVITATION

The only thing constant is change.
HERACLITUS

In times of drastic change, it is the learners who will inherit the future. The learned find themselves well-equipped to live in a world that no longer exists.
ERIC HOFFER

To encounter God is to change.
DIETRICH BONHOEFFER

Hawke's Bay is a picturesque wine region on the eastern coast of the North Island of New Zealand. Famous for its art deco architecture, vineyard bicycle tours, artisan producers, and stunning landscapes, it is a popular region with both foreign and national tourists. Yet what can be seen today is a far cry from its original shape and form. In 1931, a two-and-a-half-minute earthquake hit Hawke's Bay. Still on record as New Zealand's deadliest natural disaster, it killed 256 people and injured thousands more. The region experienced nearly six hundred aftershocks during the following month, and nearly all of the buildings in the central areas of Napier and Hastings were leveled. But the earthquake didn't just obliterate the buildings and infrastructure; within a matter of seconds, it completely changed the surrounding landscape by uplifting some twenty-five square miles of seabed and turning it into dry land.[1]

A TWENTY-FIRST-CENTURY CULTURAL EARTHQUAKE

We may not have experienced a physical earthquake, but our world's societal patterns are similarly being shaken, undergoing disruption at an ever-increasing pace. The speed of computers has been doubling every one and a half to two years since the 1960s and 1970s, and it's estimated that 90 percent of the entirety of the world's data was collected in the last two years.[2] More than 3.6 percent of the world's population live outside their country of birth, with 400 million indigenous people facing the threat of climate change destroying their homes.[3] The Hollywood writers and actors union recently settled a strike against motion picture and television producers over the threat of AI to their livelihoods in the writing, production, and even the use of their facial imagery in films and television. And if you read this book ten years from now, many of these examples will most likely be viewed as cultural artifacts of a bygone era. Whether you're a church leader or church planter, a Christian entrepreneur or organizational leader, you're no doubt experiencing these disruptive forces, and constant change is your norm. It's likely you feel you are leading in a world you weren't prepared for. Dr. Preston Cline, founder and principal at the Mission Critical Team Institute, notes that,

> A combination of increased mobility, increased information, and increased impact means that we have reached a tipping point. ... Previously, we had a historical pattern of disruption followed by stabilization—"punctuated equilibrium"—but now that pattern has itself been disrupted. Today, we find ourselves in a new equilibrium defined by constant disruption.[4]

---

[1] "1931 Hawke's Bay earthquake," Wikipedia, accessed November 17, 2023, https://en.wikipedia.org/wiki/1931_Hawke%27s_Bay_earthquake.

[2] "How Fast Is Technology Advancing? [2023]: Growing, Evolving, and Accelerating at Exponential Rates," Zippia.com, January 11, 2023, https://www.zippia.com/advice/how-fast-is-technology-advancing/.

[3] "Climate change, displacement and human rights," UNHCR, March 2022, https://www.unhcr.org/uk/media/climate-change-displacement-and-human-rights.

[4] Interview with Preston Cline, quoted in General Stanley McChrystal, *Team of Teams: New Rules of Engagement for a Complex World* (US: Portfolio/Penguin, 2015), 113.

Alongside the cultural changes around us, the Western church is experiencing seismic shifts. For the last forty years, churches such as Willow Creek Community Church (Chicago), and Saddleback Church (California), were proponents of church growth theory through attractional dynamics and captured the imagination of many in the church.[5] In a relatively stable environment, we leaned on what seemed to work—Sunday services, buildings, staff, ministry, and midweek programs—and only occasionally made simple improvements or tweaks. But across the Western hemisphere, Christianity has moved from the center of society to the margins, meaning most of us live in a culture that is largely unfamiliar with the gospel and among people who have little understanding of church. Leadership failures, denominational infighting, and political warring in the secular culture have arguably influenced the mass exodus of younger generations from formal church settings.[6] Yet rather than seeking to understand the shifting sands of our post-Christendom culture, we often see Christian leaders critiquing by engaging in polarizing political agendas and social-media bickering or retreating by disengaging with the world and becoming introspective. Meanwhile, the world looks on with an increasing intolerance for what it perceives to be an archaic and irrelevant institution.

Many church leaders are still hoping for a technique, formula, or solution that can be plugged into the church system to fix the problem … some silver bullet or killer program. We look to the experts, the latest training programs, or the models that have brought success to others. But the solutions we're offered are the answer to *someone else's problem*. Their success may have been won in a hard-fought battle, but they've been won in someone else's battle and someone else's context. This is why solutions and practices don't always translate clearly or cleanly to our setting. Even if they are effective in the short term, we rarely

---

5   "How Saddleback Church Connected and Inspired Parishioners Across the Globe," EZTexting, accessed April 3, 2024, https://www.eztexting.com/why-ez-texting/case-studies/saddleback-church; "How Willow Creek is Leading Evangelicals by Learning From the Business World," *Fast Company*, December 6, 2010, https://www.fastcompany.com/1702221/how-willow-creek-leading-evangelicals-learning-business-world; Scot McKnight, "The Legacy of Willow Creek 3," CT Blog Forum, October 7, 2020, https://www.christianitytoday.com/scot-mcknight/2020/october/legacy-of-willow-creek-3.html; Morgan Lee, "Rick Warren Mastered the Formula for Suburban Church Growth," *Christianity Today*, June 11, 2021, https://www.christianitytoday.com/ct/podcasts/quick-to-listen/rick-warren-saddleback-church-purpose-driven-podcast.html.

6   Carey Nieuwhof, "New Exodus? 4 Reasons Why People Are Leaving the Church (Including Christians)," Carey Nieuwhof, July 5, 2023, https://careynieuwhof.com/5-surprising-reasons-people-leave-church/.

understand *why* they work, and so we struggle to repeat or scale them. This technique draws us away from looking to God for his authentic work in our context. Instead of seeking to hear him and discover where he is at work, we default to human tactics. But in a changing landscape, the plug-and-play solutions just don't cut it.

Instead, we need to learn to depend on God and view life and leadership as an *adaptive challenge*—an "all-change" reality that affects everything in and around us. This reality is dynamic and continuous rather than fixed or finished. Leadership and change coach Bryan Sims notes in his book, *Leading Together*,

> The challenges facing the church and much of today's world are often referred to as adaptive challenges, because they will require us to adapt or be transformed in order to overcome them. The COVID-19 pandemic presented a very real adaptive challenge because we were faced with circumstances none of us had previously faced and none of us knew exactly how to lead through. Reaching young people with the gospel presents another adaptive challenge, given so few seem interested in church. Leaders often try to apply current know-how to face these challenges, but that seldom works, because what is actually required is for us to change.[7]

If you're choosing to read this book—whether you're a denominational or church leader, church planter, Christian entrepreneur, or microchurch leader—my guess is you're facing some of the challenges these types of disruptions have caused. I have worked with leaders for more than twenty years, but over the past five, I have noticed they are being significantly impacted by an increase in disruptive influences in various forms. Perhaps you're feeling the same. You may be experiencing the challenges of lower church attendance or a lack of engagement from your staff, volunteers, or those you work with. It might be that you're struggling to navigate the thorny terrain of cultural, political, and theological frictions. Maybe you've tried several new strategies to adapt to the ever-changing status quo, but others in your organization or denomination haven't embraced the changes, and you're back to square one. You might be

---

7   Bryan Sims, *Leading Together: The Holy Possibility of Harmony and Synergy in the Face of Change* (Cody, WY: 100 Movements Publishing, 2022), xviii.

planting a church or launching a faith-driven venture, and you feel like you've started at the worst possible time and on the worst possible terrain. Or perhaps you're wondering how to remedy a crisis of mental health, economic hardship, or systemic injustice faced by those you lead and serve.

Whether you are starting something completely new or you're trying to replant or initiate something new within your context, it's likely you feel the world you were trained for as a leader has vanished before your eyes, and you're unprepared for the challenges pressing in on every side.

HOLY DISRUPTION

In many ways, the times we're living in are a unique and unusual moment in history; but change itself isn't as new as we might think, as the biblical narrative demonstrates:

Abraham, settled and successful, was uprooted by God in pursuit of a new land. He embarked upon a journey without knowing his destination, holding onto the promise that his family line would extend for generations (Gen. 12:1–9).

Moses, raised in luxury and privilege, met God in a burning bush, and was told to return to Egypt, confront Pharaoh, and catalyze the much-needed change and freedom for his people, the enslaved Israelites (Exod. 3).

Esther, a beautiful Jewish queen, risked her life by appearing, unsummoned, before the king and changed the fate of her people (Esther 5, 7:1–4).

Nehemiah, a cupbearer in the king's court, heard a report that broke his heart and launched him to become the project manager for a God-inspired city transformation project—a huge rebuild that required the whole community's participation (Neh. 1–2).

Mary, an unmarried teenager from a backwater town, was told by an angel that she would have a baby who would become the Savior of the world. Faithful to God, and at great cost to herself, her obedience changed the world forever (Luke 1:26–38).

Simon Peter, a career fisherman, was told by a carpenter to let down his nets into deeper water. Setting aside his experience and expertise, he went from empty nets to a miraculous catch—a prophetic foretaste of the lives he would see brought into the kingdom of God (Luke 5:1–11).

Saul, on a crusade to obliterate the church, fell to the ground as a light from heaven blinded him, and he was catapulted from Saul the murderous terrorist to Paul the greatest church planter who ever lived. The punisher and persecutor became the pioneer and preacher (Acts 9:1–19).

God is in the business of change.

And he doesn't work by our rules. He doesn't respect our timescales. He doesn't fit within our constructs. He is not overly concerned with our comfort or control. He will not be put in a box or constrained by a formula.

God's story, from Genesis to Revelation is about the holy disruption he brings to our lives, seeking to redeem us and all his creation to all we were truly made to be (Rom. 8:20–21). Change isn't new; it's part of God's plan and intention for our lives, but whether we are ready to see it and embrace it is an entirely different matter.

God's greatest disruption came in the birth, life, death, and resurrection of Jesus. Every part of Jesus' life challenged the expectations of what this King would be. Born to a teenage, unmarried, refugee mother amid the mess and mire of a rundown stable, his very entry into this world bucked the status quo. This vulnerable baby was welcomed by shepherds, the most ordinary members of society. It's easy to sanitize and sentimentalize the manger scene, but if Jesus came to earth today, we might imagine him being born in a hostel or a trailer park, surrounded by empty beer bottles and pizza boxes and greeted by refuse collectors, addicts, or the homeless. It's not quite the idyllic picture most of us have of the nativity. Jesus arrived, and those who thought they'd be first to the party missed it.

It wasn't that the Jewish leaders weren't waiting for their Messiah to come; in fact, it's clear they were perfectly aware of the prophecies.[8] The Jews expected God to send their promised Messiah, but they imagined an all-conquering king, a powerful warrior general, and an overthrower of governments. They didn't envision a disrupter of the social status, a servant-king, and a lover of the outcast. Because Jesus was so different from their expectations, they refused to accept that God would work in such a way. But before we scorn the response of

---

[8] See, for instance, when Herod discovers the birth of this new king: "When he had called together all the people's chief priests and teachers of the law, he asked them where the Messiah was to be born. 'In Bethlehem in Judea,' they replied, 'for this is what the prophet has written'" (Matt. 2:4–5).

the religious leaders in Jesus' time, we need to acknowledge that our reactions might have been the same. How often have we waited hopefully for God to move in our lives and our organizations, but then reacted with panic when a curveball was thrown our way? Aren't we often set in our thinking of how the kingdom of God is going to come while missing the opportunities he is bringing through uncomfortable circumstances?

AN INVITATION TO CHANGE

Jesus embodied the holy disruption God wants to bring to our world. His very first message was an invitation to embrace disruption and engage with kingdom change. In Mark 1:15 he announced his arrival on the stage of humanity with these words: "The time [*kairos*] has come ... The kingdom of God has come near. Repent [*metanoia*] and believe [*pistis*] the good news!" Jesus intentionally uses the Greek word *kairos* rather than *chronos*. Commenting on the difference between the two words, Christian novelist and journalist Jessica Brodie notes that,

> This *kairos* is a special time, the chosen time. It's God's time, powerful and right, fixed by Him and to be used for His purposes. Note that *kairos* is different from *chronos*. *Chronos*, a more linear and quantitative sequence of moments, also refers to time, but *kairos* doesn't necessarily refer to the chronological duration of time but rather the moment itself, the season, the nonlinear and qualitative version of time. That is, *kairos* is like Time (with a capital T), not time.[9]

Kairos refers to a kingdom moment in which we are lucid, present, and aware— the birth of a child, a breakthrough at work, a deep and inspiring conversation with a friend. It is a moment pregnant with possibility. These kairos moments offer a doorway to change, for both ourselves and the world at large. *Metanoia*, the Greek word for repentance, literally means to *change* our mind, to expand our thinking, to think "above." If we harness our kairos moments by embracing metanoia, we are to put behind our old way of thinking and pick up a new one.

---

9   Jessica Brodie, "What Does the Greek Word Kairos Mean in the Bible?" Crosswalk.com, March 26, 2021, https://www.crosswalk.com/faith/bible-study/what-does-the-greek-word-kairos-mean-in-the-bible.html.

We have to embrace unlearning and relearning in order to open ourselves to a new Jesus-shaped reality. Repentance is not simply the confession of sins. It does involve that, but it is so much more. More accurately and fully translated, repentance is an invitation to *change the way we think*. And Jesus goes on to say we are to "believe" the good news, using the Greek word *pistis*, which means "to have an active faith."[10] We are to *change the way we act*. Jesus called people to go and live differently because of this faith—faith that moves us from one reality to another. Our faith is no longer a concept; it becomes active and dynamic as we intentionally apply and embody what we have heard, basing our whole lives upon this new truth. Jesus' first call is to "change your thinking" and "change your behavior."

All change.

Change was therefore a core theme of Jesus' ministry and mission. To be in Christ means to be a new creation—"the old has gone, the new is here!" (2 Cor. 5:17). We are "born again" (John 3:3), living in a new identity and transformed reality. And, as we continue to follow Jesus, we are changed increasingly into the likeness of Christ (2 Cor. 3:18). To be a movement of faithful disciples— true to God's Word and to his commissioning into the world while authentically engaging with the context in which we find ourselves—we need to become disciples who are open to change and to be people of kingdom influence and impact rather than assimilation or domination. This is the essence of what it means for us to play our part in the great Jesus movement. In their book *Brave Cities*, Taylor McCall and Hugh Halter challenge us that, "Jesus' plan was for everything to be a movement—advancing, going forward, never stalling or shrinking back. ... Thus, Jesus' most strategic move was to place this potential in the smallest, most reproducible element of his plan: the disciple."[11]

Jesus' first invitation to his disciples, then, was an invitation to a change journey where their transformation would make them agents of change (Mark 1:17). And one of his final instructions to his followers was to play their part in the Jesus movement to "Go change the world" (Matt. 28:18–20,

---

[10] Theresa Morgan, "Roman Faith and Christian Faith: Pistis and Fides in the Early Roman Empire and the Early Churches," Classics for All, June 6, 2022, https://classicsforall.org.uk/reading-room/book-reviews/roman-faith-and-christian-faith-pistis-and-fides-early-roman-empire-and.

[11] Taylor McCall and Hugh Halter, *Brave Cities: The Archaeology, Artistry, and Architecture of Kingdom Ecosystems* (Richmond, VA: 100 Movements Publishing, 2024), 49.

my paraphrase). He exhorted them to do as he had done, to go and make disciples of every people group and in every place. This all-change mandate is to unlock kingdom potential, catalyze kingdom change, and pursue kingdom transformation wherever you go and in whomever you meet—not by building empires but by mirroring the adaptive, generative, contextual, and innovative movement Jesus started, which was marked by active participation, shared purpose, and multiplication. That same commission stands today; to play our part in the great Jesus movement that continues to cascade. Christianity has always been a people movement that has expanded and extended into new frontiers and people groups—ever-evolving and ever-changing.

Sadly, rather than forming disciples, much of the Western church has created consumers, outsourcing ministry to the work of the professionalized few, and with the focus of faith becoming a weekly-church-service experience rather than a whole-life, 24/7 expression. We are managing institutions rather than making disciples. As the founder of Spirit & Truth, Matt Reynolds, notes, "We have favored pragmatism over theology, crowds over disciples, marketing over evangelism, coffee bars over catechism. We have shown greater commitment to manufacturing celebrity pastors than lifting up unseen, humble, and sacrificial shepherds."[12] As a result, many twenty-first-century Christians are not equipped to live as vibrant disciples, let alone make and form new disciples. Culture is discipling believers more effectively than the church. Consumer Christians don't own their spiritual journey, they don't contribute to the life of the church or the world around them, and they are blown around by the winds of culture.

This is a far cry from the original design of the early church that we read about in Acts. In the Gospels, we see Jesus planting the seeds of a movement, equipping his disciples to disciple others, and calling them to show and share the good news of Jesus, as active participants. It is this dynamic momentum—whether in a church, organization, nonprofit, or faith-driven venture—that this book is seeking to help you unlock and catalyze.

---

[12] Matt Reynolds, "The Death Rattle of Consumer Christianity," *Firebrand*, July 20, 2020, https://firebrandmag.com/articles/the-death-rattle-of-consumer-christianity.

LEANING INTO DISRUPTION

In 1995, the late business consultant Clayton M. Christensen coined the term "disruptive innovation." It describes the process that occurs when a new product or service transforms the marketplace by making something accessible to all that has historically only been accessible to a few. The printing press, automobiles, smartphones, personal computers, and video streaming are all examples of disruptive innovation. Christensen emphasized that disruptive innovation actually transforms the market itself. It's like reinventing the rules for soccer rather than just signing a new player for your team. For example, when the iPhone was invented, it didn't just give people a new product to choose from in the phone market; it changed the very way in which we interact with technology and the way that many of us live our lives. It was an all-change moment.

According to Christensen, disruptive innovations present us with opportunities to transform life as we know it.[13] Leadership theorists refer to our current cultural realities using the acronym VUCA—volatile, uncertain, complex, and ambiguous. But futurist Bob Johansen suggests there is reason to be hopeful. He pivots the acronym: "Volatility yields to vision, uncertainty to understanding, complexity to clarity, ambiguity to agility."[14] Moments of disruption therefore present us with exciting opportunities and can lead to innovations that change the whole landscape. It's like the process of panning for gold: the nugget is hidden in the dirt, but as the pan is shaken, the soil falls away to reveal a great treasure. If we are willing to sift through the disruption, we begin to see beyond our current reality, toward new kingdom potential. When the potential for change arises, we can either choose to embrace the moment or ignore it. We can be like the Jewish leaders of Jesus' time—pretending it isn't happening, sticking to our familiar ways, and aiming to survive; or we can allow the moment to be a catalyst—a springboard to something new. Change can often feel like a buzzword, and, to those who prefer or benefit from the status quo, it can feel threatening. But, as leaders, we are called to catalyze spiritual, systemic, and strategic change—not for the sake of change but for the good of others.

---

[13] Clayton M. Christensen, *The Innovators Dilemma: When New Technologies Cause Great Firms to Fail* (Harvard Business Review Press, 2013).

[14] Bob Johansen, *The New Leadership Literacies: Thriving in a Future of Extreme Disruption and Distributed Everything* (Oakland, CA: Berrett-Koehler Publishers, Inc., 2017), 5.

Disruptive change is almost always a painful experience, both personally and professionally. We rarely enjoy the vulnerability of becoming a novice and admitting we don't know everything; but this pain can also lead us toward a prize. We must be prepared for disruption to take us into the unknown, stripping us of the things that make us feel secure—whether they be places, people, or possessions. Our temptation is often to centralize power and function, institutionalize our models and methods, remain in the perceived safety of the status quo, or transfer our existing church culture and traditions into new missional contexts. We reduce an all-change invitation into a "some-small-controlled-change-on-my-terms" moment. We're offered a five-course meal, and yet we only nibble the appetizer. As disciples who seek God's ongoing change in us and the world around us, we must be ready to embrace the disruption that this requires and engage with the learning it brings. Despite how gritty and uncomfortable this can be, we must allow it to transform us. Jesus told us that to be a disciple would cost us everything, but in this process, we would truly find our lives (Matt. 16:25).

Perhaps you've reached the point of saying yes to change, however unknown, uncertain, or unnerving that change will be. Or maybe you're a natural change agent, but those around you are struggling to embrace the pain of change. Perhaps you feel fearful of a change being initiated within your organization. Our organizational systems are perfectly designed to achieve what they are producing, so if we want different results—whether that be in disciple making, leadership formation, team culture, or missional impact—then something needs to change. It's helpful to remember that sometimes there is more cost to staying the same than in stepping out toward something new—personally or organizationally. As spiritual director and author Ruth Haley Barton says, "When the pain of staying the same is greater than the pain of changing, we are ripe for making a move."[15] The pressure of our circumstances can provide a crucible that helps us and our organizations to pursue a new direction, reset a culture, change a strategy, or shift resource investment.[16] As we lean into these

---

[15] Ruth Haley Barton, *Strengthening the Soul of Your Leadership: Seeking God in the Crucible of Ministry* (Downers Grove, IL: InterVarsity Press, 2008), 91.

[16] A crucible can be defined as "a place or set of circumstances where people or things are subjected to forces that test them and often make them change." *Encarta World English Dictionary* (North America Edition), s.v. "crucible."

changes, we often see greater fruitfulness and kingdom breakthroughs—things we wouldn't have seen if we had done them in our own timing and methodology.

If we are to pray, "Your kingdom come, your will be done, on earth as it is in heaven" (Matt. 6:10), we are asking God to initiate an all-change process in the places we live, work, and play. We are praying, "God, change the world, so it looks more like you." We are uttering from our lips and heart, "Change the world, and start with me." If we want our new venture or existing organization to make a kingdom impact and have different outcomes, then we need to join God in a change journey for us, our team, and our organization.

To do this, we will need to trust and build our lives upon the fact that although God is a God who initiates change, he himself is the unchanging God. He is Alpha and Omega, the one "who is, and who was, and who is to come, the Almighty" (Rev. 1:8); "I the Lord do not change" he tells us (Mal. 3:6); and, summarizing the witness of Scripture, the Westminster Shorter Catechism states that God is "unchangeable, in his being, wisdom, power, holiness, justice, goodness, and truth."[17] As we step out on a journey of change, we need to remember that God is faithful and present with us. "The one who calls you is faithful, and he will do it" (1 Thess. 5:24). We stand on this firm foundation as we embrace the transformation God calls us to.

FOR GOD, FOR GOOD, AND FOR THE GOOD OF OTHERS

One of the calls on my life is to be a change agent: to catalyze kingdom change and unlock kingdom potential in the lives of others. Alongside a wonderful team, I have worked with a variety of leaders and organizations in numerous contexts and countries. Three of the initiatives I have cofounded that express this call are Movement Leaders Collective (www.movementleaderscollective. com), Creo (www.creoventures.co), and Catalyse Change (www.catalyse-change.org). Through these initiatives, we have apprenticed, trained, and empowered thousands of church leaders, Christian entrepreneurs, church planters, and marketplace leaders, as well as churches, denominations, social enterprises, organizations, and movements to have fruitful kingdom impact that

---

[17] Westminster Shorter Catechism (1674), https://www.ccel.org/creeds/westminster-shorter-cat.html.

changes the world for good. Some have been global organizations; others have been grassroots movements. Some have been individuals with a new vision and others have been teams undertaking a change-management process. Some have been pioneering brand-new ventures; others have been revitalizing existing structures. Whatever the context, I have encountered leaders who are humbly seeking to be faithful to who God has invited them to be, eagerly longing to unlock kingdom potential in every member of their organization and who want to make the necessary changes to see that become a reality.

Through all of these multiple relationships and contexts, I have learned that change is multi-faceted and multi-layered. It's never two-dimensional, and it never happens the same way twice. Some leaders know that change is necessary but don't know where to start. Others are natural change agents who need a vocabulary and guidebook to call other people in their venture or organization to change. Some are in a risk-averse context where "change" is a dirty word.

The process I am going to walk you through in this book is based on the distilled learnings of twenty years of being a change agent. The frame, content, and tools have been used in large and small churches, multiple denominations and dispersed networks, the Western church and the global South, historical organizations and new initiatives, with church planters and Christian entrepreneurs, business leaders and church volunteers. It isn't a one-size-fits-all strategy that will give you a to-do list, a model to copy, or answers for your specific context. It's more like a compass to help you on your path rather than a GPS that will detail every turn.

This book will take you through four specific phases of the change-agent journey evident in the life and leadership of Jesus. Whether you are starting a new venture or seeking to spark change within an existing organization, these phases will help you and your organization or venture to intentionally pursue kingdom transformation. In the pages to come, we will unpack the four phases and the process of how you and your team and organization can journey through them together.

Leading others through change constitutes a both/and dynamic, mirroring the both/and God we serve and with whom we partner. It is *both* spiritual *and* strategic, *both* momentary *and* ongoing, *both* seen *and* unseen, *both* in our thinking *and* in our behavior. Often—in our linear, individualistic, binary brains—we think in terms of either-or and look for one person, one factor, one ingredient, one strategy, or one process. But God's creative diversity means we all bring a different element to kingdom transformation. There's a beautiful tension in this both/and. If we're to respond to the adaptive challenges we see around us, we need frameworks to help us rather than formulas. The four phases in these pages offer a framework for you to mobilize your community, venture, or organization to unlock its kingdom potential and pursue a God-sized dream.

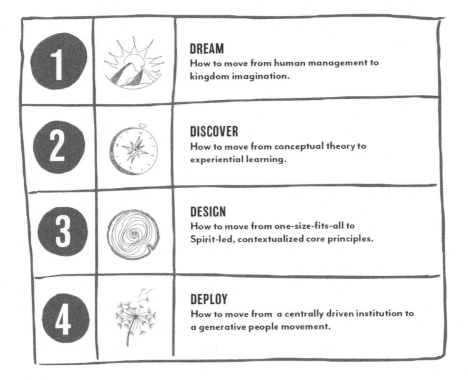

DREAM
How to move from human management to kingdom imagination.

DISCOVER
How to move from conceptual theory to experiential learning.

DESIGN
How to move from one-size-fits-all to Spirit-led, contextualized core principles.

DEPLOY
How to move from a centrally driven institution to a generative people movement.

So, is this book for you?

It's for you if you have leadership influence in your context, whether you are planting a church, overseeing a nonprofit, serving in a microchurch, pioneering a faith-driven venture, pastoring a church, or leading a denomination.

It's for you if

... there are dreams within you still to be realized, and you have a nagging sense there is more for you and those you lead to live into.

... you believe there is raw material in your life and in the lives of those around you that God can multiply for his kingdom.

... you have grown weary of managing the status quo, or the autopilot of life and organizational leadership has almost snuffed out the flame that once burned passionately for Christ.

... one too many flesh wounds find you playing it safe rather than taking risks for Jesus.

... you feel like you're dragging your organization forward to a place they don't want to go.

... your internal narrative is, *I could never*, or *That's not for me*.

... you have a kingdom vision, but you don't know where to begin or what next steps to take.

...you need to believe again that every Christian has a part to play in the great Jesus movement, and every believer has the kingdom potential to lean into God's will being done on earth.

God can bring change.

But first, we need to be willing to abandon change as a to-do list, peripheral pursuit, or negative reality and instead allow God to change our hearts and minds and transform our systems.

Will you allow God's hands to shape everything in your reality—including you—for his good and his glory? Will you respond to his invitation to unlock kingdom potential in a world you weren't prepared for?

Will you play your part in his all-change story?

THE ONLY WAY UP IS DOWN

A BRIEFING FOR THE JOURNEY

Progress is impossible without change; and those who cannot
change their minds cannot change anything.
GEORGE BERNARD SHAW

Truly, the best thing any of us have to bring to leadership
is in our own transforming selves.
RUTH HALEY BARTON

True transformation of the world, and ourselves, will only happen as we are
conformed to the image of Jesus Christ—his way becomes our way, his source
of power becomes our source, and his patterns of life become our patterns.
ANDY CROUCH

Nestled in the mountain range between Nepal and Tibet, standing at nearly 30,000 feet, and in existence for more than sixty million years, is the formidable Mount Everest. For the last one hundred years, thousands of attempts have been made to conquer its summit, with the first known successful expedition being made by Sir Edmund Hillary and Tenzing Norgay in 1953.[1] Today, even with

---

[1] "Mind-blowing facts about Mount Everest," Global Adventure Challenges, October 1, 2019, https://www.globaladventurechallenges.com/journal/mind-blowing-facts-about-mount-everest.

advances in modern equipment and knowledge of the terrain, climbing Mount Everest requires a kit list of more than eighty items, takes around two months to achieve (with a third of people failing to reach the summit), and costs between $30,000 and $100,000.[2]

As Christian leaders, it can feel like we're tasked with climbing Mount Everest. It's costly, there's a limited chance of success, and nothing comes quickly or easily. But just like the thousand or so people who attempt to climb Everest every year, we do it anyway. We do it because we have a deeply held conviction that God is redeeming his world back to himself and that he's inviting us to partner with him in enacting that change. We don't know whether we'll be the ones who live to see these transformations or if we'll reach the summit, but we believe it's something worth giving our lives for.

As we prepare to embark on the leadership journey ahead of us, we might be inclined to think first about training, tactics, and techniques; but instead we need to cultivate depth of character, start with the end in mind, and journey with the right team. Consider these three elements that are critical for change agents seeking to unlock kingdom potential in themselves and others and to move their organization toward a God-given vision:

- Who you are (*your identity as a disciple*)
- Where you are going (*your journey as a change agent*)
- Who you will take with you (*your people as a leader*)

WHO YOU ARE (YOUR IDENTITY AS A DISCIPLE)

Our change-agent journey starts with our identity as a disciple and requires conviction, humility, and courage as we take others through the difficult terrain ahead. As we approach this change journey, there are two essential dynamics we need to engage with: *Awareness* and *Application*.

---

[2] "Everest Gear List," Alpine Ascents International, accessed November 8, 2023, https://www.alpineascents.com/climbs/mount-everest/gear-list/; Nicole Chavez, "If you're dreaming of climbing Mount Everest, this is what it takes," CNN Travel, June 2, 2019, https://edition.cnn.com/2019/05/28/asia/how-to-climb-mount-everest/index.html#; Michelle Ma, "Mount Everest summit success rates double, death rate stays the same over last 30 years," University of Washington, August 26, 2020, https://www.washington.edu/news/2020/08/26/mount-everest-summit-success-rates-double-death-rate-stays-the-same-over-last-30-years/.

At the end of the Sermon on the Mount (Matt. 7), Jesus tucks in one last parable—about wise and foolish builders. It's a pivotal piece of Scripture and gives us a significant key to the process of operating as mature change agents. Preceding this parable, Jesus sets out a detailed manifesto for living a counter-cultural kingdom life. But he doesn't just leave his listeners with some powerful words to meditate on. By telling the story of the wise and foolish builders, he gives them a challenge: "Therefore everyone who hears these words of mine [Awareness] and puts them into practice [Application] is like a wise man who built his house on the rock" (v. 24). He is calling them to both hear (Awareness) and obey (Application).

Awareness is the ability to listen and look carefully at what's going on around us. Through the lens of Scripture, we reflect on what we hear and see theologically and theoretically in culture, in our organizations, and in our churches. Awareness also involves the ability to reflect on what is happening within our own hearts and minds as disciples, which helps us uncover the areas where we need to more fully align with God and his purposes. When we don't see these things in ourselves (or they are not pointed out to us by God or others), we are unable to mature. We can't fix the problems we don't know about.

People who are gifted in Awareness are meaning-makers. They see themes and patterns, discern what God is saying, and ask deep questions. They love to explore concepts and create frameworks that help themselves and others to understand and engage with the world.

Application is the orientation toward action and learning by doing. It's about "figuring it out on the way" as ideas are road-tested in real time and real life, with continual action, forward movement, and iteration through practice rather than through considered thought. Without healthy Application, we can become set in our ways, cynical about change, defensive of what we know best, or stuck in the status quo. People who are gifted in Application embrace experimentation and exploration and aren't afraid of getting things wrong. They interact with the many possibilities God presents, and in doing so, they discover the new things God is doing.

Without a healthy engagement with these two dynamics, change will remain a pipe dream, an idea in your head, or a scribble on a whiteboard. Or, you will launch into a change process and become isolated, rejected, or in a constant loop that fails to bear kingdom fruit.

Leaders that are high on Awareness but low on Application can drift toward *Concept*. At their worst, they get stuck in endless cycles and death by a thousand conversations or committees. Because they lack Application, they muse, reflect, think, and muse some more because there is always another angle to be considered, more data to gather, and another exploratory conversation to be had to refine their thinking.

Leaders that are high on Application but low on Awareness can be driven by *Instinct*. At their worst, they become one-generation leaders, where the work flies when they're present and dies when they leave, as their instincts cannot be scaled or reproduced. Or they become reactionary leaders who jump into activity without stopping to think or listen to what God has said. Because they lack Awareness, they often cannot explain to others the principles behind the practices or stop to ask why.

In all the years I have worked with leaders and organizations, the primary reason they have failed to initiate or embed lasting, transformative change has been due either to a lack of Awareness or Application. This is mission critical. Will we hear the word God wants to speak to us (Awareness) *and* obey by putting this word into practice (Application)?

Harnessing both of these dynamics as a disciple is a bit like channeling all the wisdom and insight of the sage in their eighties with the curiosity and zeal of a five-year-old. All of us will have a natural leaning toward either Awareness or Application, but maturing in both is key to leading yourself and others through this journey of change. Leaders must go on a discipleship journey themselves in the change process, framed by Awareness and Application.

This journey toward maturity also applies to organizations or ventures. Some are stronger on Awareness, deeply engaging with reflection, theology, and theory, and tend toward a more conceptual culture. Others are stronger on Application—with an orientation toward effort, activity, and initiatives— and therefore tend toward a more instinctive culture. In every organization or venture, both the conceptual and instinctive will be present, although usually one is dominant. But imagine the synergy that occurs when maturity is expressed through both high Awareness and high Application.

For more guidance on how to grow in both Awareness and Application, see appendix one—"Awareness and Application: The Journey to Maturity" (pages 273–79).

WHERE YOU ARE GOING (YOUR JOURNEY AS A CHANGE AGENT)

As we explored in the previous chapter, change is usually initiated by some form of disruption. Disruption awakens us and pushes us (often unwillingly) into identifying where there is a lack, what's falling short, or a problem that needs to be fixed. Disruption can also reveal passion, hope, and vision that pulls us toward a preferred future.

The all-change journey begins by leaving what is familiar and known. In order to reach the peak, we must embrace hardship, enter the "valley," and go through the phases of Dream, Discover, Design, and Deploy. Change itself is not the point. It's a means to an end, to allow us to unlock kingdom potential and pursue kingdom transformation and to allow God to work in and through us for his purposes. The journey is important, but it's vital to remember the destination we are heading toward.

In the Gospel of Luke, we see Jesus navigate these four phases with his disciples. He functioned as a change agent, sparking a movement that we are still part of today. As we examine each phase, we will unpack the change-agent dynamics of Jesus and the footsteps we are seeking to follow. But for now, let's briefly examine each of the phases to give us a bird's-eye view of the journey we are about to embark upon.

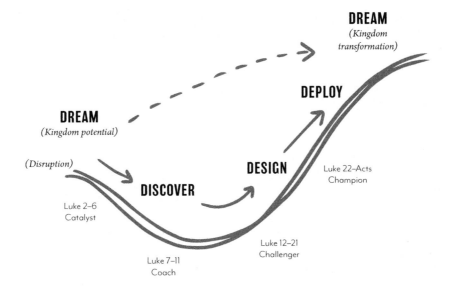

DREAM

In the Dream phase, we purposefully and prayerfully ask God to spark our imagination and compel us to move toward the vision that he is revealing. We lay aside our own agendas, fears, and insecurities and begin to dream a God-sized dream. It's a dream that centers on God, is expressed communally as a shared purpose, and makes a kingdom impact in the world. This dream could be to pioneer and plant a new venture or spark change and renewal within an existing organization. The dream is like a North Star that keeps us heading in the right direction together, driving us to put one foot in front of the other when all we want to do is sit down in the dirt, bury our head in the sand, or maintain the status quo. The prize ahead fuels the perseverance needed for the whole organization or venture to face the difficulties on the journey. For Jesus, the dream of humanity reconciled to God ("the joy set before him") enabled him to endure the cross, scorn its shame, and sit down at the right hand of the throne of God (Heb. 12:2). Some leaders are more inclined to dream than others, but nevertheless it is a skill that can be learned and, as sheep that hear the Shepherd's voice (John 10:27), we have all been given the capacity to hear what God is saying.

Dream—Jesus' Change-Agent Journey: The Catalyst

In Luke 2–6, Jesus functions as a *Catalyst*, sparking the imagination of ordinary people, disrupting the status quo of the religious elite, unearthing latent potential, and beginning to plant the initial seeds of the dream of a Jesus movement.

DISCOVER

Once we have begun to envision the dream, we need to move into the valley. Though we may wish there was a magical rope bridge to carry us straight across to fulfilling the dream God is calling us to live out, the only way up is down. The Discover phase is about initiating the journey of change as we cross the threshold of safety and security. In this phase, we learn as we go, as Abraham did when he set out to discover a new land (Gen. 12) and as Simon Peter did when he shifted from being a fisherman to a fisher of people (Luke 5). Whether in an existing organization or a pioneering venture, we galvanize a small band of pioneers and adventurers, armed with working hypotheses and prototypes. As in the parable of the sower (Luke 8), we look for responsive people and places as we experiment, gather insight, and unearth key principles that in time will influence and benefit the whole organization. We work at the edge of the organization to test under the radar rather than implementing our ideas system-wide. In these initial efforts, we stretch the boundary lines of our own and our organization's thinking and practice. Success at this stage is based on unlearning and relearning. This phase makes us feel vulnerable because we are allowing God to strip away the known and familiar and reveal fresh paths and insights about the way forward.

> **Discover—Jesus' Change-Agent Journey: The Coach**
> In Luke 7–11, Jesus calls together a small group and acts as their *Coach*, providing experiential learning as they stand at his shoulder and walk in his dust. He teaches, heals, and interacts with individuals and the crowds, and the disciples have a front-row seat. They learn through discussion and hands-on experience. Over time, Jesus increases their responsibility, and they discover as they go.

DESIGN

The Design phase flows on from the Discover phase. Here, we identify what's worked and what hasn't from our initial prototypes. We gather all the initial experiential learning and work to create more focused pilot projects and design a strategic frame that can integrate core principles across the whole organization in the next phase (Deploy). The small pioneering group begins to discern principles and patterns that can be contextualized in many people and places, and they begin to think about how this can be communicated effectively. Jesus did this through parables that revealed kingdom design principles he wanted every Jesus-follower to live out, such as sacrifice (Luke 14:25–33), persistence (Luke 18:1–8), and childlike faith (Luke 18:15–17). He also demonstrated kingdom design by providing the disciples with recurring practices, such as the Lord's Prayer (Matt. 6:9–13) and Communion (Matt. 26:26–28). This same design process is expressed in the apostle Paul's many letters as he shares the blueprints for the early church. The Design phase enables us to engineer a sustainable and scalable process for change. We are preparing to make accessible to many what used to be the domain of a few.

> **Design—Jesus' Change-Agent Journey: The Challenger**
> In Luke 12–21, Jesus begins to talk of the future. As a *Challenger*, he uses parables to move the disciples toward becoming leaders as well as disciples. Core principles embedded within the parables frame the worldview and behaviors of the disciples and are the design of the movement that he will commission them to extend.

DEPLOY

In the Deploy phase, we pass on our learning, embed and reproduce our DNA in others, and scale in a healthy and sustainable way. The Deploy phase is where the initial pioneering dream is becoming a practiced reality for many in our organization or venture—what was once novel becomes normative. Recovering our Genesis identity of fruitfulness (Gen. 1:28), embodying the Great Commission (Matt. 28:16–20), and mirroring the early church (Acts 1:8), in this phase we are on our way to becoming a Jesus movement. In an existing organization, the work becomes organization-wide as the yeast works its way through the dough (Matt. 13:33) and becomes self-generating and self-replicating. In a pioneering venture, this is the threshold moment where we move from "scrappy start-up" to solidifying our venture so that it is ready to scale. Many leaders are activated and extend the vision on their own initiative rather than being forced or managed. However, our organizations are never a finished product. By embracing this journey, we learn how to continuously change, as we respond to the ongoing disruptions and opportunities for transformation God gives us.

Deploy—Jesus' Change-Agent Journey: The Champion

From Luke 22 onward and into Acts, through Jesus' death, resurrection, and ascension, he becomes a *Champion* as he resources his disciples with everything they need to further the work without his physical presence. The disciples shift from apprentice leaders to movement makers empowered by the Spirit. They are commissioned to extend the movement themselves, taking the kingdom dream Jesus had planted and the kingdom design he had taught them to new people and places.

Although these are phases of a transformative process, the dynamics are interwoven and overlapping rather than a linear, step-by-step formula. If you have ever seen a 4 x 100 meter relay race, you know there is a changeover box where the runner on the existing leg continues to run, but they slow down, readying themselves to pass on the baton. The runner who will take the next leg does not have a standing start, but they begin to run and speed up to perfectly receive the baton in the middle of the changeover box. While one runner is slowing down, the other is beginning to speed up. The four legs of a relay race are similar to the four phases in our process, so rather than one phase stopping and then another one starting, there is an overlap between the phases.

As well as being found in the Gospel of Luke, biblical examples of this journey of change are also found in Psalm 23 and the Exodus journey. We all want the blessings of the Promised Land of Canaan (Joshua 3–24) or the prepared table and green pastures (Psalm 23), but there is no shortcut through the desert or the valley. Change always comes by going down and through. The work God can do in us in the desert and the valley is different from what he can achieve in the Promised Land or the green pastures.[3] In the desert or the valley, there is an

---

[3] In *A Shepherd Looks at Psalm 23*, Phillip Keller notes the following as he unpacks the meaning of "You prepare a table before me" (v. 5): "In thinking about this statement it is well to bear in mind that the sheep are approaching the high mountain country of the summer ranges. These are known as alplands or tablelands so much sought after by sheepmen. In some of the finest sheep country in the world, especially in the western United States and southern Europe, the high plateaus of the sheep ranges are always referred to as 'mesas'—the Spanish word for 'tables.' ... So it may be seen that what David referred to as a table was actually the entire high summer range." W. Phillip Keller, *A Shepherd Looks at Psalm 23* (Grand Rapids, MI: Zondervan, 2007), 125–26.

awareness of our frailty and humanity that God uses for our learning, health, and growth. Ruth Haley Barton refers to this process as "the roundabout way."

> God in his kindness leads us in such a way that at this stage we don't face challenges that are more than we can handle. God intentionally led the Israelites by "the roundabout way" rather than the most direct route, because God knew that they weren't ready to take on the challenges that a more direct route would have brought: "When Pharaoh let the people go, God did not lead them by the way of the land of the Philistines, although that was nearer; for God thought, 'If the people face war, they may change their minds and return to Egypt.' So God led the people by the roundabout way of the wilderness" (Exodus 13:17–18). Even though they might have preferred a more direct route to their dream, it was actually a great kindness that God prevented them from encountering more than they were ready to handle. The *roundabout way* may not be the most direct route, but it represents a wonderful era in the spiritual life when God shows up in a very tangible way that assures us of his presence on the journey.[4]

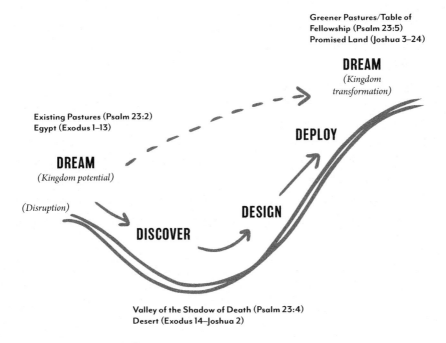

Greener Pastures/Table of
Fellowship (Psalm 23:5)
Promised Land (Joshua 3–24)

DREAM
(Kingdom transformation)

Existing Pastures (Psalm 23:2)
Egypt (Exodus 1–13)

DEPLOY

DREAM
(Kingdom potential)

(Disruption)

DESIGN

DISCOVER

Valley of the Shadow of Death (Psalm 23:4)
Desert (Exodus 14–Joshua 2)

---

4   Haley Barton, *Strengthening the Soul of Your Leadership*, 93–94.

WHO YOU WILL TAKE WITH YOU (YOUR PEOPLE AS A LEADER)

The process of enacting change must start in us as change agents, but then extend to those we bring with us on the journey. In his book *Strong and Weak*, Andy Crouch says,

> Leadership does not begin with a title or a position. It begins the moment you are concerned more about others' flourishing than your own. It begins when you start to ask how you might help create and sustain the condition for others to increase their authority and vulnerability together.[5]

The process of enacting change in an existing organization is more like a marathon than a sprint. Normally when we consider this metaphor it relates to perseverance and managing our speed over the long term, which is, of course, applicable to the change process. However, here we are using the metaphor not about perseverance but about participation. When competing in a large event, such as the London, Boston, or New York marathons, entrants are categorized according to how long it is likely to take them to complete the race. There will be those who are elite runners and professional athletes, competing to achieve a personal best or a place on the podium. Some will have run hundreds of marathons; others will be competing for the first time. Most will wear specialized sports gear, but some will raise money in character costumes. Marathon organizers will assess all of these factors and enact a staggered-start process. That way, you don't have someone dressed as a giant teddy bear getting in the way of a world-record-holder. In a 100-meter sprint, there are eight lanes, and one start line; and when the gun goes off, every single runner starts at the same time and immediately sets off toward full pace. But in a marathon, you cannot have every runner lined up, shoulder-to-shoulder on the start line. When the gun goes off, some sprint off the line and out ahead while others have to shuffle along slowly until they eventually get to the start line. It can take the runners at the back several minutes to even reach the start line, while the groups at the front have covered many miles in the

---

[5]   Andy Crouch, *Strong and Weak: Embracing a Life of Love, Risk & True Flourishing* (Downers Grove, IL: InterVarsity Press, 2016), 111–12.

same timeframe.[6] Everyone is running the marathon but at a different pace. This is what it means to help everyone flourish across the organization. This mirrors Jesus' approach to involve everyone through public teaching and the Sermon on the Mount while also relationally investing in a small core group of disciples who went first in obedience and exploration. It's an all-change journey but not an all-at-once change journey.

In an existing organization, we need a similar staggered-start approach to ensure everyone participates in the journey of change. Devised by Professor Everett M. Rogers in his book *Diffusion of Innovations*, the Diffusion of Innovations Curve gives a helpful framework for understanding this process.[7]

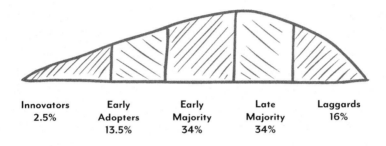

| Innovators 2.5% | Early Adopters 13.5% | Early Majority 34% | Late Majority 34% | Laggards 16% |

The innovators are those who easily and quickly embrace risk, experiment with new ideas, and are open to change, followed by the early adopters and so forth. The further to the right, the less open a group is to adopt change. Each group most easily relates to the group on their right and their left, but they are influenced by the group to their left.

In a pioneering venture, you will probably initially attract mainly innovators and early adopters because they are the groups most likely to engage with a new opportunity or idea. However, you will need to find and engage the early and late majority later in the change journey. As you move toward the Design and Deploy phases, these individuals will be needed to solidify and scale the new venture.

6 "The first runners usually start at around 9.40am and the last runners at 11 am." Nick Harris-Fry, "London Marathon Start Time: When Does the 2023 Race Begin," Coach, April 12, 2023, https://www.coachweb. com/fitness/running/london-marathon-start-time.

7 Everett M. Rogers, *Diffusion of Innovations*, 5th ed. (New York, NY: Free Press, 2003).

Throughout the chapters to come, we will explore who to engage at which phase in the change journey, so for now we simply need to understand that not everyone needs to be involved at every stage of the process; trying to make that happen can actually hinder the process of change.

When seeking to bring about change in an existing context or when a new venture is pioneered, we need to consider the flow of how the process is disseminated across these different groups. There will be times when they are moved closer to one another, as well as times when the groups are stretched out as they move toward the new.

When an existing organization initiates a change process, one of three mistakes is often made.

The first mistake is to start by attempting to get buy-in from those most resistant to change (the late majority and laggards). Expending energy trying to get the most sedentary group to move causes everything to bunch up or stall. These organizations end up on the back foot before they even start, using huge amounts of energy arguing, cajoling, and struggling to convince a group that is not even ready to engage with the conversation, let alone put anything into practice.

The second mistake is to aim for the biggest target—going for both the early- and late-majority groups, in the misguided belief that if the masses get on board, then sheer weight of numbers will prevail. This often occurs in organizations led by more pastoral leaders, who want to ensure that everyone is involved, and no one is left behind. While this is well-intentioned, the early- and late-majority approach is like taking a herd of sheep and trying to move them to a new field. With a huge amount of skill and experience, it is possible, but you will be constantly pulling stragglers forward and chasing strays.

The third mistake is to give the innovators and early adopters either too much freedom or not enough agency. If given free rein, they can disappear off to the frontiers, never to return; or their pioneering efforts can stretch and stress the organization. They inject too much risk into the existing system or push the whole organization to move too fast or go too far. But if they aren't given enough responsibility, they can get so frustrated that they leave the organization, or they remain but disengage with the change process. Organizations can stall if the innovators and early adopters leave or are marginalized—without them, we lose the impetus and spark for forward movement and change.

The natural movement of a caterpillar is a helpful metaphor for engaging the whole organization in a change process. On the caterpillar below, each circle represents a different group from the Diffusion of Innovations Curve.

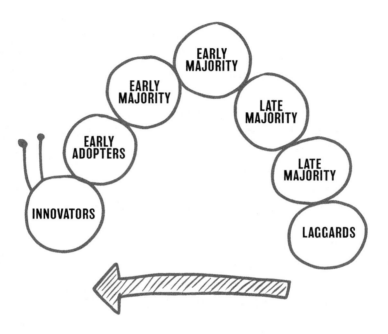

A healthy change journey for an existing organization is a coordinated stretch-consolidate-stretch-consolidate process, where the front stretches the caterpillar forward, then pauses to let the back catch up. The pause allows the whole to constrict and consolidate, and then the front moves out again, and so on. By proceeding in this way, you will move everyone forward without fracturing the groups.

A pioneering venture will only initially have the head (innovators and early adopters). The pause and consolidation will therefore need to happen as early majority individuals are invited to participate in later phases to strengthen and solidify the venture.

I   Innovators
EA   Early Adopters
EM   Early Majority
LM   Late Majority
L   Laggards

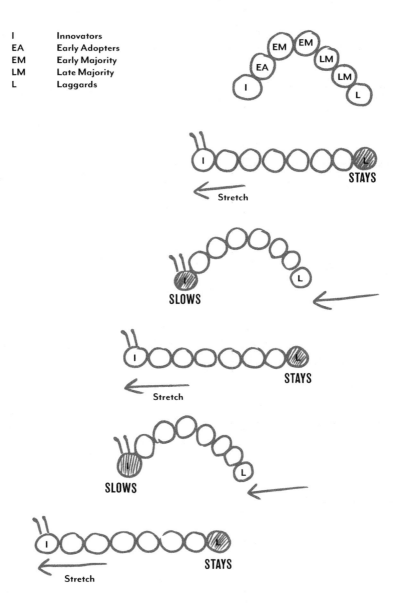

Regardless of whether it is an existing organization or a new venture, the coordinated stretch-consolidate-stretch-consolidate process applies. This process avoids the three mistakes mentioned earlier of trying to get the back to move (getting behind the caterpillar and pushing forward); targeting the largest group (trying to get the middle of the caterpillar to move first); or giving the pioneers too much freedom (the head moving out so far that it stretches the caterpillar to breaking point). As the team and I have trained Christian entrepreneurs through the work of Creo, as well as network, church, and denominational leaders through the work of Movement Leaders Collective, we have seen this process effectively used in numerous contexts.

We will explore more of which groups need to be involved throughout each of the phases. And in the Deploy phase, we will also double-click on the caterpillar dynamics. So, for now, hold these as general principles you will need to carry forward.

DON'T FORGET ...

As you embark on the journey of change ahead, remember to keep *who you are, where you are going,* and *who you will take with you* as a constant refrain that will help orient you in each of the phases ahead.

And, as you begin to take your first steps as a change agent, remember if your leadership drift is toward *Awareness,* you'll need to get out of your own head and give things a go; and if you lean toward *Application,* you'll need to create time and space to stop and reflect.

Think of all the above principles like the last words a coach gives to their team as they head onto the field to start the game—they are a frame to carry through each of the phases as you move forward.

The all-change journey begins by leaving what is familiar and known. In order to reach the peak, we must embrace hardship, enter the "valley," and go through the phases of Dream, Discover, Design, and Deploy. Change itself is not the point. It's a means to an end, to allow us to unlock kingdom potential and pursue kingdom transformation.

PHASE ONE
DREAM

/driːm/
"to imagine something you would like to happen"

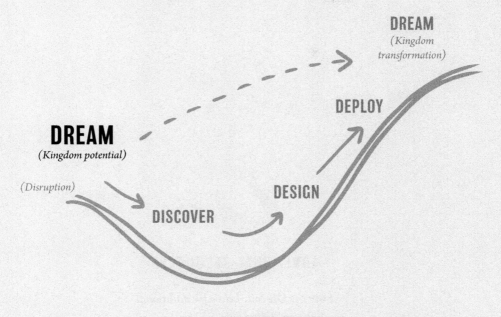

DREAM
(Kingdom
transformation)

DEPLOY

DREAM
(Kingdom potential)

(Disruption)

DISCOVER

DESIGN

PROBLEM

Instead of being innovative and creative, the Western church often relies on plug-and-play approaches and simplistic solutions that fail to connect with our culture and are heavily reliant on a solo leader.

We tend to manage the status quo rather than take a courageous faith journey together.

PROCESS

Move from human management to kingdom imagination.

PRIZE

Unlock kingdom imagination to discern where God is currently at work and where he is leading us in the future.

ADDITIONAL RESOURCES

Scan the QR code below for additional resources, including videos, practices, and a toolkit to accompany the Dream phase.

allchangejourney.com/resources

THE BIGGER STORY

CREATED TO DREAM

We need an incarnational imagination, a Jesus-soaked
imagination, so that every truth becomes a lived truth.
EUGENE PETERSON

There is nothing like a dream to create the future.
VICTOR HUGO

For too long we've read scripture with nineteenth-century eyes
and sixteenth-century questions. It's time we get back to reading
with first-century eyes and twenty-first-century questions.
N. T. WRIGHT

The 2016 Olympic Games in Rio de Janeiro, Brazil, made history for several reasons. They were the first to be held in South America, and the first to include golf and rugby sevens. Michael Phelps earned his twenty-eighth Olympic medal; and Usain Bolt won the 100-meter and 200-meter races for the third consecutive games—the only athlete ever to do so. But it was the story of one previously unknown competitor that captured international attention. By the close of the Olympics, Yusra Mardini only ranked fortieth in the 100-meter butterfly, but another of her swims was truly worthy of a medal.[1]

Mardini had been invited to compete in Rio 2016 as part of the first Refugee Olympic Team, having fled Syria the previous year by making a treacherous twenty-five-day journey with her older sister, Sara.[2] In August 2015, as they and eighteen others embarked upon the sea crossing from Turkey, their small dinghy became waterlogged and began to sink. Faced with the possibility of death and a boat full of non-swimmers, Mardini and her sister tied ropes around their waists, jumped into the water, and swam for hours, pulling the boat to safety. Incredibly they all survived and, upon reaching Greece, the sisters made their way to Germany where they were eventually granted asylum.

Mardini's inspirational story, now documented in the Netflix film *The Swimmers*, points to her dream of swimming at the Olympics.[3] Like many of the millions of refugees around the world today, Mardini was forced to leave her home country amid the threat of war and chaos. But for Mardini it was more than just the safety of a new life that motivated her to make such a dangerous journey—it was her dream of competing in the Olympics. When she reached Germany, the basic living conditions didn't stop her from tenaciously pursuing that dream; and the offer of competing as a refugee, with all its associated stigma, didn't deter her from realizing her goal.

WAKE UP!

We live in a world where the disruptions we face vary, depending on our geographical, cultural, and economic context. There are those, like Mardini, who experience seismic upheaval as they face war, extreme poverty, or climate-related catastrophe. There are also those, perhaps closer to us, who face life-changing turmoil such as illness, economic hardship, or systemic injustice. Although disruption is all around us, almost paradoxically many of us drift

---

[1]   Yusra Mardini, Olympic Biography, accessed April 4, 2024, https://olympics.com/en/athletes/yusra-mardini.

[2]   Brooke Theis, "The real story behind Netflix's *The Swimmers*," *Harper's Bazaar*, December 1, 2022, https://www.harpersbazaar.com/uk/culture/culture-news/a41983020/the-swimmers-netflix-real-story-yusra-mardini/.

[3]   *The Swimmers*, directed by Sally El Hosaini (Working Title Films/Netflix, 2022).

along in a state of inertia, either because we feel overwhelmed by the amount of change or because we would rather craft a life of comfort. The same is often true for our organizations and communities. The problem with inertia is that it dulls us to what's going on around us, so we're never aware enough to break out of the norm. We rely on personal and organizational defaults, often expressed in throwaway comments such as, "That's just the way it's always been." Like a tidal drift slowly dragging us along, we move toward a future destination, but it's not one we have chosen.

The systemic issues of our time and the biases within our systems are like air or water to us; we know they are there, but we seldom think about them. If we do face these problems, we often merely remedy the symptoms rather than dealing with the root causes. We look downstream for a fix rather than upstream to the source of the issue.

As we said in chapter one, a "kairos moment" often wakes us up. These moments can be of our own initiative, through prophetic and prayerful engagement, reading Scripture, or interacting with our community; or they can be external, brought about by a cultural or circumstantial shift that disrupts our status quo. In April 2019, Swedish climate activist Greta Thunberg addressed the Parliament in London, issuing a wake-up call and creating a kairos moment on the realities of climate change—not only for those in the room but also for many around the world. "We children are doing this to wake the adults up," she said. "We children are doing this for you to put your differences aside and start acting as you would in a crisis. We children are doing this because we want our hopes and dreams back."[4]

If we allow it, the Dream phase can similarly wake us up, jolting us from our slumber, so that we start to believe that just because things have always been a certain way, it doesn't mean they always have to be. We start to believe change is possible.

The disruption of the kairos moment in the present and the dream of a preferred future—the "what could be"—creates the stimulus for us to move out and move forward. This could be sparking change within an existing context or the conviction to step out and launch a new faith-driven venture or church plant. Without dreaming, we end up reactionary and responsive, taking other people's

---

[4] Deborah Coughlin, *Outspoken: 50 Speeches by Incredible Women: From Boudicca to Michelle Obama* (London, UK: WH Allen, 2019), 261.

knowledge and applying it, or being blown around by emotions, circumstances, and culture. Without imagination, we simply take what worked somewhere else or an answer from the past and apply it to our present problem. If the call of Jesus is to hear his words and put them into practice (Matt. 7:24–27), the Dream phase is about opening ourselves to first hear what God is saying before we obey. As we step down into the valley—through the hard process of enacting change that will be outlined throughout these pages—we need the motivation of the dream to help us continue to pursue what is ahead rather than shrink back to what was before. The dream is the mountaintop we're aiming for or the wicked problem[5] we're trying to solve. Like Yusra Mardini, we need the dream of something more to help us persevere through the potential hardship we will face on the journey.

A BIGGER AND BETTER STORY

With the world changing around us, we know something needs to give … so what's stopping us from dreaming of a different future? Perhaps part of the problem is that we let others do the dreaming for us. We watch Netflix and live vicariously through other people's dreams and adventures. We stare at our phones and are told what to think. Algorithms sift through the news and highlight headlines for us; a code calculates what we want to know or should hear; echo chambers are created both digitally and relationally, reinforcing our narrow worldview and our small circle of information and influence. Other people are defining the story we live and the stories we hear.

Dreaming can lead us in one of two directions: *escapism* or *empowerment*. We either get lost in a story someone else writes for us, or we are motivated to live a different story for ourselves and others. There's a reason Jesus used stories to explain what his kingdom coming would be like—stories are a powerful way of engaging our ability to dream. And, when redeemed, stories are a powerful force for good. However, many of us have allowed ourselves to be so consumed

---

[5] "A wicked problem, according to Rittel, is a social or cultural issue or concern that is difficult to explain and inherently impossible to solve. These are the crises that we long for answers to, but answers do not come easily." Shaline Wayne and Beth Hendricks, "Wicked Problem | Definition, Characteristics & Examples," Study.com, November 21, 2023, https://study.com/learn/lesson/wicked-problem-overview-characteristics-examples.html.

by the stories of others that we've forgotten how to dream the bigger and better story of God.

Our understanding of the bigger story is vital if we are to dream effectively with God. In their book *Reframation*, Alan Hirsch and Mark Nelson highlight how in the Western church we have greatly reduced God's great story, our place in it, and the story we tell others.

> When we reduce God and truth, what naturally follows is a reduction of the story of God that we tell. The telling of a reduced story takes the always impressive and authoritative story of Jesus and siphons it of its transformative power, drains it of its restorative influence, or simply bleeds it dry until it is lifeless. … It is these reductions and the shrouding of truth that have left us completely unprepared for the missional moment and context we find ourselves in.[6]

It is hard to take responsibility for a big dream if we have a small God and a small story. When we reduce the story God is inviting us into, we limit our dreams and enact change in incremental, safe steps. We drift toward a "middle-of-the-road," passive existence rather than dreaming and living into the kingdom mandate God has called us to. Alternatively, when we engage with God's big story, we enter into something far more than we could hope or imagine. We are inspired to step forward and dare greatly, and we have a drive within us to take responsibility for our part in this great story. As Hirsch and Nelson go on to say, when we dream and tell the bigger story of Jesus,

> It provokes questions and thoughts, such as: how would my life change if I lived in a world where it was truly better to give than receive? What would it be like to live in a world where the first shall be last and the last shall be first? If I really did believe that God had power over death, would that alter the way I lived? What would it be like to live in a world where death didn't have the final word?[7]

Jesus told this bigger story everywhere he went, whether it was on the road, around the table, on the shore of a lake, up a mountain, or conversing at a

---

6   Alan Hirsch and Mark Nelson, *Reframation: Seeing God, People, and Mission Through Reenchanted Frames* (Cody, WY: 100 Movements Publishing, 2019), 63–64.

7   Hirsch and Nelson, *Reframation*, 66.

well. Through parables, allegories, and questions, he continually pointed to an alternative vision for the future and invited others to respond and to be part of pursuing this new kind of life, to dream of something different. He pointed to a life that was completely outside of most people's experience. He spoke of a kingdom where sinners were welcomed (Luke 15), where the last would come first (Matt. 20:16), where the smallest and least significant would be championed (Matt. 25:40–45), and where the lost would be found and celebrated (Luke 15). Jesus gave agency and responsibility to those to whom the world gave none (Luke 5:1–11). He painted a picture of his kingdom through challenging analogies: faith as small as a mustard seed (Matt. 17:20); enemies who tend to us in our hour of need (Luke 10:25–37); honor being bestowed upon a disgraced son (Luke 15:11–32). He captured people's imagination (head) and engaged people's emotions (heart), which pulled them into a bigger story (hands).

And yet, instead of telling this beautiful story and being on the forefront of breakthroughs and innovations, churches and Christian ministries often apply management programs, looking for efficiency and pragmatism and hiring consultants to provide answers and quick-fix or plug-and-play solutions. We run churches like a business and wonder why the world outside our walls finds us outdated and irrelevant. As we navigate the difficult terrain of our world, we need more than good ideas. We need God ideas.

But to receive these God ideas we need to be what James K. A. Smith refers to as "regularly recentered in the Story."[8] "It is in the worship of the Triune God that we are restored by being restoried," he says. "It is the practices of Christian worship that renarrate our imagination so that we can perceive the world *as* God's creation and thus hear his *call* that echoes within it."[9] Being open to dreaming can help us discover what God is revealing—to play our part in God's great story.

Below are examples of organizations that have articulated and are embodying their dreams, playing their part in God's story.

---

[8] James K. A. Smith, *You Are What You Love: The Spiritual Power of Habit* (Grand Rapids, MI: Brazos Press, 2016), 174.

[9] Smith, *You Are What You Love*, 174–75.

- *"Every student should have an opportunity to find hope in Jesus and home in the local church"* (Fusion, student ministry).
- *"Ending homelessness in Scotland, one person at a time"* (Bethany Christian Trust, homeless nonprofit).
- *"Together, we can build a safer, more just world"* (International Justice Mission, global justice movement).
- *"We help you build flourishing churches that make disciples of Jesus Christ in an ever changing world"* (ECO: A Covenant Order of Evangelical Presbyterians, denomination).
- *"To see the gospel of Jesus Christ transform lives and impact cities"* (Redeemer City-to-City, nonprofit organization).
- *"KC Underground exists to equip and empower ordinary people to flourish in their souls and family, spilling over into mission where they live, work, learn, and play"* (Kansas City Underground, microchurch network).
- *"We aim to see 10,000 Christian entrepreneurs globally who are empowered to create, build and scale ventures that advance the common good"* (Creo Ventures, training ministry).[10]

The writer to the Hebrews describes faith as "being certain of what you hope for and sure of what you do not see" (Heb. 11:1), and this is our posture as we dream—being open to hope for what we do not yet see. Dreaming helps us to see what's right in front of us in a new light and to gain the perspective of God, as it illuminates the possibilities of what's much further ahead. Compelled and propelled by the dream, we begin to navigate our current reality to shape the future. We rewrite and reform the contours of tomorrow by unlocking our imagination today.

WRESTLING FOR OUR GENESIS IDENTITY

In Genesis, God created human beings in his likeness—in the likeness of our creative, Creator God. Dreaming, or engaging imaginatively, is thus hardwired into humanity's design. In the words of Kristin Joy Taylor, "Creativity is not a fringe thing

---

[10] https://www.fusionmovement.org; https://www.bethanychristiantrust.com; https://www.ijm.org/our-work; https://eco-pres.org; https://redeemercitytocity.com/about; https://kcunderground.org; https://creoventures.co.

but is central and of infinite worth, because we are made in the image of God."[11] Adam was given the creative role and responsibility to name every living creature (Gen. 2:19–20). And, together with Eve, he was given the mandate to "Be fruitful and increase in number; fill the earth and subdue it" (Gen. 1:28). Fruitfulness and filling the earth involved creativity, pioneering, and the pursuit of something beyond what they could see. It was a mandate that involved dreaming. God has designed us to be those who can imagine potential and see new things become reality.

Our ability to dream is part of what makes us uniquely human. According to psychologist and professor Thomas Suddendorf, our "open-ended ability to imagine and reflect on different situations" is one of the key features that sets us apart from the rest of the animal kingdom.[12] This is expressed in our capacity to empathize—a uniquely human characteristic. Empathy is essentially imagination, as it's the ability to consider how it feels to be someone else. Research shows that the greater a person's imagination, the greater their capacity to empathize.[13] For us to be those who can bring about kingdom change, we need to be able to understand what it's like to be in the shoes of others. That's part of what Jesus called us to do when he shared the second commandment to "love your neighbor as yourself" (Mark 12:31).

Of course, our identity as dreamers—given to us in Genesis 1 and 2—is also wrapped up in the tragedy of Genesis 3. We fight to recapture what was lost in the garden, but without embracing the true identity God has given us, we will either forget to dream or fail to dream in the way he intended.

Before the fall, humanity was given three key elements, and each of them affects our ability to dream:

- Relationship
- Resource
- Responsibility

---

[11] Quoted in Jordan Raynor, *Called to Create: A Biblical Invitation to Create, Innovate, and Risk* (Grand Rapids, MI: Baker Books, 2017), 24.

[12] Thomas Suddendorf, "What Separates Us From the Animals?" *Slate*, March 3, 2014, https://slate.com/technology/2014/03/the-science-of-what-separates-us-from-other-animals-human-imagination-and-our-ability-to-share-imaginative-scenarios-with-others.html.

[13] Aaron Rabinowitz and Lea Heinhorn, "Empathy and Imagination," *Imagination, Cognition and Personality*, vol. 4, no. 3 (March 1985), https://doi.org/10.2190/43DX-UKUF-NVP5-ALTP.

In Eden, we were given a covenant *Relationship* with God (Gen. 1:27; 2:25), the source of all creativity. This covenant relationship gave humanity the freedom to dream and for our imagination to flourish without the fear of rejection or failure.

In Eden, we were given abundant *Resource* from God (Gen.1:15–17, 29–30), the One who can provide all we need to realize our God-given dreams. This abundant resource meant that no idea was restricted, every need was met, and all possibilities could be explored.

In Eden, we were given the kingdom *Responsibility* (Gen. 1:15, 26, 28; 2:19), under God, to be fruitful, to name, to oversee, and to develop. This kingdom responsibility meant humanity could pursue the mandate to benefit others, without impure motives or insecurities.

- Covenant Relationship *with* God
- Abundant Resource *from* God
- Kingdom Responsibility *under* God

Before the fall, the Garden was an environment designed for humanity to dream freely and to thrive and was the perfect reflection of the creative and imaginative God. This meant that Adam and Eve had the perfect conditions for authentic relationships, abundant resources, and meaningful responsibility for their work. But the effects of the fall mean we are now cut off from these perfect conditions.

EMPIRE OR KINGDOM?

Throughout history, the effects of the fall have led to a dark side of dreaming. Hitler's imagination led to the Holocaust, Osama Bin Laden's to mass terror attacks, Al Capone's to a criminal empire, and Jeffrey Dahmer's to the murders of multiple people. Those with the gift of imagination and creativity can become spin doctors and create social media "bots," churning out fake news and distorting what we trust and who we believe. The imagination can be used for inventions that yield profit, regardless of the potential pain experienced by those involved in their production.

This dark side of dreaming is the inverse of our original design. After the fall, humanity has been left with a hole we long to fill.

- *Without living in Relationship with our Creator, we seek approval from others.* Our dreams become about deifying ourselves or winning the affirmation of the crowd.

- *Without looking to God for our Resource, we hustle for provision.* Our dreams become more about making things happen in our own strength or trying to conserve resources.

- *Without knowing the Responsibility entrusted to us, we strive for success.* Our dreams become about exerting unhealthy power and pursuing personal gain, or, conversely, simply becoming apathetic.

We're not immune to the influence of these pitfalls in our leadership roles and organizations. We need to secure our identity before we initiate activity. At moments we may have dreamed of our organization being flooded with new members, becoming known for the best programs and services, or receiving abundant financial provision to enhance our assets and facilities. Or, on an even more personal level, we may have dreamed about receiving recognition as an outstanding leader, being known for our gifting, knowledge, or skill set, and being looked up to and loved by those we work with. The desires God built into us in creation are as strong as ever. We're just looking to fulfill them in the wrong ways.

Even if we've avoided these weaknesses personally, many of us have worked with leaders who seem more concerned with achieving their own personal dreams than engaging in pursuits that will benefit others. This can result in huge amounts of pain and frustration, not to mention wasted money, time, and effort. Individuals might dream of becoming celebrity leaders, of exerting power over others, or of increasing their own wealth and personal comfort. Sometimes these misguided goals are subtle in their expression and difficult to detect, especially when they are pursued under the guise of seeking "success" for God's kingdom. Leaders can become more concerned about looking good than about obediently serving God, and their abilities can be used to obtain and retain resources, without trusting in God or the contribution of others. Or they can function as sole decision-makers who don't invite the opinions of others because they believe they should make all the decisions. Wrestling with these issues is essential.

In the Dream phase—whether we are seeking to spark change within an existing organizational context or initiate change through pioneering a faith-based venture, nonprofit, or church plant—we are setting foundations and a direction that will significantly affect outcomes later down the line. If we're walking a long journey, being just one degree off course will take us to the wrong destination. In the same way, if our dreams are not aligned with God at the start, by the time we get to the Deploy phase we may find ourselves building our own empires rather than seeking the kingdom. If we are to unlock kingdom potential and catalyze kingdom transformation, the work has to go beyond our influence and control, as it did with Jesus. We are called to invest our lives sacrificially in others and be the seed that goes to the ground to produce a great harvest:

> "Very truly I tell you, unless a kernel of wheat falls to the ground and dies, it remains only a single seed. But if it dies, it produces many seeds. Anyone who loves their life will lose it, while anyone who hates their life in this world will keep it for eternal life. Whoever serves me must follow me; and where I am, my servant also will be."
>
> JOHN 12:24–26

If there is an element of celebrity or control, the work will not fully mature beyond the scope of an individual leader. A kingdom-focused movement lasts beyond its founder and goes to places way beyond the original footprint.

Because all leaders are human, we have all operated from impure motivations and have also worked with other leaders who have done the same. The imagery Jesus uses to describe this is the difference between "hired hands" and "good shepherds":

> "The good shepherd lays down his life for the sheep. The hired hand is not the shepherd and does not own the sheep. So when he sees the wolf coming, he abandons the sheep and runs away. Then the wolf attacks the flock and scatters it. The man runs away because he is a hired hand and cares nothing for the sheep."
>
> JOHN 10:11–13

When we lose sight of the dream being for God, for good, and for others, we can easily become like hired hands, pursuing something that's essentially for ourselves. Whereas a good shepherd lays down their life for the sheep, the hired hand runs away because they care more for their own life than those they lead. Through our narrow cultural lenses, we often associate shepherding with soft, pastoral interactions. However, people in the time of Jesus knew that shepherding was a dangerous role that included sacrifice, resilience, courage, and commitment. Hence, when David was about to face the fearsome Goliath, he said, "The LORD who rescued me from the paw of the lion and the paw of the bear will rescue me from the hand of this Philistine" (1 Sam. 17:37). Jesus was ultimately *the* Good Shepherd, but as those called to follow in his ways, we too are called to lead others through the valley as good shepherds rather than hired hands.

When we are thinking about enacting change, we have to regularly audit our motives. Are fear, pride, escapism, or boredom driving the desire for change in you as a leader? We need to be change agents who initiate change for meaningful purposes, not change for the sake of change or our own gain. If we're just coming up with a new idea or initiative to be clever or to mask our fear by controlling or changing our circumstances, then change will be unfruitful. When we dig down into the truth of our motivations, we must be ready to give ourselves back to God's great story and surrender our hopes of personal acclaim.

I DO BELIEVE; HELP ME OVERCOME MY UNBELIEF!

In the Dream phase, we must name and own our disappointments and doubts. To be human is to dream; but to be human is to also know the pain of unrealized or unfulfilled dreams. Maybe it was a personal ambition, work project, or a vision for collective change with those you led. Maybe it was the dream set out by someone you followed, where you were encouraged to "buy-in" and get behind making the vision a reality. There are many reasons dreams don't come to fruition. Sometimes it's because we've misinterpreted what God was saying, or because the vision was based on one person's agenda or ego. It may have been that we went too fast, too soon, or too slow. Sometimes dreams don't work out because we live in a fallen world. Sometimes God has something better for us.

Our doubts and disappointments whisper, "Will this vision really come to pass?" "What if we try but lose more than we started with?" "What if the whole thing falls flat on its face and feels like a waste of time?"

When we tune into God's bigger story, we need to be prepared for it to not always look like the dream we may have imagined for ourselves. Jesus dreamed in such a way that he painted an incredible picture of our future—but one that completely defied expectations, reworked people's ideas of success and failure, and had many twists and turns. The disciples were imagining a kingdom that overthrew the Romans, but instead they got a Savior who was crucified, brought back to life, and imparted his Spirit to empower them to do all he had done. Mary dreamed of marrying Joseph, but instead she became pregnant out of wedlock and gave birth to the Savior of the world. Peter dreamed of leading a new-found Jewish movement but ended up with God showing him that both Jew and Gentile were to be included in his kingdom. For each of them, what they dreamed of and what they ended up with were very different. God is always writing a bigger, better, brighter story, even when we can't see it or comprehend it fully. Life is easier to understand looking backward than it is to predict looking ahead. I'm sure, like me, you can look back on many instances in your life, and now, with hindsight, realize what God was doing. At the time it may have seemed like your plans were thwarted or you didn't enjoy the outcomes or circumstances, but God was forming you more deeply so you could accept and inhabit more responsibility with him in the future.

The real danger isn't that the dream might not work out; it's choosing to never dream again. As Adam Grant notes in his book *Originals*, "The drive to success and the accompanying fear of failure have held back some of the greatest creators and change agents in history."[14] Fear, insecurity, and fatigue can set in, and we're not sure if we should even begin to imagine a different future.

A dream always starts with an internal conviction, hope, or drive but has to be externalized in a first step toward the preferred future that God reveals.

Dream on, Dreamer!

---

[14] Adam Grant, *Originals: How Non-Conformists Change the World* (London, UK: Penguin, 2016), 11.

SQUARE PEGS IN
ROUND HOLES

LEARNING TO DREAM

If I were to wish for anything I should not wish for wealth and power, but for the passionate sense of what can be, for the eye, which, ever young and ardent, sees the possibility. Pleasure disappoints, possibility never.
SØREN KIERKEGAARD

In change, you have to find a story that gives people hope for where you are going to be.
BETH COMSTOCK

There are far, far better things ahead than any we leave behind.
C. S. LEWIS

The world is selling us dreams. We like to think we are rational, logical beings, but the three Eden dynamics of Relationship, Resource, and Responsibility drive us more than we know. Perhaps this is no more evident than in the sphere of marketing. Marketing connects deeply with these core desires and is big business. In 2022, the United States alone spent $481 billion on marketing, all because advertisers know we want to be the hero; to change the world; to be known, accepted, and loved by others; to find deep peace, joy, happiness, intimacy; and to live in a better world.[1] They know we want the lead role in our lives and to receive five-star reviews and a standing ovation. They know we want life to be full of meaning and purpose, rather than something we manage, dread, or simply survive. In *Winning the Story Wars*, cofounder of Free Range Studios Jonah Sachs emphasizes the power of story in marketing:

> Today's best marketers are creating cause and brand loyalty by telling stories that deliver a pattern of meaning for a society in need of just that. They build communities of purpose and give people an empowering sense of *us*. … Our hunger for these stories explains many of the greatest marketing successes of our time.[2]

Marketers know if they can sell us that dream, we will buy their product. Not just once, but over and over again.

Marketing consistently speaks to at least one of our desires for Relationship, Resource, and Responsibility. Every product that is sold comes with the promise of deeper community (Relationship), the opportunity to obtain more (Resource), or a doorway to a new and better world for yourself (Responsibility).

Think about the following slogans:

- Bank of America: "Life's better when we're connected" (*Relationship*)
- Airbnb: "Belong anywhere" (*Relationship*)
- Dollar Shave Club: "Shave time. Shave money" (*Resource*)
- Target: "Expect more. Pay less" (*Resource*)
- Adidas: "Impossible is nothing" (*Responsibility*)
- Apple: "Think different" (*Responsibility*)
- Coca-Cola: "Open happiness" (*Relationship, Resource, Responsibility*)

---

[1] "Marketing in the United States—statistics and facts," Statista, accessed November 8, 2023, https://www.statista.com/topics/8972/marketing-in-the-united-states/#topicOverview.

[2] Jonah Sachs, *Winning the Story Wars: Why Those Who Tell—and Live—the Best Stories Will Rule the Future* (Boston, MA: Harvard Business Review Press, 2012), 29.

Tag lines are simple phrases that unlock pain and prize for us—the deficit of what is missing and the desire for more.

If we're being sold a product or service to make us more beautiful, more connected, or more loveable, the advertising taps into our *relational* desire.

If it increases or saves us money, time, or effort, the advertising taps into our desire for abundant *resources*.

If we're being sold something to make us more influential or successful, the advertising taps into our desire for purpose and meaningful *responsibility*.

We therefore need to be cognizant of the influence our desires have on us and how they may impact our ambitions and dreams. In their book *Switch*, Chip and Dan Heath draw on research from the University of Virginia psychologist Jonathan Haidt. Haidt describes our emotional side as an "Elephant" and our rational side as its "Rider" and reflects on how these two interact and impact our decision-making.

> Perched atop the Elephant, the Rider holds the reins and seems to be the leader. But the Rider's control is precarious because the Rider is so small relative to the Elephant. Any time the six-ton Elephant and the Rider disagree about which direction to go, the Rider is going to lose. He's completely overmatched.[3]

Our desires and our emotions significantly impact our direction of travel. As we think about being change agents, Relationship, Resource, and Responsibility are all forces we can harness for good or, when mishandled or misunderstood, can be forces that either prevent change or enact harmful change.

REDEEMING DREAMING

What the first Adam lost in the Garden of Eden, Jesus as the Last Adam (1 Cor. 15:44–49) won back for humanity. Although we live in a now-but-not-yet reality, Jesus' resurrection has achieved for us covenant Relationship, abundant Resource, and kingdom Responsibility. Rather than viewing life and ministry through our fearful, limited mindset, we are free to dream kingdom dreams and

---

[3] Chip Heath and Dan Heath, *Switch: How to Change Things When Change is Hard* (London, UK: Random House Business Books, 2010), 7.

partner with God in the making of all things new—our Father is pleased to give us the kingdom (Luke 12:32). This is not a "prosperity gospel," where we get everything we want for our benefit. Instead, this is an invitation to know our identity as children of God, to trust God for his provision, and to intentionally partner with God in his work on earth. It's a life defined by faith, not fear.

- **Relationship**—*No fear of isolation* because we are known and loved in our covenant relationship with God (Rom. 8:31–39)
- **Resource**—*No fear of lack* because we have been given the abundant provision of God-given resources (2 Cor. 9:8)
- **Responsibility**—*No fear of failure* because we always have a kingdom mandate to work, name, and develop in partnership with God (Matt. 28:16–20).

Jesus lived a limitless life, with access to all the goodness of heaven, and he perfectly modeled overcoming temptation in these three areas in the desert (Luke 4:1–13). In his book *In the Name of Jesus*, Henri Nouwen unpacks these temptations as the crucible of testing, exposing both the darker side of these dynamics and how Jesus overcame all three.[4] In order to be a kingdom change agent and to initiate a kingdom dream, we too must name and fight these battles, both personally and as leaders. Doing so is the difference between being a catalyst or a celebrity; it determines whether we partner with God in a kingdom dream or work hard to build our own empire. All three temptations will be battlegrounds. We will have seasons when one is more predominant than the others; however, there will also be one temptation that seems to rise above the other two on a more regular basis and so, as leaders, we must be mindful of the recurring patterns below.

DREAMING IN COVENANT RELATIONSHIP—NO FEAR OF ISOLATION

Relationship temptation: "If you are the Son of God," he said, "throw yourself down from here. For it is written: 'He will command his angels concerning you

---

4   See Henri J. M. Nouwen, *In the Name of Jesus: Reflections on Christian Leadership* (New York, NY: The Crossroad Publishing Company, 1989).

to guard you carefully; they will lift you up in their hands, so that you will not strike your foot against a stone'" (Luke 4:9–11). Nouwen talks about this as the temptation for the Christian leader to be spectacular and gain approval through their action and activities. This counterfeit dream makes us the hero. Nouwen names resisting this temptation as a move from "popularity to ministry."[5]

As we seek to be kingdom change agents, we need to pursue intimacy with our heavenly Father who defines our identity and purpose, so our activity comes from our relationship with him rather than a human effort to win God's affections and the attention of others.

Jesus was the perfect embodiment of what it means for a human to be in relationship with God. All that Jesus said and did came from the context of that relationship. He wasn't trying to *win* relationship with the Father or popularity with the crowds through his activity. His ministry was a *byproduct* of the relationship itself.

Jesus often retreated from the disciples and the crowds and went up a mountainside to pray and be with his Father. This solitude and elevation gave him the chance to connect with the Father to receive a different perspective and heavenly insight. Relationship is the context in which revelation comes.

> "Very truly I tell you, the Son can do nothing by himself; he can do only what he sees his Father doing, because whatever the Father does the Son also does. For the Father loves the Son and shows him all he does. Yes, and he will show him even greater works than these, so that you will be amazed."
>
> JOHN 5:19–20

It can often feel like we're just too busy to find time to take a moment by ourselves or to stop and survey the land. If our head is down or we're running hard, we struggle to connect with God. If we're not listening or looking for God at work, we neuter our capacity to dream healthily. Jesus understood this challenge as he faced continual pressure from the crowds and the religious leaders who hounded him. Yet he still chose retreat, silence, prayer, and an

---

[5] Nouwen, *In the Name of Jesus*, 49–70.

unhurried existence. We too need to pray and embrace silence and solitude and find ways to still our internal world to be able to hear and see clearly.

In 2022, I worked with Redeemer Downtown (RDT) in New York on a vision and values process. Pete Nicholas was taking up the role of senior pastor, and he wanted the community to assess who they were, what they stood for, and what they were passionate about before dreaming about where they were going in the next five to ten years. Pete could have just brought in some "experts" on church strategy to come up with an assessment of RDT. He could have chosen to only listen to senior leaders in a boardroom or those from one demographic in the church. He could have felt the pressure to hustle hard, move fast, set out a compelling vision himself, and galvanize people's engagement in his first one hundred days. But instead, he asked me and my team to gather insight from multiple stakeholders across the church. At the same time, Pete initiated a listening process, which involved prayer gatherings, listening prayer, intercessory prayer, and discussions around spiritual themes for the past, present, and future of RDT. The participating stakeholder group included different ages, ethnicities, and genders, and ensured that we spoke to those across the leadership spectrum of staff, elders, deacons, and volunteer leaders. Over many months, these stakeholders discussed, discerned, and expressed the vision and values that were latent in the RDT community. From this prayerful listening process, the members of RDT were able to craft a vision statement, name three core values, and communicate a phrase, picture, and practice attached to each of the core values that felt authentically "them." The community was empowered to dream together, to listen to God together, and to imagine the future they saw for the city of New York and for RDT.

DREAMING WITH ABUNDANT RESOURCE—NO FEAR OF LACK

Resource temptation: "The devil said to him, 'If you are the Son of God, tell this stone to become bread.' Jesus answered, 'It is written: "Man shall not live on bread alone"'" (Luke 4:3–4). Nouwen refers to this as the temptation to lead in our own strength, satisfy our own appetites, and utilize our own resources. This is a dream *we* have to accomplish. Nouwen names resisting this temptation as a move from "relevance to prayer."[6]

---

6   Nouwen, *In the Name of Jesus*, 25–48.

We recently sent our eldest son off to university, and one of his dawning realizations was that he would have to cook for himself. Every day. The responsibility to budget, shop for ingredients, cook meals, wash up, and repeat was one of the revelations of living independently. Our son grew up in a home where, when he opened the fridge, there was food. There are a saddening number of children for whom this is not true, but our children never even had to wonder whether there would be resources in the fridge to satisfy their appetites. It was just there. This is how Jesus lived with his Father. He knew there would be resources. And yet as leaders, many of us do not have an abundance mindset. We lack faith that God will provide for the work he has called us to do. Jesus wasn't afraid to spend everything for the sake of those around him and to dream big, trusting in the provision of the Father to give him all he needed to fulfill his calling and mission. He wasn't worried about whether he'd have enough to go around, and he proved that by feeding more than five thousand people with a young boy's brown-bag lunch of bread and fish (Matt. 14:13–21).

Whether we are leading a start-up, pioneering venture, or existing nonprofit or church, we often struggle to raise funding, wrestle with our budgets, and agonize over how we can steward the resources we have in the best possible way. Our dreaming is often eclipsed by the sense that there aren't enough resources to do what we feel called to do. However, the remedy to a lack of resources isn't to attempt things in our own strength or to dream smaller. It's the very opposite of this. Jesus tells us to trust that our heavenly Father will provide (Matt. 6:25–34).

George Müller understood this reality. Müller was a nineteenth-century Christian evangelist who founded schools and orphanages in Bristol, England, that cared for more than 120,000 orphan children. He repeatedly saw miracles of God's provision, despite never asking people for money. A well-documented example of this occurred one morning when one of the orphanages had no food in the larder and no money to buy food. Müller lifted up his hands and prayed,

> "Dear Father, we thank Thee for what Thou art going to give us to eat."
> There was a knock at the door. The baker stood there, and said, "Mr. Müller, I couldn't sleep last night. Somehow I felt you didn't have bread for breakfast, and the Lord wanted me to send you some. So I got up at 2 a.m. and baked some fresh bread, and have brought it."

Mr. Müller thanked the baker, and no sooner had he left, when there was a second knock at the door. It was the milkman. He announced that his milk cart had broken down right in front of the orphanage, and he would like to give the children his cans of fresh milk so he could empty his wagon and repair it.[7]

We may not all see miraculous provision in quite this way, but remember Resource is not just financial. Resource can also be spiritual, relational, physical, and intellectual, or any other raw material we need to live out the mandate God has given us. In many church congregations, businesspeople are an underutilized resource, as are parents, teachers, and social workers. The list goes on. Sometimes we don't have the resources for our dreams because we have not asked in prayer; at other times the resource is hiding in plain sight, but we fail to see and realize it.

If we have a finite view of resources, then every resource that someone else has is one that we ourselves do not have. This win/lose dynamic is one of the main reasons churches end up competing with one another. If churches are fighting over the same scarce resource (volunteers, attendees, and givers) while ignoring the vast numbers of lost souls in their area, then their dreams will shrink to what they, as individual churches, can accomplish rather than seeing themselves as part of a kingdom collaboration for the good of the city. A finite mindset for resources means we also have a finite mindset for relationships, and they become functional and transactional. As Simon Sinek says in *The Infinite Game*, "When we lead with a finite mindset ... it leads to all kinds of problems, the most common of which include the decline of trust, cooperation and innovation."[8] However, when we truly trust God's heart and character as our provider, then we are free to dream without fear or restraint.

I often say that the leaders we have the privilege to work with as part of Movement Leaders Collective and Creo have "an imagination bigger than their budget," and this is true of many pioneers, who seem to have faith in an abundant God. When God has stretched the imagination of a pioneer, he has

---

[7]   "George Müller: Trusting God for Daily Bread," Harvest Ministry, accessed December 6, 2023, https://harvestministry.org/muller.

[8]   Simon Sinek, *The Infinite Game: How Great Businesses Achieve Long Lasting Success* (London, UK: Penguin Business, 2019), 5.

often brought them to a place of conviction so that they take responsibility to "step out of the boat" and trust God for the provision of the future he has revealed (see Matt. 14:28–30). This also frees them to collaborate generously with others.

DREAM WITH KINGDOM RESPONSIBILITY—NO FEAR OF FAILURE

Responsibility temptation: "The devil led him up to a high place and showed him in an instant all the kingdoms of the world. And he said to him, 'I will give you all their authority and splendor; it has been given to me, and I can give it to anyone I want to. If you worship me, it will all be yours.' Jesus answered, 'It is written: "Worship the Lord your God and serve him only"'" (Luke 4:5–8). Nouwen talks about this as the temptation to use power to exert dominance and control and fulfill human ambition. This is a counterfeit dream where we "win." Nouwen names resisting this temptation as a move from "leading to being led."[9]

As Jesus walked on earth, he was clear on his purpose and responsibility. He turned the worldly scorecard of leadership and success upside down. Instead of lording it over others (Matt. 20:24–28), he washed their feet (John 13:1–20). Instead of depending on his own power, he humbled himself (Phil. 2:1–8). And instead of being the center, he commissioned others to take the work further (Matt. 28:16–20). At his baptism—before he had taken responsibility, achieved or changed anything—the words of affirmation spoken over him from the Father set his identity in place (Matt. 3:17). And his ministry activity and the ensuing fruit was subsequently built upon this foundation of identity. Often, we have it the wrong way round—we take responsibility in an attempt to win or succeed and to earn our identity. But God has already won. When we operate with a mindset of kingdom responsibility, we can play our part in seeing his kingdom come. From a place of wholeness and intimacy, pursuing a dream isn't about a pass or fail but instead is an expression of partnership with God. We no longer need to be the one in charge, the smartest person in the room, have all the answers, or make all the decisions. Instead, we are led by God and appreciate the contributions of others.

---

[9] Nouwen, *In the Name of Jesus*, 71–85.

This means that the invitation to dream becomes about something bigger than us; it is not dependent on us or about us. We can dare more greatly and step out more courageously.

When Alan Hirsch and I launched Movement Leaders Collective (MLC) in 2018, it was born out of our conviction that the church needed to reimagine itself as a Jesus movement. Our dream was to see the church remember and recapture its first-century design and to reimagine and release this in our twenty-first-century context. As Alan and I were discussing the formation of MLC, one of our key observations was that if we were to realize this dream we needed to create and convene a collaborative environment for pioneering leaders who refused to buy-in to the competitive culture of the Western church.

We therefore intentionally brought together leaders from different organizations in a setting of camaraderie, peer coaching, encouragement, and sharing of best practices, as well as a collaborative space where we dreamed together. Often these pioneering leaders came into an MLC environment and described it as "feeling at home," "finding their people," or "breathing oxygen" alongside other pioneers also taking responsibility to ideate and innovate in their context. We have seen individual organizations not just interact but form collaborations and networks, such as Brave Futures Collective (several microchurch movements working together to deliver training and a microchurch conference), Reimagine (a global collective of female church planters and organizations who are now training other church planters across the globe), and the City Leaders Collective (leaders from over sixty US urban networks who gather for retreats and are creating a training system and tools for city impact). This environment has released leaders to dream kingdom dreams so big that only God could enable them, and they cannot be achieved without the help of others.

CORE BUSINESS OR ADDED EXTRA?

In the Dream phase, kingdom dreaming with Relationship, Resource, and Responsibility harnessed effectively creates huge dynamism for you and your organization or venture. In many Christian ministries, however, dreaming is often treated as an add-on or optional extra. It's something we might do for fun or as a "brainstorming" exercise, but we rarely see its value or place in our everyday working practices. Dreaming can be narrowed to either a prayer meeting and prophetic words or a strategic planning session and business management system. But healthy dreaming should be both a *spiritual* and *strategic* engagement. If we simply view dreaming as an add-on or as either a solely spiritual *or* strategic exercise, we lose the incredible catalytic power it holds. Einstein once said, "The mind that opens to a new idea never returns to its original size."[10] We need to learn how to let dreaming expand our brains and change who we are and how we move forward into our future.

The English scientist Edward de Bono wrote about lateral and vertical thinking.[11] Vertical thinking is reality-adjusted thinking, or what we would refer to as logic, whereas lateral thinking is a process that unlocks possibility through imagination and is therefore vital in the Dream phase. De Bono claims that, since the time of Aristotle, vertical thinking (logic) has been given the place of supremacy in Western culture. But he proposes all truly new ideas, by which new eras of reality have come into play, have been products of lateral thinking (imagination). Lateral thinking involves seeing differently; it creates new paths, possibilities, and worlds. Initial breakthroughs come from lateral thinkers (imaginative dreamers) and are developed further and deeper by vertical thinkers (logical developers). Once lateral thinking has shifted our perspective, the vertical thinkers can busy themselves for generations by adding, deepening, strengthening, and iterating. De Bono likens the activity of vertical thinkers (logical developers) to digging holes deeper and deeper, along the lines established by those who bring lateral breakthroughs (imaginative dreamers).

Whenever Anna and I have moved into different neighborhoods over the years, we have tried not to go with answers or to start with a developmental plan (vertical thinking/logic) of how we will engage in mission. Instead, we have sought to unlock imagination in the Dream phase before initiating any activity—embracing the vulnerability of lateral thinking through prayer, listening to God, relational engagement and listening to the community, and gaining a perspective on the culture itself. Allowing ourselves to dream in this way has led us to clean up dog poop, form soccer (what we call "football")

---

[10] "Top 500 Albert Einstein quotes" (2024 Update), Quote Fancy, accessed April 4, 2024, https://quotefancy.com/albert-einstein-quotes.

[11] Edward de Bono, *Lateral Thinking: A Textbook of Creativity*, reprint ed. (London, UK: Penguin, 2009).

clubs, hold bingo and cake evenings, host local Alpha courses, and deliver parenting classes—all of which were creative and contextual ways to meet the needs, or engage with the hopes, of a community.

As leaders, we are wired to make things happen, and sitting around waiting for ideas to drop from the sky or discussing imaginative scenarios can feel frustrating and pointless. We can busy ourselves with vertical thinking, developing and iterating what's in front of us so that we feel we're getting something done and progress is being made. As a "recovering activist," I know the deep temptation to skip the dreaming and get to the "real stuff." But the importance of unlocking imagination can't be overstated.

Bill Gates, founder of Microsoft, is known to take a twice-annual "Think Week," where he spends seven days of solitude in a cabin in the forest, engaging in active dreaming, "letting new ideas flood into the quiet space he's cleared for them."[12] Gates attributes some of his best thinking, and many of his Microsoft innovations, to these weeks.

Reflecting on the habits of "successful" people, entrepreneur Michael Simmons notes that,

> Despite having way more responsibility than anyone else, top performers in the business world often find time to step away from their urgent work, slow down, and invest in activities that have a long-term payoff in greater knowledge, creativity, and energy. As a result, they may achieve less in a day at first, but drastically more over the course of their lives.[13]

Simmons refers to this as "compound time" because "like compound interest, a small investment yields surprisingly large returns over time." He gives the example of Warren Buffet, who estimated that he spent 80 percent of his career reading and thinking—in other words, dreaming. If our culture's top business leaders understand this reality, how much more should those of us who are following Jesus embody this principle?

---

[12] "How to do a Think Week Like Bill Gates," Runaway Suitcase, accessed November 8, 2023, https://www.reservations.com/blog/resources/think-weeks/.

[13] Michael Simmons, "Why Successful People Spend 10 Hours A Week On 'Compound Time,'" LinkedIn, August 14, 2017, https://www.linkedin.com/pulse/why-successful-people-spend-10-hours-week-compound-time-simmons/.

Despite its clear and proven benefits, our culture often stigmatizes dreaming. In organizations, the dreamers are often the square pegs in round holes. "You're a dreamer" is a pejorative statement. (Remember Joseph, the classic dreamer, with his technicolor coat and his exasperated brothers!) The term can be used to suggest someone who has grand ideas and no follow through, or someone who lives in a world that doesn't exist and is unable to make that world a reality. There can be a grain of truth to that. There are also people who have a hundred ideas before breakfast and flit from one harebrained scheme to the next. Many of us have known leaders who leave a trail of half-baked plans and projects in their wake, and we've regretted giving them our time, money, or effort. But despite the immature expressions of dreaming that can exist, we need to recapture and redeem the vital nature of dreaming—and to become mature dreamers.

CHANGING THE CONVERSATION— THE 100 MOVEMENTS PUBLISHING JOURNEY

As we journey through each of the phases of catalyzing kingdom change, I will draw from many different examples to show how each phase lands in organizations and ventures. However, I will also highlight one ministry example—100 Movements Publishing[14]—throughout the book to show how each stage builds on the previous phase. Many of the other examples throughout this book will refer to new initiatives started within existing organizations; however, this is an example of pioneering a brand-new venture. The publishing arm of Movement Leaders Collective, 100 Movements Publishing (100MP), was birthed seven years ago with a dream to "change the conversation" by equipping leaders and inspiring missional disciples to play their part in catalyzing Jesus movements.

Like most ministry endeavors, whether completely new or a new initiative within an existing organization, 100MP began with a dream. In 2016, Alan Hirsch, Anna Robinson (who leads 100MP), and I happened to be at the same Scottish Christian conference and ended up discussing the content creation of Alan's forthcoming book, which he intended to self-publish. Anna brought her

---

[14] https://100Mpublishing.com.

previous publishing experience into the conversation, and I brought my training perspective. As conversations developed over the months that followed, we discussed the current publishing industry, which is often forced to function more like a commercial business than a Christian ministry in order to survive. This means that missional resources—which may not always be considered sufficiently profitable or have a large enough readership or author platform—can be overlooked. We began to dream about what it might look like to create a publishing house where missional and movemental authors could have their manuscripts professionally edited and produce resources that equip the church to imagine itself as a Jesus movement. We also dreamed of a publishing house that encouraged a diverse range of voices and allowed authors to keep their intellectual property. A year later, 100MP published its first book and has continued to grow in influence and titles since that initial publication. As is the case with any dream, 100MP was birthed in the hopes, frustrations, and conversations of a few dreamers. As we continue through these pages, we will explore the change journey of 100MP in each phase.

THE ULTIMATE DREAMER

Jesus' victory over sin and death ultimately restores to us what was lost in the Garden, although we still live today in a "now-but-not-yet" reality. Often, we are still trying to win back our Creation identity—seeking approval, hustling for provision, and striving for success. Our efforts are usually less about dreaming and more about present-day survival, leaving many of us stressed and worn out. We choose to carry a heavy burden when Jesus offers us a light yoke (Matt. 11:28–30). What if we viewed dreaming not as an add-on or something that creates more work with high chances of failure but instead as a doorway into internal and external change that leads us to a more intimate, fulfilling, and fruitful walk with Jesus as a disciple and leader?

When Jesus called his first disciples, he simply said, "Come, follow me, and I will send you out to fish for people" (Matt. 4:19). It wasn't exactly a detailed PowerPoint presentation or a strategic roadmap for what would happen. There was a lot left to the imagination. But it was an invitation rich with adventure. It gave a rag-tag group of would-be disciples a glimpse of a better future—for themselves and for others. They were invited to dream and discover, with an invitation into Relationship, the assurance of Resource, and a commissioning into greater Responsibility.[15]

We might not consider him as such, but Jesus was the ultimate Dreamer— he had a vision of something much better, bigger, and greater for humanity to experience.[16] He came to share this dream of a better world with anyone and everyone he interacted with, and he invited his disciples to join him in realizing the dream.[17]

Many of us know John 3:16 by heart. But consider the dream that was driving God's initiative to send Jesus: "For God so loved the world that he gave his one and only Son [disruption], that whoever believes in him shall not perish but have eternal life [dream]."

We are called to follow in the footsteps of a Savior who denied himself, took up his cross, and died to self. The dream may cost you everything, but if it's a kingdom dream, it will be worth it. God calls us to humble ourselves, submit our dreams to him, allow them to die, and see what he resurrects for his glory and his kingdom.

---

[15] See, for example, Matt. 28:18–20: "Surely I am with you always" (Relationship) and "Therefore go and make disciples of all nations" (Responsibility); and Acts 1:8: "You will receive power when the Holy Spirit comes on you" (Resource).

[16] See, for example, John 10:20 and Matt. 20:28.

[17] See, for example, Matt. 4:19, Luke 5:10, and Matt. 28:16–20.

IMAGINEERING TOGETHER

EQUIPPING OTHERS TO DREAM

If your dreams do not scare you, they are not big enough.
ELLEN JOHNSON SIRLEAF

Do not call people back to where they were (they were never there).
Do not call people to where you are, as beautiful as it may seem to you.
But travel with them to a place neither of you have been before.
VINCENT DONOVAN

Loosen up your life enough to be ready for interruptions. Don't structure your days
so rigidly that you lock out God from working with you in the middle of them.
CHRISTINE CAINE

On April 15, 2019, the Notre Dame Cathedral in Paris, France, experienced a fire that raged for around fifteen hours. The fire devastated the infrastructure, and experts predict it will take over twenty years to fully restore. The people of Paris and the world united, with more than $670 million pledged to the restoration project.[1] It seems that great tragedy and beauty can elicit a significant

---

[1] Iain Martin, "French Billionaires Pledge $670 Million to Restore Notre Dame," *Forbes*, April 16, 2019, https://www.forbes.com/sites/iainmartin/2019/04/16/french-billionaires-pledge-340-million-to-restore-notre-dame/.

response in people. But consider for a moment, not the fire of 2019, but the breaking of ground in 1163. The Notre Dame Cathedral project was initiated by Bishop Maurice de Sully, and it took nearly two hundred years to build the cathedral. It was finally completed in 1345.

Those who began the project perceived the vision and the future structure, but they never saw the completed cathedral or got to stand at the top and enjoy the vista across the whole of Paris. It's a sobering reminder that our dreams may involve starting something that we may never get to fully enjoy and experience. Remember the heroes of the faith in Hebrews 11 who "did not receive the things promised; they only saw them and welcomed them from a distance, admitting that they were foreigners and strangers on earth" (v. 13). The Dream phase is not only about seeing the future but also about faithfully initiating the first steps of the journey to make that potential a reality—regardless of whether we get to see its full realization.

In chapters two to six of Luke's Gospel, Jesus communicated the dream of the coming kingdom with stories, but he also catalyzed the initial engagement of a small core group. His early disciples took the first steps to embody this dream. Jesus didn't just paint a picture of a preferred future; he demonstrated that different future in the present through how he lived, what he did (and didn't do), whom he engaged with, and how he engaged with them. He showed them who God was.

The founder of IKEA, Ingvar Kamprad, said, "If there is such a thing as good leadership, it is to give a good example. I have to do so for all the IKEA employees."[2] This statement came from a billionaire who flew economy class, drove a 1993 Volvo, and encouraged IKEA employees to use both sides of the paper to write on. When we're inspiring those we lead to dream of a different future, we need to *show* them something of what that future might look like.

WHO'S IN THE ROOM?

Going back to the Diffusion of Innovations Curve (see page 28), in the Dream phase, we are primarily working with the innovators and early adopters.

---

[2] John Dudovskiy, "IKEA Leadership: effective application of leading by example," Business Research Methodology, August 14, 2022, https://research-methodology.net/ikea-leadership-effective-application-leading-example/.

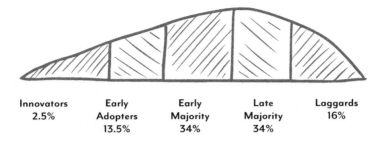

Innovators	Early Adopters	Early Majority	Late Majority	Laggards
2.5%	13.5%	34%	34%	16%

They are the ones who will be able to take the possibility, uncertainty, and opportunity of this phase and fill that space with imagination and innovation. The early and late majority are much less likely to imagine something new. They tend to be happy with the status quo and therefore don't perceive a need to dream of something different, which initially seems like a loss.

As Seth Godin says in his book *Tribes*, "At first, the new thing is rarely as good as the old thing was. But if you need the alternative to be better than the status quo from the very start, you'll never begin."[3] The early and late majority tend to take something that exists and build on that. For example, if you are casting a vision for missional communities or microchurches that haven't yet been launched in your context, the late-majority leader will usually interpret these models as a bigger version of a small group or a smaller version of a church service. They will take what they know (a small group or church service) and expand it rather than create a brand-new expression. It's therefore critical in this phase that we have the dreamers in the room—those who have a childlike faith, are willing to take risks, and possess the drive to ideate and experiment.

The dreaming of this group can create and clarify a picture or vision for the future that can bind the whole organization together and pull the whole organization forward. So, at this stage, the vast majority of the core group should be made up of pioneers (innovators and early adopters), although it's important to have some organizational stakeholders present to connect this pioneering energy with the life of the main organization. These individuals form a guiding coalition that either drives the formation of a new initiative (e.g., church plant, faith-driven venture, or microchurch) or serves the whole organization or

---

[3] Seth Godin, *Tribes: We Need You to Lead Us* (London, UK: Piatkus, 2008), 93.

community (e.g., church, denomination, or existing venture) by imagining what is possible in the future that is not yet real.

Remember, Jesus communicated the dream with the crowds through the Sermon on the Mount, but he initially created momentum toward that dream with only a small core group of disciples. In our contexts, as the core group dream together, it's important to socialize the macro-idea of this dream to the whole organization or wider community, but we don't require every individual to participate yet.

CREATING A CULTURE OF DREAMING

Jesus-centered dreaming is characterized by fixing our eyes on Jesus in the present and looking toward where he is leading us into the future. We pray God's kingdom comes, and that his will is done on earth as it is in heaven ... right now and also tomorrow and into the future. Like those who built the Notre Dame Cathedral, we not only dream about what will benefit our generation but also the generations to come. And we don't just dream in isolation; we dream in community. We have to think long-term, multi-generational, and intergenerational. Our dreaming focuses on Jesus, not ourselves. We're not trying to build a bigger, better, stronger organization; we're attempting to stretch toward kingdom impact, cultural transformation, and systemic change.

We live in a world where it's easy to become hard-hearted and hard-headed; we see the problem and critique the other. Our tendency to be individualistic and self-centered prompts us to rely on our own strength, intellect, and ability. To engage with dreaming, we need a healthy understanding and expression of Relationship, Resource, and Responsibility. We need to unlock faith, recapture hope, and be motivated, together, by love. These are the qualities and commitments that drive healthy innovation and change.

Childlike faith is essential in this phase. Children see the world with curiosity and possibility. To me and most adults, a chair is just a chair, something functional that you sit on. But to a child, a chair can be a den, an anti-aircraft gun, a zoo cage, a house, or a climbing frame. Children dream, explore, and create worlds with their imaginations. Jesus urged us to "Be like little children" (see Luke 18:15–17), but somewhere along the way we "grow up," and curiosity, childlike faith, and trust in him go by the wayside. The ever-increasing and never-ending demands of "adulting" mean we simply try to survive the day rather than look for opportunities or possibilities. We seek techniques and solutions rather than ask questions. Whereas adults tend to rationalize, analyze, and fix, children tend to hope, dream, and explore.

Old Testament scholar Walter Brueggemann says, "Our culture is competent to implement almost anything and imagine almost nothing."[4] The challenge of organizational change is that we often shoot down ideas before they've even been given a chance. A child says, "How might that be possible?" whereas an adult says, "That'll never work."

We need to allow ourselves to be challenged by the simplicity, clarity, and magnitude of Jesus' truth and to dream big, take a risk, and pursue something worthy of the transformative power of God's kingdom. We need to be more like children if we are to open ourselves up to the possibilities God is leading us to imagine, rather than adults managing and improving the status quo.

Here are three postures that will help you create a *culture* of kingdom dreaming with your core group.

POSTURE #1: BE AWARE

How often have you turned up somewhere, parked the car, removed the key from the ignition, and had the fleeting thought, *How did I get here?* You've taken the trip so many times you've driven on autopilot, with no clear recollection of the landmarks you've passed or the turns you've taken. We can "drive" through life in much the same way—drifting to and from places, unconscious of what's happening around us. To become kingdom dreamers we must become aware and foster that awareness. We need to look anew at the world and open our minds to what God is saying and doing.

Usually, we find ourselves on autopilot for one of two reasons: either because we're in an over-familiar environment or because we are going too fast. The pace of life many of us operate under means we are stressed and overworked, struggling to survive the week. Under stress, we default to tried-and-tested methods because this takes the least mental or physical energy. We get the job done, narrow our focus, and our brains go into survival mode. We are not fully present

---

[4]   Walter Brueggemann, *The Prophetic Imagination*, 2nd ed. (Minneapolis, MN: Fortress Press, 2001), 40.

in our relationships, and we are often reactive in the areas of responsibility. There is no time to dream, exercise our imagination, or be aware of possibilities.

In a busy, ever-connected, technology-driven world, it's vital to steward our resources well and to cultivate the practice of creating mental, emotional, physical, and spiritual space. In his Becoming Minimalist blog, Joshua Becker notes that,

> Being busy is a choice. It is a decision we make. We are never forced into a lifestyle of busyness. The first, and most important, step to becoming less busy is to simply realize that our schedules are determined by us. We do have a choice in the matter. We don't have to live busy lives.[5]

Of course, there will be seasons when we are inevitably busier, but a lifestyle of constant busyness is a choice we make. Many of us live our lives at top speed, running past our emotions, our questions, and our musings, never slowing down long enough to allow them to impact us. Just think how hard it is to hear someone talking to you as you run past them. If you are jogging, you may pick up some content, but if you are sprinting, you have no chance. This is what we are like with God, others, and even ourselves. If the main component of the Dream phase is to hear God and look for where he is at work, we must create space, or it will not happen. As leaders, we need to encourage ourselves and our teams to slow down and make room for the capacity to have a conversation, sit a while, or simply listen to one another.

The practices below aim to help you and the core group become more aware of your surroundings and your interior world, switch off your autopilot, and break your inertia. Embracing these practices will develop the raw materials for dreaming.

- **Switch off:** Regularly turn off your phones and close your laptops as a practice of creating space to hear God.
- **Review your world:** Take an audit of your schedules, online interactions, friendships, Scripture reading, rest time, work rhythms, reading,

---

[5] Joshua Becker, "A Helpful Guide to Becoming Unbusy," Becoming Minimalist, accessed November 8, 2023, https://www.becomingminimalist.com/un-busy/.

and hobbies to make sure there is a good pace and regular times and spaces to restore mind, body, and soul.

- **Look for patterns:** Record what you sense God highlighting to you throughout the day. Note the curiosities, questions, anomalies, possibilities, feelings, and thoughts from each day, to look for patterns of how God may be speaking to you. Share your notes with the rest of the team.

POSTURE #2: BE CURIOUS

Some of the best conversations I've had started with a question: "What if … ?"; "Why don't we … ?"; "Have you ever thought about … ?" Remember the example of 100 Movements Publishing I introduced in chapter four. It started with a simple "What if we were to disrupt the traditional model of publishing and start a hybrid publishing house for missional practitioners?" The ensuing experimentation took months and years to evolve, but it grew out of a series of questions. We refused to shut down possibilities and remained curious about what could be.

The opposite of being curious is being closed. No doubt we've all been in environments where the unspoken message is, "This is how we do it around here." We've all been in places where we can see things aren't working, but the consensus is to double down and keep quiet. Organizations are often experts at maintaining tradition—potentially to their downfall. On top of all this, online algorithms create echo chambers, meaning all we see and hear are people who are like us, who think like us, or who like us. Opposing opinions or different perspectives are silenced, and this sucks the curiosity out of us. But when we mix with people who have different opinions, it stretches our thinking and helps us to see new possibilities and consider different perspectives. And we become curious as a result.

We interact with myriad people, data points, and situations every day—all of which God can use to reveal himself and his truth to us. If we keep an open, curious mind, believing every interaction holds the potential to provide revelation, God will speak through them. Like onions, dreams are often peeled one layer at a time, and these layers may come in a flash of inspiration or a fleeting thought. For me, moments like that often involve a frantic rush to scribble down a note, or a pause to type into my phone or to put the iron down and capture that moment. The "aha" moments are rarely a full revelation of the whole picture but are more like pieces of the puzzle. We need to examine them with others to discern what God may be trying to show us.

The practices below aim to help you and your core group cultivate a culture of asking questions rather than providing answers, of exploring rather than explaining, and of dreaming together rather than accepting the opinions of others.

- **Step out of your comfort zone:** Read an author you wouldn't normally choose to read—and maybe even don't agree with—and look for what you can learn. Spend time in an environment you don't naturally enjoy or usually engage with. Read or listen to a different Bible translation. Seek out a person with a different life experience from yours and engage relationally by listening to their story.
- **Learn from reality:** Throughout the day, jot down any surprises you encounter. Learn from the times when things played out differently than you expected. Observe the questions that were raised in your interactions. Return to these at the end of the day with the posture of a learner to look at where God might have been at work or what he might want to reveal to you.
- **Reflect on what God is doing in the everyday:** Pray that you can see and hear what God is saying and doing in every interaction, and intentionally journal, reflect on, and discuss what you are learning. Create a process to record, steward, and develop the learning and dreams intentionally and faithfully as they slowly emerge and become clearer.

POSTURE #3: BE COMMUNAL

Dreaming is a team sport. To become a dreamer again and to recapture our imagination, we must be communal. We need to listen to, learn from, and be inspired by and with others. Like an orchestra with numerous players that together create a beautiful symphony or a jazz band riffing off each other, we need to hear one another, combine with others, and learn and grow together, to create something that we could not do on our own. Whether our preference is introversion or extroversion, action or reflection, we need to engage with others if we are to unlock our imagination and our ability to dream.

The opposite of community is isolation. If we are stuck in an office or inside our own heads, fruitlessly trying to work everything out ourselves, we won't ever truly step into the dreaming phase. The idea that we must be a solo-heroic leader who single-handedly comes up with all the good ideas is exhausting, impossible, and unbiblical. This unrealistic expectation is one of the reasons why stress levels are so high in pastors. We weren't made to do it alone. Encouragement and creativity are essential for dreaming—and they are found and fueled in relationships.

The practices below aim to unlock the power of differing perspectives, harness the experience and intelligence of the core group, and help foster the creation and ownership of a communal dream.

- **Change your environment:** Get out of the office and create and initiate conversations about possibilities, the future, and key problems to solve.
- **Ask for a different perspective:** Ask the opinion or insight of someone on your team in an informal context, such as a phone call, a walk, or a coffee. Ask questions, muse, and discuss together.
- **Include everyone:** Be intentional about inviting the voice of the introverts as well as outside wisdom into your team meetings, planning, or activities.

ACTIVATING DREAMING IN YOUR ORGANIZATION OR VENTURE

Whereas the postures and practices above are about creating a *culture* of dreaming, below are three specific practices that help to initiate the *activity* of dreaming. These will enable your core group to learn by doing together and create a shared experience of what it means to dream communally.

As we explored in the previous chapters, it's important at this stage for each of you in the core group to check your motives. A personal dream puts ourselves at the center rather than Jesus. As organizations, we need to be careful that the dream doesn't center our organization as the hero. The other danger at this point is that the dream (vision and mission) can become diffuse, vague, or overly conceptual. When the picture is unclear, we become unsure of our progress and whether we've achieved what we set out to.

Below are a few questions we can ask—as individuals and as teams—to ensure that we don't center ourselves or allow unhealthy expressions of Relationship, Resource, and Responsibility to be the motivation; instead, we collectively pursue a well-defined, kingdom dream.

- What aspect of Jesus and his good news does this dream reflect and express in the world?
- Who will benefit from seeing this dream accomplished? And how will they benefit?
- How will the world be different and better if the dream becomes a reality?
- How will we know if we are heading in the right direction, and how will we know the dream has become a reality?
- How will we show others a foretaste of this future through our present example?
- What Scripture and prophetic words undergird our dream?
- How do we overcome the fear of isolation (Relationship), the fear of lack (Resource), and the fear of failure (Responsibility)?

As we ask these questions and discuss and dream together, here are a couple of frames to help channel the energy and possibility into something more cohesive in the Dream phase.

Dream Frame 1
- **3 Impacts**—What three future impacts will our dream have on the people group or place we're called to serve?
- **3 Symbols**—What three symbols describe our future identity (who we will be) and impact (what we will see)?
- **3 Sentences**—What three sentences describe the desired future we envision together?
- **3 Words**—What three words define our future identity and impact?

Dream Frame 2

- **Identity**—Who do we want to become as an organization?
- **Activity**—What will we do as an organization?
- **Impact**—What difference will we make as an organization?

PRACTICE #1: PICK YOUR CORE GROUP

In an existing organization, the core group that drives the change process will act like yeast in the dough as a guiding coalition to initiate and navigate change. In a pioneering initiative, this core group is the embryo of the venture itself and the driving energy that initiates the process of launching or planting. Either way, the core group's initial efforts, although small, will have a deep and lasting influence on the organization. Who joins you on the change-agent journey is vital, so you therefore need to be prayerful and wise in your choices.

As I mentioned above, the majority of this group needs to be pioneering (early adopters and innovators), but there also needs to be a sprinkling of organizational stakeholders. Too many middle managers and organizational stakeholders will kill the Dream phase and neuter the power of exploration in the Discover phase because they are risk averse and too entrenched within the existing system. However, a group of solely pioneering leaders (innovators and early adopters), will struggle in the later phases—with the discipline required in the Design phase and the intentionality needed in the Deploy phase. In an existing organization, without involving some organizational stakeholders, the change that is proposed will only affect the organization's periphery. Like adding salt to a recipe, it's a delicate balance.

Your guiding coalition for the change process needs to include members who are committed to the organization's future but not wedded to its existing system. They need to have the following characteristics.

- **Integrity—they are sacrificial.** They are not seeking to use power and influence to benefit themselves. Instead, they look to serve others and desire a healthy future for the organization. They are not trying to be heroes but are servant-hearted and have a kingdom worldview and practice.

- **Humility—they are learners.** They are not proud, thinking they have all the answers or the perfect product or pathway. Open to experiential learning and aware of their need for others, they have an open and infinite mindset rather than a closed, finite mindset.
- **Agility—they are flexible.** They don't hold to a one-size-fits-all formula or a tactical or technical solution. Instead, they can respond adaptively and experiment intentionally to iterate and improve. They are not so in love with their systems or tools that they are unwilling to change them.
- **Creativity—they are innovative.** They don't merely seek pragmatism, efficiency, and managing the status quo. Instead, they look for where God is at work and listen to what he might be saying. They are motivated to create new worlds and ways rather than manage existing realities and pathways.
- **Ingenuity—they are dynamic.** They don't merely live in the world of sensory detail. Instead, they work actively, often intuitively and entre-preneurially, to gather data and use circumstances and resources as raw material for catalyzing change. They are reflective practitioners, who see themes and patterns and unravel the threads of the present to start to knit together a better future.

PRACTICE #2: RUN A DREAM LAB

A Dream Lab aims to create an intentional environment where the core group can undertake the process of dreaming together. The lab helps this team dream about particular problems, opportunities, or situations.

Preparation: As a leader, create time with the core group in an environment conducive to dreaming (not at your desks with laptops and inboxes open, where you will be regularly interrupted by the everyday stresses of ministry or work). Encourage your team to sit with the following questions first silently and prayer-fully, and then take time to share answers, making sure every team member has a chance to add their perspective. It can be helpful to give the team these questions before the Lab, so they have time to reflect on them.

The discoveries made in this discussion will prepare you as you go through each of the phases of catalyzing change.

Questions:

What is our dream—our defining prize or wicked problem?
- What kingdom change do we desire to see in the world?
- What question are we seeking to answer, what problem are we seeking to solve, or what prize is pulling us forward?
- What do we consistently revert to as a cause that we champion, value, or pursue?
- What, if we solved it or changed it, would have the greatest kingdom impact?
- What kingdom change are we passionate about and committed to pursuing?

What are our organizational priorities?
- What are our organizational strengths in Relationship, Resource, and Responsibility that we can leverage for greater kingdom impact to make the dream a reality?
- What are our organizational weaknesses in Relationship, Resource, and Responsibility that might hinder our kingdom dream/vision?
- What is missing in our organization (e.g., leaders, wisdom, strategy) that we need to pursue the kingdom dream/vision?
- What one pivotal thing in our organizational culture and practice could unlock the potential for us to move forward?
- What could "sink the ship" or "blow us off course"? (The pre-mortem exercise below will help teams flesh out this question in detail.)

What are my personal priorities?
- What's my dream as a disciple for my own life?
- Which area of my spiritual life needs more intentionality or intensity to grow?
- What mindset and skill sets do I need to become a change agent?
- What is God currently speaking to me about?
- How are the kairos moments from God bringing encouragement and challenge for me to go further and deeper?

Dream Labs can be repeated regularly to socialize new team members to the shared dream, to sharpen and clarify existing elements of the dream, and to refresh the dream itself with new revelation and conviction.

This communal process of dreaming fuels the energy and activity to move the team toward the next phase. Dreaming together about the future you believe God is revealing creates a conviction and stimulus for the core group to embark on the first steps of the Discover phase and drive you toward initial pioneering efforts.

PRACTICE #3: CONDUCT A PRE-MORTEM

The Dream phase can be full of excitement and expectation. As you imagine the change you desire to see in the world, it's helpful to think ahead and dream about success, fruitfulness, and impact. But it's also vital at this stage to embrace the possibility of failure. As the saying goes, to be forewarned is to be forearmed.

A *post*-mortem is carried out after someone dies. The coroner examines the corpse and determines a cause of death. This exercise is a *pre*-mortem—an examination *before* death. As a team, this exercise challenges you to dream about fatality rather than possibility, pulling you away from idealism to realism. Take time to do this sobering exercise together. It will save you a lot of pain in the future!

- **Imagine three or five years from now.** You got fired up and started something, but sadly, it died. It didn't work, didn't catch, or didn't hold.
- **Imagine what went wrong.** Visualize and name all the reasons why it died. They may be obvious or obscure, internal or external, relational or resource-related, or too much or too little of something. Whatever they are, brainstorm them all. What were the battles you lost that hindered the process, the decisions you didn't make, or the things you missed that eventually took you down, blew you up, or blew you off course?
- **Analyze why it went wrong.** Take the time to collect all of the data and opinions of each member of the core group. Allow your team the chance to pull things apart and for *each person* to give their perspective on the three most likely reasons they think you failed. In this collective

analysis, look for themes, commonalities, and anomalies. As a group, discuss all of the options presented and from all the reasons given, *collectively identify* the three most significant or likely reasons that you will fail in the future.

- **Invite God into what you identified as causes of death.** Explore with the team what God is revealing in the areas you diagnosed. Review what you can do in the present to avoid your projected catastrophe. Where does your organization's direction, culture, or structure need a reimagination or a reset?

Identifying potential future failure helps you to be innovative and intentional in those areas in the present. It helps to channel your dreaming energy not just for the future but also for the present in areas that are essential for your organization's health and growth. It helps to address these issues in the short term and as part of the dream, rather than being surprised by them. It also enables you to be prayerful and purposeful in these key areas rather than reactionary as you move into the Discover and Design phases.

LEAD LIKE A GOOD SHEPHERD RATHER THAN A HIRED HAND

As we head toward the Discover phase, we step out and go deeper into "the valley." We encounter terrain that is unknown and uncertain, so it's important to note that change efforts can fail and dreams can die because they are led by "hired hands" rather than "good shepherds" (see chapter three). As shepherd-like leaders, we need to give ourselves on behalf of the sheep. We need courage to step out beyond what is known. As former First Lady Rosalynn Carter said, "A leader takes people where they want to go. A great leader takes people where they don't necessarily want to go, but ought to be."[6] Those we lead need to know that we are with them. When it gets tough in the valley, and those we are leading are tired on the journey, we will need to be the kind of leaders they can trust not to abandon them.

---

[6] "Historical Women Leaders ... Rosalynn Carter," Arden Coaching, accessed December 21, 2023, https://ardencoaching.com/historical-women-leaders-rosalynn-carter.

To lead as a good shepherd from the Dream and into the Discover phase and beyond requires three key elements. These all start to seed a vision for a Jesus movement where there is larger participation further down the line.

Cause: Those you lead need a cause (a dream) they can become passionate about and pursue—a way to imagine a better future. As a leader, you need to help people see they have a great adventure ahead, they are doing something of value together, and they each have a vital part to play. Having a shared cause means the dream is no longer solely owned by the leader but instead is shared by everyone on the team.

Care: Good leaders prioritize people, and the flow of benefit runs downstream (toward the people) not upstream (toward the leadership). This creates an authentic community through the Dream phase. When people are prioritized, the potential for a leader to co-opt the dream toward their own ends is neutered. Because the process of change will be costly, the team needs to know "we are in this together" and have a high degree of ownership.

Commitment: The shepherd-like leader demonstrates loyalty in the Dream phase, helping group members trust that there will be a commitment to the group through the journey to come. If there's any sense that the dream is a pipe dream or a personal dream, the chances of it becoming a shared dream and communal adventure are vastly reduced. The commitment of the shepherd to both the core group and the cause encourages the group's commitment, allowing them to not only visualize and personalize the dream but to also take practical steps toward making it a reality.

The journey into the Discover phase needs to be led with faith, hope, and love and navigated by a leader who is a good shepherd rather than a hired hand. We need to follow in the footsteps of *the* Good Shepherd.

DREAM 101

PRIZE

Unlock kingdom imagination to discern where God is currently at work and where he is leading us in the future.

PEOPLE

Primarily innovators and early adopters, with some organizational stakeholders.

LEADERSHIP EXPRESSION

A mature Catalyst who is an *inspiration* and *irritant*.

SHADOWSIDE

An immature Catalyst who creates disillusioned people through an endless trail of ideas, empty words, and pipe dreams.

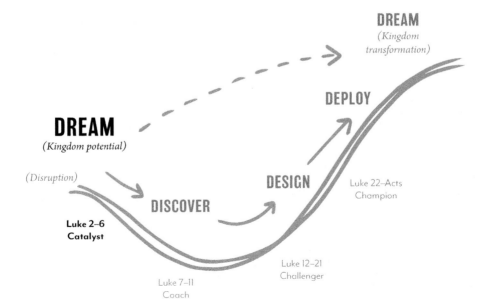

SCRIPTURE: LUKE 2-6

In these chapters, Jesus as a Catalyst functions as an *inspiration* and an *irritant*, sparking the imagination of ordinary people, disrupting the status quo of the religious elite, unearthing latent potential, and beginning to plant the initial seeds of the dream of a Jesus movement. Tested in the wilderness, he rejects the counterfeit dreams offered by the devil for the ultimate dream of humanity restored (Luke 4:1–12). Everything he does is about unlocking dreams in ordinary people, challenging where the dream of the Messiah had become misaligned, and embodying a dream of humanity restored. He speaks in the synagogue at Nazareth and is rejected (Luke 4:14–30), drives out demons (Luke 4:31–36), heals the sick (Luke 4:38–44), casts vision and calls his first disciples on the shore (Luke 5:1–11), eats with sinners (Luke 5:27–31), redefines the Sabbath (Luke 6:1–10), and shares the essentials of kingdom living (Luke 6:17–49). To those who want to engage in a new dream (e.g., the twelve disciples), he is an inspiration; but to those who are invested in the status quo (e.g., the Pharisees), he is an irritant.

YOUR CHANGE-AGENT JOURNEY

- Where do you need to operate as a Catalyst to be both an *inspiration* and an *irritant* within your organization or venture?
- How can you communicate a dream through word and deed and invite a small core group to come and dream with you?

We rewrite and reform the contours of tomorrow by unlocking our imagination today.

PHASE TWO
DISCOVER

/ dɪˈskʌv.ɚ /

"the act of finding something that had not been known before"

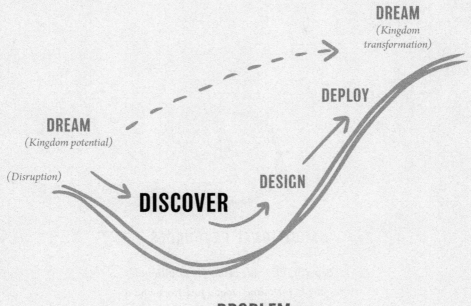

DREAM
*(Kingdom
transformation)*

DEPLOY

DREAM
(Kingdom potential)

(Disruption)

DESIGN

DISCOVER

PROBLEM
___

Instead of being courageous and embracing new frontiers,
the Western church does not like to fail, shies away from
vulnerability and uncertainty, and rejects risk.

We tend to rely on existing systems, tried-and-tested models,
and the technical solutions of experts rather than being open to
exploring new frontiers, considering possibilities, and initiating
active learning.

PROCESS
___

Move from conceptual theory to experiential learning.

PRIZE
___

Grow in clarity and conviction of God's leading as we gather
insight and unearth principles through experiential learning.

ADDITIONAL RESOURCES

Scan the QR code below for additional resources, including videos, practices, and a toolkit to accompany the Discover phase.

allchangejourney.com/resources

BUT BECAUSE YOU SAY SO

CREATED TO DISCOVER

*A church which pitches its tents without constantly looking out for
new horizons, which does not continually strike camp, is being untrue
to its calling. ... [We must] play down our longing for certainty,
accept what is risky, live by improvisation and experiment.*
HANS KÜNG

Creativity is allowing yourself to make mistakes. Art is knowing which ones to keep.
SCOTT ADAMS

*A great deal more failure is the result of an excess of caution than of
bold experimentation with new ideas. The frontiers of the kingdom
of God were never advanced by men and women of caution.*
J. OSWALD SANDERS

Imagine a world without fire, paper, the wheel, or the compass; a world without
planes, trains, and automobiles; or a world without surfing the internet, "click
and collect," texting, or video calls. What we now take for granted started life as
an idea, an experiment, or a possibility. Someone, somewhere, at some point,
thought creatively and tried something new that no one else had tried before.

Likely it failed the first time, and many other times, until, through many generations and iterations, it eventually became something we deem essential.

CURIOSITY KILLED THE CAT

Astrophysicist Mario Livio says, "Only humans are worried and curious about reasons and causes for things. Only humans really ask the question, 'Why?'"[1] This unique ability is one of the primary drivers that lead humans to make new discoveries. To discover is to find something that has not been known before. By its very nature, discovery requires us to go beyond our comfort zone and chart new territory. In the Dream phase, we unearthed a problem to solve or a prize to pursue. In the Discover phase, we gather data about the prize or the problem through dynamic experimentation. The exploratory activity of the Discover phase helps us to understand underlying threads and themes, opening ourselves up to possibility and potential. Our curiosity pushes us beyond our current limits and forces us to explore beyond the boundaries. Curiosity will often lead to discovery. And discovery is an essential component of change—because without its stimulus, the status quo will remain.

THE CURSE OF KNOWLEDGE

Maybe you consider yourself an expert in a particular field—sport, IT, astrophysics … or TV crime dramas. As an authority on that topic, it can be irritating if a newcomer tries to give their opinion on something they seemingly know nothing about. In his book *Think Again*, Adam Grant talks about the "curse of knowledge"—a problem we experience when we are entrenched in our own expertise: "The curse of knowledge is that it closes our minds to what we don't know. Good judgment depends on having the skill—and the will—to open our minds."[2] This is critical in the Discover phase. If we think we know everything, there's no stimulus to discover anything new. Knowledge puffs up (1 Cor. 8:1), and if we're not careful we can become those Jesus challenges for having a

1   Adam Wernick and Christie Taylor, "Why are humans so curious?" *The World*, August 27, 2017, https://www.pri.org/stories/2017-08-27/why-are-humans-so-curious.
2   Adam Grant, *Think Again: The Power of Knowing What You Don't Know* (London, UK: WH Allen, 2021), 31.

closed mind and hard heart (Mark 3:1–6) rather than having an open mind and soft heart. We need to choose to become active learners again.

In Luke 5, we see Simon Peter overcoming his curse of knowledge. The disciples had been fishing all night without catching a thing. They weren't novice fishermen who'd found a new hobby; they were professionals who'd likely been fishing since they were children. So, when Jesus, a carpenter's son, told them to push out into deep water and let down their nets for a catch, their response may not have been quite as accommodating as the text implies. Perhaps there was an eye roll … a look of incredulity … a whisper of "*Seriously?*"

But Simon Peter was open to discovering something new. He hadn't closed off his heart or mind. He recognized he didn't know everything. And he also had an inkling that maybe, just maybe, Jesus might be who he said he was. And so Simon Peter says, "Master, we've worked hard all night and haven't caught anything. *But because you say so,* I will let down the nets" (Luke 5:5, emphasis mine). These five words make a world of difference and give language to what it means to be a disciple: But because *you say so* … I will trust you beyond what seems logical or reasonable, beyond my experience and training. But because *you say so* … I will trust more than my eyes can see. Simon Peter is effectively saying, "Yes, Jesus; I will join you on a journey of discovery beyond what I already know, toward what you are revealing."

In the Gospels, it seems there are two broad categories of people: the humble, who are open to Jesus; and the proud, who aren't. Some come to Jesus with humility, recognizing they are dependent on him; and only through him are they able to see and discover new things. The French novelist and critic Marcel Proust said, "The real voyage of discovery consists not in seeking new landscapes, but in having new eyes."[3] The humble have soft hearts and open minds, looking at things with "new eyes." They haven't arrived at a foregone conclusion on every matter. The demoniac (Luke 8:26–39), the leper (Matt. 8:1–14), those who cut a hole in the roof to get their friend to Jesus (Mark 2:3–11)—none of these would have appeared on a "Who's Who" list of cultural influencers or dynamic leaders, but all of them came to Jesus knowing that just one word from him could change everything. Their desperation and childlike

---

3   Marcel Proust, *La Prisonnière* (Paris: Le Livre de poche, 1923).

faith brought humility and openness. They chose to trust God, and they chose to say, "But because you say so," with both their words and their lives.

And they're held in stark contrast with those too proud to accept that they needed Jesus' help—the religious elite. The scribes and Pharisees were the experts in their field, cursed by their knowledge. So much so that they couldn't see the forest of grace for the trees of law. They were too busy nit-picking on the details to discover anything new. They couldn't engage with the repentance Jesus called them to because it required a change in mindset. And their minds were most certainly set. They were too proud to say to Jesus, "But because you say so." They stood in front of Jesus with an attitude of *because **I know so**.* They were the center of the story, and their minds were closed. They were too proud to move from the shallow waters of law and try fishing in the deeper waters of grace.

In the Discover phase we must admit we don't know everything. We must open ourselves and those we lead to new possibilities. We have to be prepared to accept that we don't always know best, and we can't always see the whole picture. It takes humility, faith, and courage to say, "But because you say so."

A UK church leader and friend recently described to me some of the personal challenges he faced during the COVID-19 pandemic when he battled with leading a church alongside dealing with his mental health struggles. He described it as being catapulted into the valley, where he was no longer able to rely on his own strengths and understanding. He aptly put it that when we're in the valley we realize it's no longer about us "holding it together." We learn to depend on God and let go of our need to achieve in our own strength. Without the painful unlearning that is required in this phase, we're unable to harness the benefits of the learning God is opening up to us; and without the humbling experience of the valley, we link any future success to ourselves and our own strength. Unless our hearts admit that we don't know it all and can't do it all, we'll never receive the full extent of God's grace, nor will we experience the fullness of kingdom fruitfulness: the huge catch of fish.

We can sometimes miss the way God is choosing to engage with us; or we can reject it because it doesn't fit our experience or worldview. In the Gospels, Jesus often quietly draws near, without fanfare or grand entrance, and interjects a simple statement, question, or a single word. God even speaks through silence. Pete Greig, founder of 24-7 Prayer, says, "The Bible is a book about a

God who speaks! But it does not portray Him as one who speaks incessantly to His people …. Instead, we often endure Holy Saturdays in which God's word is muted and His presence is veiled."[4] In the Discover phase, we can be so tired, overwhelmed, and frustrated we can't hear anything; or we can disregard the Rabbi's fishing advice because we think we've got the skill, strength, and capacity to do it ourselves. Jesus' words are drowned out by our intellect, expertise, baggage, or opinion.

SOFT EYES AND OPEN EARS

When stargazing, scientists recommend looking just to the side of a star so that it becomes clear in your peripheral vision. If you don't look straight at it, you will see it more clearly.[5] The Discover phase works similarly. As Detective Bunk on *The Wire* says, it's about having "soft eyes."[6] "Hard eyes" see nothing but the object of their focus, but having "soft eyes" enable us to see something as a cohesive whole rather than looking at fragmented parts or jumping to conclusions.

Our physical bodies are designed to both look and listen, and our spiritual beings are the same. While on earth, Jesus called people to truly see in the physical and to perceive in the spiritual: "Do you still not see or understand? Are your hearts hardened? Do you have eyes but fail to see, and ears but fail to hear? (Mark 8: 17–18). His parables were a way to force his hearers to discover truth for themselves—to truly see. In his book *Rewilding the Church,* Steve Aisthorpe makes these observations about Matthew's Gospel:

> Jesus did not tell us, as many translations suggest, just to *look* at the birds and *consider* the lilies. The words he used literally mean "fix your eyes on these things" or "take a really good look". Commenting on these passages in

---

4   Pete Greig, *God on Mute: Engaging the Silence of Unanswered Prayer* (Eastbourne, UK: David C. Cook, 2007), 240.

5   Martin Moberly, "Averted vision: how to get a better view of night-sky objects," *BBC Sky at Night Magazine,* January 29, 2021, https://www.skyatnightmagazine.com/advice/how-to-master-the-art-of-averted-vision.

6   The term "soft eyes" was popularized from a line in the American crime drama series, *The Wire.* Detective Bunk tells Detective Gregg that it's "soft eyes" that are required for a crime scene. *The Wire,* season 4, episode 4, "Refugees," directed by Jim McKay, October 1, 2006, on HBO, https://www.hbo.com/the-wire.

Matthew's Gospel, Bible scholar and keen ornithologist the late John Stott writes "... he meant more than that we should notice them ... the Bible tells us that the birds have *lessons to teach us*".[7]

We need to have soft eyes *and* open ears to perceive where God is at work. As Christians, we are sheep that hear the Shepherd's voice (John 10:27), and so we can not only look for where God is at work but can also hear his direction and revelation through Scripture, prophecy, and the body of Christ.

As we lean into the Discover phase and see the kingdom opportunities before us with soft eyes and open ears, we need to entertain anomalies and curiosities, search for patterns, explore possibilities, and seek to find a sense of meaning or resonance within the mass of information and interactions. As design consultant Marty Neumeier says in *The 46 Rules of Genius,*

> Sift through threats for hidden possibilities. Every threat carries with it the potential for innovation. The problem of obesity contains the possibility of new kinds of nutrition. The problem of global pollution contains the possibility of new energy sources. The problem of high unemployment contains the possibility of new educational models. The list is endless, if you can learn to see what's not there.[8]

We must be okay with not knowing or seeing everything straight away. This can be both releasing—bringing a sense of lightness or joy in the exploration—and anxiety-inducing, as it creates uncertainty and vulnerability.

The Discover phase is also about more than just observation; it requires activation, experimentation, and documentation. Whether you are starting a new church or faith-driven venture or sparking change in an existing organization, this phase is about testing hypotheses, connecting the dots, and seeing the themes through actively gathering information. Multiple, small discoveries cohere and lead to an "aha" moment when everything suddenly makes sense. It's like the many broken pieces of a mosaic suddenly coming together to create the bigger picture.

---

7   Steve Aisthorpe, *Rewilding the Church* (Edinburgh, UK: Saint Andrew Press, 2020), 13, emphasis mine.

8   Marty Neumeier, *The 46 Rules of Genius: An Innovator's Guide to Creativity* (Indianapolis, IN: New Riders, 2014), 21.

Like a TV detective drama—where the pinboard in the situation room is covered in lists, photos, maps, theories, and mugshots—there's a lot of information to be analyzed and explored. The detectives working on the case are searching, musing, and looking for the hidden connections. They are not just seeing the data; they are seeking to perceive the patterns.

COMPETING FORCES

We need to understand that the Discover phase is both exhilarating and exhausting for ourselves and our core group. This phase often requires us to dismantle or let go of the previous methods that have brought us the leadership success and position we currently hold. We will need to experiment and fail multiple times in our learning process. Even the most secure and confident pioneers can be shaken by the attrition of this phase. To navigate it effectively, we must confront this vulnerability head-on and acknowledge its challenges. We need to stand on the Rock and allow God to give us his peace, knowing that even if all around is uncertain on our journey of discovery, we have a sure footing. In the midst of change, God remains the unchanging God. As the late pastor and theologian Timothy Keller said,

> If you have ever been on a coast in a storm and seen the waves come in and hit the rocks, sometimes the waves are so large that they cover a particular rock, and you think, "That is the end of that rock." But when the waves recede, there it is still. It hasn't budged an inch. A person who feels the "peace that passes understanding" is like that. No matter what is thrown at you, you know it will not make you lose your footing.[9]

If we find our security in being clever and competent, we will struggle in the Discover phase. As we step out of our areas of expertise and embrace new learning, we must remind ourselves of our primary identity as disciples, so that no matter what waves crash against us, we can stand in peace. Pursuing kingdom discovery can create a sense of fear of rejection or fear of lack—we'd prefer to hold onto our sense of competence and security rather than move into territory

---

[9] Timothy Keller, *Walking with God through Pain and Suffering* (London, UK: Hodder & Stoughton, 2013), Kindle edition, Kindle location 4723 of 5811.

that exposes our inability. Virginia Rometty, who became the first woman to head up IBM and appears on many of the "most influential people in business" lists, once said: "I learned to always take on things I'd never done before. Growth and comfort do not coexist."[10]

As we step out of our comfort and competencies, we undertake a process of moving from unconscious competence to conscious incompetence. When you pick up a pen with your natural writing hand, you don't even really think about what you're doing—that's unconscious competence. But when asked to write with your other hand, things suddenly feel awkward. You might struggle to even pick up the pen, let alone form letters coherently on a page. This is conscious incompetence, and it's the experience we often have when we lean into the Discover phase.

I often hear leaders express excitement, waxing poetic about the change they want to bring about—but many of these comments prove fleeting and progress is minimal. Potential never changed the world. Catalyzing change involves hard work, failure, and setbacks. Venturing into unchartered territory means people will misunderstand us, refuse to engage or value our efforts, and accuse us of being on the wrong course. As Michelle Kao Nakphong, a contributor to *Voices Rising*, notes,

> Implicit in every attempt at success is the possibility of failure. Without the potential of failure, success is meaningless. Would attaining an educational degree be as significant if it did not take focused effort to pass tests, gain competencies, and earn grades? Would you be ecstatic if you already knew that the person you asked on a date would certainly say yes? This possibility for failure, rejection, and disappointment makes every endeavor suspenseful and risky.[11]

Our internal, God-given drive for change needs to be greater than our need for affirmation, comfort, or control. Until the force for change outweighs these, change will only exist as a pipe dream.

---

[10] Tony Woodall, "QoD-039: Virginia Rometty—I learned to always take on things I'd never done before," Goal Getting Podcast, August 8, 2015, https://www.goalgettingpodcast.com/qod-039-virginia-rometty-i-learned-to-always-take-on-things-id-never-done-before/.

[11] Shabrae Jackson Krieg and Janet Balasiri Singleterry (eds), *Voices Rising: Women of Color Finding & Restoring Hope in the City* (Pomona, CA: Servant Partners Press, 2018), 391.

THE CURSE OF COMFORT

Throughout the Bible, we see individuals called by God to step into the unknown in order to discover something new and receive something greater. We see the courage of Abraham, called by God to, "Go from your country, your people and your father's household to the land I will show you" (Gen. 12:1). God promised blessing, but to step into that blessing and discover what was ahead, Abraham had to trust God and leave behind what he knew. No doubt Abraham was fearful of facing a new culture; no doubt his heart was filled with sadness at leaving behind his father's family; and no doubt he was apprehensive about leaving the place of security for the unknown. To move forward into discovery always involves leaving something behind. But the promise of what Abraham was moving toward was far greater:

> "I will make you into a great nation,
>   and I will bless you;
> I will make your name great,
>   and you will be a blessing.
>
> I will bless those who bless you,
>   and whoever curses you I will curse;
> and all peoples on earth
>   will be blessed through you."
>
> GENESIS 12: 2–3

Abraham's move was for God, for good, and for others. The promise (dream) given was worth the pain of change. Abraham, "trusted what God said more than what his eyes could see,"[12] and took the steps to discover what God had in store for him.

On our change journey, it's easy to hope for a shortcut to take us to our destination or opt to stay in the perceived safety of what is known. But if we are seeking to unlock the power of movemental Christianity, rather than one-generational ministry activity, we will need to prepare for the long haul. In the Discover phase, we embark on a journey that is greater than our own

---

[12] Sally Lloyd-Jones, *The Jesus Storybook Bible: Every Story Whispers His Name* (Grand Rapids, MI: Zonderkidz, 2012), 69.

imagination and initiative. Humanly, we want to avoid the valley, but the valley is exactly where discovery is made. Just think of the challenges of Moses, Deborah, Esther, Daniel, Mary, and Paul … to name but a few. Change comes as we go "down and through" the valley. It's only when we embrace the difficult path of unlearning and relearning that we can be awakened to something new and better.

When we treat the process of change simply as a journey with a positive trajectory, we fail to fully discover what God is calling us to pursue. Great discoveries have been made and courageous stories are lived when people experiment and step outside of their familiar and previously held understanding and experience. The Discover phase is about intentionally stepping into the valley, exploring unchartered places, and allowing our minds to go beyond our existing frame of reference. As leaders, we tend to look for a cast-iron guarantee of success or a clear road map before we step out; but instead of a management handbook helping us to maintain existing systems and techniques, we need a compass, the desire to explore new frontiers, and to trust in God as we push out into the unknown.

Hebrews 12:2 says, "For the joy set before him [Jesus] endured the cross." He kept his eyes focused on what would be won on the other side of victory. What's the joy set before you (dream), that will push you to discover, to leave your place of comfort, and not settle until you've found the kingdom break-through God is calling you to pursue?

What you dreamed about in the first phase is what you are about to begin exploring, but only if you are willing to say, "But because you say so."

FACTORY OR FIELD?

LEARNING TO DISCOVER

Questions, more than answers, are the pathway to collective wisdom.
DANIEL CHRISTIAN WHAL

Creativity is the discipline you use when you don't know the answers,
when you're traveling to parts unknown. On this type of journey, missteps
are actually steps. Every mistake brings you closer to the solution.
MARTY NEUMEIER

Experimenters delight in how fast they can take a concept from words,
to sketch, to model, and yes, to a less than polished prototype.
TOM KELLEY

The Industrial Revolution of the eighteenth and nineteenth centuries continues to affect twenty-first-century leadership. Over the last two hundred years, rapid changes in industry, business, and technology have conditioned us to approach life with a linear mindset. We tend to view our churches, ministries, and organizations like an industrial production line—if there's a problem, we only need to understand which part of the process to fix, and, once addressed, the whole production line will continue to run smoothly. In his book *A Non-Anxious Presence*, church leader and cultural commentator Mark Sayers uses the

COVID-19 pandemic as an example of a disruptive event that challenged our ingrained linear and industrial mindset:

> We are engaged in linear projects and see change as an event that may interrupt our progress but ultimately can be managed. This is how many people approached the pandemic—initially interpreting it as an "event," a temporary interruption that may pause our linear projects for a period, but then life would return to normal as it was before. However, the pandemic was a complex event occurring within a complex world.[1]

In a factory production line, there may be lots of stages to the process, with complicated procedures and knowledge required. However, it is ultimately a linear process that can be understood, adapted, and tweaked accordingly. If a single part breaks, that one part is fixed, and the production line works again. The default setting in this world is a "technical solution."

Even in our churches and ministries, if we can "plug in" a new program, create a pipeline for the production of leaders, or find an expert to tell us the right technique or answer, then the problem is fixed, and the "factory" continues to function. However, as we explored in chapter one, the reality is we live in a disrupted world, and this inevitably affects kingdom ministries. The interconnected nature of our social, spiritual, economic, and ecological systems means we can't approach life's problems looking for a simplistic solution. Instead, we need an "adaptive response." We need to delve into the discovery of our complex world, being curious and operating with soft eyes and open ears to see and hear where God is on the move.

AGRICULTURAL NOT INDUSTRIAL

Jesus didn't approach his mission with an industrial mindset, looking for a technical solution. His storytelling and agrarian-based culture continually point us back to the natural way God has designed us to live and work. Jesus' mindset was adaptive; the parables he told drew his followers into a narrative of experiential learning, encouraged questioning, and led them to embed the learning for

---

[1] Mark Sayers, *A Non-Anxious Presence: How a Changing and Complex World will Create a Remnant of Renewed Christian Leaders* (Chicago, IL: Moody Publishers, 2022), 131.

themselves—as they encountered this new kingdom amid their everyday lives. There is a messiness in the agrarian reality that is different from the precision of the industrial approach. When Jesus told the parable of the sower (Matt. 13:1–24), he wasn't speaking to those who bought food at the supermarket or ate in restaurants, consuming products grown thousands of miles away. He was speaking to those who knew the toil of sowing seeds and who understood the frailty of the crops that were dependent upon good soil, favorable meteorological conditions, and protection from predators. Only 25 percent of the soil produced anything in the long term. Imagine a production line that wasted 75 percent of its input. Our post-industrial, efficiency mindset cannot fathom that failure rate. But the natural world and its multiplex of integrated ecosystems is a truer picture of the environment God has invited us to live within than an industrial manufacturing line. The Discover phase is far more like a gardener scattering seeds looking for good soil than an engineer working on machines looking to produce the same product every time.

There are endless books on factory-like leadership with code, system, and process, breaking the world down into rules, frames, and lists as manageable, linear chunks. But if you consider leadership, family, parenting, relationships, teams, ministry, or business—none of them are solely defined by a factory-like linear process with a fixed set of rules, production-line rhythms, and intended outcomes. All these realities are far more agrarian because they are variable, uncertain, unpredictable, multi-faceted, and interconnected—more like a garden than a factory. We need to stop treating discovery as a simple game of "find the solution" and start facing the complexities of the landscape we're navigating.

As I sit here writing, I have my smartphone next to me. When I get distracted, I can open it, go to my Amazon app, purchase something digitally, and it can be on my doorstep by the end of the day. We must be aware of how much this consumer reality shapes our leadership paradigm. We want to microwave leadership formation or growth—expecting a 1+1 system that offers shortcuts and speed and results that are instantaneous. The late Eugene Peterson regularly challenged the church for our quick-fix, sugar-rush approach to spirituality. In *A Long Obedience in the Same Direction*, he notes that the culture of our world has led Christians to now believe that "anything worthwhile can be acquired at once." He goes on to say that,

> We assume that if something can be done at all, it can be done quickly and
> efficiently. Our attention spans have been conditioned by thirty-second
> commercials. Our sense of reality has been flattened by thirty-page abridg-
> ments. ... There is a great market for religious experience in our world; there
> is little enthusiasm for the patient acquisition of virtue, little inclination to
> sign up for a long apprenticeship in what earlier generations of Christians
> called holiness.[2]

We must resist the pervasive culture of our world. Rather than acting like
a religious factory foreman who oversees the production line, we need to
embrace the mentality of a spiritual farmer, who sows the seed, waits, tends,
and over time reaps a harvest. Kingdom transformation takes time, patience,
and commitment—and is always messy!

In terrain that is stable, certain, and known, efficiency and management will
triumph. But in terrain that is unstable, uncertain, and unknown, we are forced
into the realm of adaptive challenges and adaptive responses. These challenges,
scenarios, and problems we face need a spiritual and strategic response. They
carry with them both a threat and an opportunity.

Here's a checklist to help you consider whether you're in an "adaptive
challenge" moment:

- There are no known solutions.
- There are many possibilities and parts.
- Numerous people/stakeholders are involved.
- It's necessary to learn in new ways or areas.
- Existing mechanisms and thinking need to be refined and improved.
- Experiential learning is required.
- Iterative processes and progress must be embraced.

If you checked "yes" to many or all the items on this list, then you are facing an
adaptive challenge. This means it is vital that you don't approach the challenge
and the Discover phase with a linear mindset that reaches for a technical

---

2   Eugene H. Peterson, *A Long Obedience in the Same Direction: Discipleship in an Instant Society* (Downers
Grove, IL: InterVarsity Press, 2000), 16.

solution (e.g., "Let's just implement a new discipleship curriculum to 'fix' our small groups!"). Whereas managers will tweak an existing system, leaders will embrace discovery and seek adaptive responses. In the Discover phase, it's important to be open to testing and learning rather than seeking to find a formula, because it allows us to gather data, test hypotheses, and unearth core principles. These will help us to move toward our dream by creating frameworks in the Design phase that will enable our leaders to navigate multiple terrains or scenarios. We need to be willing to give things a go and just make a start. As David Ehrlichman says in *Impact Networks*, "Starting in exactly the right place is not as important as just starting—experimenting, learning, and adapting as you move forward with new partners. Then, when promising experiments catch on, you can help them to scale."[3]

THE KEY TO DISCOVERY

The most strategic way to initiate the Discover phase is to prototype in a few places with your small core group. This strategy applies whether you are starting a new venture or sparking change within an existing organization. A prototype is defined as, "a first or preliminary version of a device or vehicle from which other forms are developed."[4] The aim of the prototype is to test a hypothesis related to our dream. "A hypothesis is an assumption, an idea that is proposed for the sake of argument so that it can be tested to see if it might be true. … A hypothesis is usually tentative; it's an assumption or suggestion made strictly for the objective of being tested."[5] For example, if our dream is to spark a disciple-making movement that impacts our neighborhoods, our hypotheses might be that 1) we need to mobilize more people; 2) we need to equip those people to take their discipleship more seriously; and 3) mission is the most effective environment for fruitful disciple making. Prototyping to test these hypotheses might look like training a group of leaders in Jesus' methods for disciple making or attempting a new ministry or outreach

---

[3]   David Ehrlichman, *Impact Networks: Create Connection, Spark Collaboration, and Catalyze Systemic Change* (Oakland, California: Berrett-Koehler Publishers, 2021), 67–68.

[4]   See *Oxford English Dictionary*, s.v. "prototype," accessed November 8, 2023, https://columbiacollege-ca. libguides.com/chicago/encyclopedias.

[5]   Merriam-Webster Dictionary, s.v. "hypothesis," accessed February 14, 2024, https://www.merriam-webster.com/dictionary/hypothesis.

activity to engage a new people group in one place. Instead of the whole organization being mobilized, you can experiment with a smaller number in a more measured way. These prototypes allow us to test our hypotheses, which will ultimately help us to refine and realize our stated dream. This requires accepting some risk, experimentation, and change in a small area, with the aim of gathering data and learning around our hypotheses to benefit the whole organization later in the process. Think about prototyping not as developing a product but instead as embracing a discovery process. We're not looking for the final solution or a short-term fix; instead, we're seeking to try something that will enable us to learn in order to influence the organization in the longer term or discern a clear way forward for our new initiative.

If we are closed in this phase or seek a simplistic formula or answer, we can be lulled into a specific, one-size-fits-all solution that works in some contexts but not across the whole organization. Imagine, as part of your Discover phase, you've tried and tested new discipleship principles and practices in a few of your small groups, missional communities, or microchurches. Some have flown and grown, and others have stumbled and faltered. Through your prototyping you may have discovered different ways to pray and build community; you may have tried new missional outreach activities; perhaps you've tested different times of the week to gather or a different physical space in which to meet; or it may be you've tried different formation content. Through this prototyping process, some key principles have been revealed. For example, one principle might be the recognition that if the leadership doesn't embody key principles, then the community doesn't follow. Another principle unearthed might be the need for concrete practices—without this, the missional expressions are too conceptual, and people don't live them out in their everyday lives. Or it may be that you learned the importance of having a shared language with key terms and words clearly defined.

The Christian entrepreneurs I work with in Creo are often prototyping around their value proposition, gathering data for the market they are seeking to break into or how they can have the most effective social impact. And the network leaders who are part of Movement Leaders Collective might be prototyping around collaborative environments, compelling messages, pioneering projects, or the most effective training process for their leaders.

We only fully realize what our core principles are and what core practices we need when we prototype and experiment in a real-life context rather than theorizing or remaining instinctive and intuitive.

In the Discover phase, we will unlearn and relearn in areas that are familiar to us—such as discipleship, leadership, community, mission, church, or theology—as well as learn in areas that are unfamiliar. We rediscover what has been lost and forgotten as well as discover new insights or learning. Prototyping, by definition, is not about maintaining the status quo or extending existing conventions. It's trying, testing, and experimenting in something new. In his book *Originals*, Adam Grants talks about conformity and originality. "Conformity means following the crowd down conventional paths and maintaining the status quo. Originality is taking the road less traveled, championing a set of novel ideas that go against the grain but ultimately make things better."[6] He goes on to say that,

> Originality starts with creativity: generating a concept that is both novel and useful. But it doesn't stop there. Originals are people who take initiative and make their visions a reality. ... The starting point is curiosity: pondering why the default exists in the first place. ... We face something familiar, but we see it with fresh perspective that enables us to gain new insights into old problems.[7]

In the Discover phase we have to unlock curiosity and creativity in ourselves and others. The mistake most organizations make is responding to problems or prizes with temporary solutions based on conventional paths, but after the program has been run or the training is over, the organization snaps back to its prevailing paradigm and embedded culture. This leads to a lurching back and forward with numerous short-term projects or program initiatives rather than embarking on a longer-term, deeper process of change.

EXPERIENTIAL LEARNING

Much like Jesus' parable of the sower, prototyping in the Discover phase can feel like we're scattering a lot of seed without the guarantee of a profitable return. But only by experimenting generously can we receive the wealth of information

---

[6] Grant, *Originals*, 3.
[7] Grant, *Originals*, 3, 7.

we need for the next part of the journey. Interestingly, the principles under-girding Jesus' parable are now commonly accepted in management theory. Management consultant Joseph M. Juran developed the Pareto Principle—also known as the 80/20 rule—named after Italian sociologist and economist Vilfredo Pareto. Juran proposed that 80 percent of consequence, effect, or output, is caused by only 20 percent of input.[8] I'm sure many of us can attest to this when we see that the majority of what happens in our organizations or ventures is initiated and delivered by the minority, and a few key projects and efforts define most of our organization's activity. Though we might sometimes despair at this reality, in the Discover phase we need to feel encouraged by it. As we scatter seed widely through our prototypes, even if only a small minority of ideas and initiatives give a return, these results allow us to identify the few key leverage areas that will affect the whole endeavor significantly. We're looking for the good soil. As you think about developing prototypes, it's important to consider numerous areas that will help you and your team gain insight into what is already happening, both inside and outside your organization or venture, and where God is at work.

We must embrace the mess and uncertainty of this process through personal, firsthand experience. We need to be actively involved in order to glean the information around us and unearth the core beliefs that are within us so that we become part of the story. Too many leaders will hypothesize from behind a desk or conceptualize on a whiteboard, rather than stepping out and learning in their own context. We unlock vital learning by embracing risk, looking with soft eyes, and listening with open ears. We need to be *experiencing* something ourselves as a leader so we can generate and gain feedback as a learner rather than pontificating or projecting as an expert.

Jesus encouraged his disciples to discover through experience rather than through studying concepts separated from the action. Whether you are an organizational leader, Christian entrepreneur, or church leader, consider the following pattern of Jesus' ministry in the Gospel of Luke, in which he initiates a process that helps his disciples to learn for themselves.

Modeling and Explaining. First, Jesus models his kingdom through visual

---

[8]   See "Pareto Principle (80/20 Rule) & Pareto Analysis Guide," *Juran*, March 12, 2019, https://www.juran.com/blog/a-guide-to-the-pareto-principle-80-20-rule-pareto-analysis/.

demonstration, healing a man with leprosy, forgiving and healing a paralyzed man, and calling Levi and eating with sinners (Luke 5:12–29). He then communicates through verbal explanation, talking about love for enemies, judging others, a tree and its fruit, and the wise and foolish builders (Luke 6:27–49). The disciples listen, observe, and interact with Jesus' example up close. Jesus utilized the rabbinic approach in which disciples spent concentrated periods of time with their teacher, enabling immersion as well as instruction. Through proximity and relationship with Jesus, they are apprenticed and begin to actively discover the vision for themselves.

Imitating and Embodying. Next, the disciples imitate Jesus—having a go themselves and learning on the job—and begin to embody what they have seen him living and speaking out. When Jesus sends out the Twelve (Luke 9), they begin to do what they have seen Jesus do, and they embrace discovery by seeking out the "people of peace" (Luke 10:5–9). The disciples experience provision for themselves during the feeding of the five thousand, as Jesus pushes them with, "You give them something to eat" (Luke 9:13). They hustle to find the one person who brought their lunch, and then partake in the miracle by handing out the multiplying loaves and fishes.

Reflecting and Questioning. Then the disciples reflect with Jesus and question areas of their learning with him, gaining a deeper understanding of what has happened and its significance. After Jesus sends out the Seventy-two with the same frame and commission as the Twelve, they return with joy (and learning!), as they've discovered for themselves what it's like to operate in the authority given to them (Luke 10). Finally, Jesus privately reflects with his disciples on the discoveries they have made: "Blessed are the eyes that see what you see" (Luke 10:23) as he signifies that their hands-on experience has taken them beyond lofty concepts or theories into personal testimony. They later ask Jesus how to pray (Luke 11:1), but he doesn't give them a lecture on the philosophy of prayer. Instead, he prays a simple prayer (vv. 2–4) and encourages them to actively and regularly do the same (vv. 5–13).

It is only as the disciples discover and experience the kingdom firsthand that they realize what they don't know. It's therefore no surprise that it's only *after* the disciples have been sent out on mission that they suddenly begin to understand the importance of prayer and ask Jesus to teach them how to pray. This revelation would likely never have come if they hadn't gone on the journey of discovery. Similarly, it was only when they were faced with a hungry crowd that they began to discover their need for and the reality of God's provision.

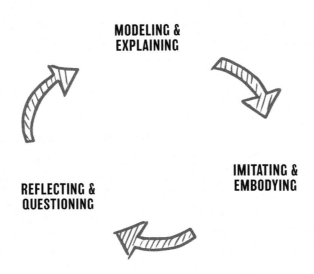

MODELING &
EXPLAINING

IMITATING &
EMBODYING

REFLECTING &
QUESTIONING

The process that Jesus took his disciples through is the very same process you can use with your initial core group of leaders as you embark together on the Discover phase. Learning in this phase doesn't happen in familiar, safe, or sanitized environments; it happens when we are taken out of our comfort zones and move into new terrain. Jesus took the disciples into areas that would have felt complex and demanding. The disciples' assumptions were challenged, and their lives were disrupted at every level. This meant they were far more open to learn from Jesus instead of relying on their own experiences, personal information, or instincts. As Joseph Henrich asserts in *The Weirdest People in the World*, "When problems are difficult, situations are ambiguous, or individual learning is costly, people should rely more heavily on learning from others."[9]

As leaders today, we need to walk in the footsteps of Jesus, making space

---

9   Joseph Henrich, *The Weirdest People in the World: How the West Became Psychologically Peculiar and Particularly Prosperous* (Dublin, Ireland: Penguin Random House, 2020), 64.

for ourselves and our teams to discover together. To position us well in the Discover phase, we need to posture ourselves as learners rather than experts, capturing what we are learning and making room for these experiences to be shared as we reflect together.

ON THE FIELD OR IN THE STANDS

To release a culture of discovery and experiential learning in your core group, it's essential to allow individuals to experience hands-on learning. We often pass on information to others via a sanitized classroom environment—it might be someone's living room, a boardroom, a Zoom call, or even a coffee shop, but it's essentially a classroom. We "teach" concepts and information "at" people. Instead, we need to allow our core group to experience something so they can realize what they don't know, ask questions, participate, and make their own active discoveries.

A dynamic, virtuous cycle forms when we allow people to get on the field and play rather than sit in the stands and listen. Participation creates progress, which brings greater motivation. In his book *Essentialism*, Greg McKeown says, "Research has shown that of all forms of human motivation, the most effective one is progress. Why? Because a small, concrete win creates momentum and affirms our faith in our further success."[10]

In the early 2000s, I worked on staff for a church where I was responsible for the missional communities. During that time, I started to work one day a week away from the church office. Every Wednesday, I set myself up in a coffee shop in my local community. Over time I built up a rapport with the staff as they all worked the same shift pattern, so we had our weekly connection point. There were also regular customers with whom I interacted. Over the next few months, I became the unofficial-but-very-much-encouraged chaplain to this little coffee shop—talking to the regulars and staff about faith, life, pain, hopes, and dreams. I didn't start with this as a master plan, but these relationships emerged through our week-in, week-out engagement. Through that simple act of being out of the office and present in the coffee shop, I was changed, informed, and shaped as a disciple and a leader; and it also helped

---

[10] Greg McKeown, *Essentialism: The Disciplined Pursuit of Less* (London, UK: Virgin Books, 2014), 196.

me to discover new possibilities in mission and evangelism. I had numerous opportunities to build relationships, serve non-Christians, and pray for people. Eventually, this was the coffee shop that allowed our missional community to use their space free of charge to run an Alpha course for our local neighborhood. My firsthand experience of discovery in the coffee shop informed my thinking around missional communities across our entire church and gave me insight that helped me to coach other leaders as part of my role overseeing this ministry. This didn't happen overnight; it was a culmination of many months, conversations, and interactions, and it was born out of the lived experience I gained. It might have sounded like a great idea if I'd merely thought about it intellectually, but it was only when I went and spent time with people that I learned what was really needed and how I could serve and connect in that space.

Similarly, I know of one church in Norway that locked their offices one afternoon a week and sent all their staff into the city center to pray for people, demonstrate acts of kindness, and explore how they could serve the community more effectively. Another church in the UK has created an indoor jungle gym at the back of their large sanctuary to serve the neighborhood because, as they interacted with local people, they heard families were struggling to find safe, affordable, and enjoyable spaces to go with their children. A US church I coach has invested in a coffee shop offering free coffee for local residents so they can use it as an accessible workspace. These were all solutions to problems that could only be discovered by spending time with people in the community, and they all started from simple prototypes of giving something a go, iterating, and experimenting.

It is only when communities are listened to and engaged with, and when we are "on the ground" that real-life experience and interaction shape the process of discovery. Too often we assume we know the answers for what people need. We start at a distance with our assumptions and solutions, rather than humbly engaging and asking questions of others. We need to start with connections and conversations where we ask questions and allow those we lead to experience discoveries for themselves. If you simply supply information—functioning as the "expert" and attempting to fix everything for them—or provide a to-do list, they will forget because there is no struggle or ownership; but if they discover something for themselves, it will stay with them.

If you offer answers or control the direction of discovery, you will end up with "my answers" in response to "the problems I see" rather than collating diversely informed answers to the actual complex problem you're seeking to address. Set parameters, give direction, provide encouragement and reflective insight, but allow the prototyping process to unfold for itself. You don't want a team that is disempowered or dependent, but you also don't want a disillusioned team.

LEARNING FROM OUR MISTAKES

Years ago, Anna and I lived and ministered in an under-resourced community, with a dream to see the gospel impact those around us. As part of our Discover phase, we prototyped various ministry activities which included a weekly community cleanup. We went door-to-door and offered to clean our neighbors' yards and take away their trash. We painted fences, moved fridges, and worked hard! Our hypothesis was that if we offered a service and those in our community had a nicer environment, we would:

1. make *relational connections in the community*;
2. increase *our missional effectiveness*; and
3. create a more *vibrant discipleship in a missional context* as the Christians in the group stepped out into a missional frontier.

The hypothesis was that these three shifts would expose those around us to the gospel and therefore move us closer to the Dream we had for this community. But, after months of work, we realized we had essentially become "Christian Social Services." In the British system, numerous government agencies were functionally offering services to our neighbors, and they perceived us as simply another service to keep their yards clean. We were not able to discern who were the "people of peace" (Luke 10:5–9) because they had all become "community clients." Going back to the three aspects of our hypothesis, here's what we learned:

1. **Relational connections in the community:** Although some genuine relationships were developed, the prototype revealed that

the relationships were primarily shallow, functional, and transactional because they were based around a service.

2. **Missional effectiveness:** Although a few people appreciated the sacrificial effort, many simply viewed this as a weekly service they were entitled to.

3. **Vibrant discipleship in a missional context:** We did confirm that discipleship was more vibrant. Stepping out of our comfort zone, embracing vulnerability, and practically expressing core convictions meant we were more engaged in our personal faith journey.

We took this learning from the discovery process and tested a more refined hypothesis in other communities, eventually unearthing a core principle that mission should not be "to" people or "at" people as a service that meets a need (e.g., your front yard has trash; I will take it away). Instead, it should be "alongside" and "with" people as a communal effort toward a shared goal (e.g., how can we clean up the neighborhood together?). We realized we needed to include words of proclamation and deeds of demonstration of the gospel in a humble, collaborative, and prayerful way. The key principle was that mission should be relational, reciprocal, and communal. In the years to come, I used this principle in training missional community leaders, using the following language: "Mission should include contextual proclamation and demonstration and, rather than doing activity for or at people, should make a difference shoulder-to-shoulder *with* people around an issue that the community together has identified as important."

This relational, reciprocal, and communal nature of mission is seen in Luke 10, as Jesus sends the Seventy-two out as "lambs among wolves" and commands them not to take "a purse or bag or sandals" (vv. 3–4). He then instructs his disciples to stay and be served by the houses of peace that accept them (vv. 5–8), as well as offering value to those in the town (v. 9). Note how the above core principle we deduced was grounded in Scripture. In the Discover phase, any core principles unearthed that will shape your organization moving forward must have biblical resonance. The principles you are finding now will be the DNA that is embedded and replicated in many people and places in the Deploy phase. Therefore, to unlock the power of movemental kingdom transformation in the future, what is discovered in this phase needs to be rooted in Scripture and in the words, works, and ways of Jesus. For an existing organization, these learnings should also resonate with the heritage of the organization so there is continuity in identity and language from the past to the future. We are looking for principles that have system-wide impact and affect the whole organization rather than a particular people group or part of the organization.

When Anna and I moved to our current community, we took this "shoulder-to-shoulder" approach and asked questions of our neighbors to unlock the shared problems or prizes. Two key issues emerged: 1) The area was full of young families, many of whom felt unsupported in some of the pressures of family life. 2) Being a community close to the North Sea meant that lots of people walked their dogs on the beach and many tourists dropped their litter— so there was a problem with dog poo and litter.

In response to concerns about family pressure, in partnership with the local coworking space, we ran Sunday morning parenting sessions that facilitated conversation, discussion, and a communal journey around family issues.

In response to the matter of dog poo and litter, as part of a local Facebook group, we mobilized the community to do various litter pick-up days. But this time round, it wasn't just Christians picking up trash for other people; it was the whole community owning the endeavor. During one cleanup day, we happened to have a group from the US visiting us as we were planting wildflowers around the primary school. The local community was actively involved, and this activity was designed to make the environment more appealing to the kids and parents. Our American friends were amazed at the informal but deep, relational conversations, and the shared communal effort as we planted the flowers. One of the visitors commented, "If this was us in the States, we would have come with branded church t-shirts, planted all the flowers ourselves, and done it *to* the community." I smiled to myself at the irony that our first Discover phase prototype ten years earlier had been exactly that.

Through prototyping, the goal of the Discover phase is to test our hypothesis of what key actions will move us toward our stated dream. We need to test different assumptions, understand what key elements would be present if we were to realize our dream, and use all the information at hand to continue to prototype—allowing us to test and refine our hypothesis. We must explore possibilities before we reach any level of certainty. We are not seeking perfection; perfection is the enemy of prototyping. Instead, we are simply attempting something that allows us to see where the gaps and holes are in our thinking and practice. We're looking for clues to what will enable us to iterate, and eventually (in the subsequent phases) to strengthen and design something that can flourish and scale.

CHANGING THE CONVERSATION— THE 100 MOVEMENTS PUBLISHING JOURNEY

Let's return to our example of 100 Movements Publishing, as an example of launching a new venture. In the Discover phase, the prototyping stage involved the publication of just one book. This allowed us to test the hypothesis that a hybrid publishing model with the same quality as a traditional publishing house and the flexibility of self-publishing would enable us to pursue our dream of changing the conversation toward movemental Christianity. Within this prototype were several small experiments and lots of reflective questions: What was the best way to communicate the book's key ideas? What basic elements would be needed for the book to be published, including cover design, interior design, editorial, ISBN, and barcode? What was the best way to communicate with the core group and contractors involved, and at what stage should they be invited into the project? Which contractors were reliable and might be useful for future projects? Which weren't?

Mistakes were made, processes took twice as long as they should have, and the finished product wasn't as polished as it could have been. But, through our prototype, we discovered some core principles. One principle, refined now over many books, was that we wanted the subject matter and tone of the books to be "prophetic and winsome." The initial manuscript contained challenging concepts and content, so the team wanted to temper this with a winsome tone, in the same way that the apostle Paul talks about balancing love and prophetic truth in 1 Corinthians 13:1–3.

In testing the hypothesis, we gathered valuable learning on how to create a stronger editorial process in line with the caliber of a traditional publishing house. Another key element of the hypothesis that was tested and later refined related to setting clear expectations between author and editor. As a result, we had a clearer hypothesis and validated learning that we were able to take into publishing the second and third books.

RENEWING THE OLD

100 Movements Publishing is an example of a completely new venture, but prototypes are just as effective in an established institution. A few years ago, I worked with Mennonite Church Eastern Canada (MCEC). They had 110 churches, and the leadership team wanted to see each of them grow in missional fruitfulness. However, instead of trying to get every church to do something new, we suggested picking ten churches to run a first prototype. This small group of pioneering churches went through an initial learning community over two years, and we coached them to embed a missional discipleship culture into their existing small groups. Part of the prototyping was encouraging the leaders of these churches to experiment, seeking to be missional in their everyday lives and mobilizing people into discipleship, while unearthing key principles that they would eventually pass on to other churches within the denomination. Each time they tried something new, they had the coaching and learning community as places to process and reflect on their learning; to evaluate what was effective, what wasn't, and why; and to clarify the key principles that were being discovered. All this learning was later taken into the Design phase and eventually—in the Deploy phase—was rolled out more widely across the denomination in their own contextualized expression of the training.[11] By practicing and prototyping, this small, pioneering group had the freedom to experiment. Nothing in this stage was viewed as a failure because it was all about gathering information and learning. And, crucially, because the prototype was only implemented in a handful of churches rather than as a wholesale edict for all 110, there was freedom for a smaller group to test freely, without having to deal with the fall-out of forcing everyone to do something they didn't understand or want to do.

Another organization I coached identified that they needed greater diversity on their senior leadership team. They had an aging, white, male leadership group, and this urgently needed to change. Instead of jumping to technical solutions

---

[11] See https://www.innovatebethechange.ca.

("We will hire a younger leader, female leader, leader of color") or making a knee-jerk, short-term practical response, they paused. With reflection, prayer, and careful consideration, they developed prototypes in numerous areas. They created a listening exercise that engaged younger leaders in the organization around key questions. Rather than the senior team spearheading a particular project, they allowed a mixed team (gender, color, and organizational position) to lead it. And they invested in a short, six-week program for a small group of female leaders from across the organization. All of these prototypes disrupted the status quo and helped them gather vital data, insight, and engagement that was used to strengthen and inform the leadership as they looked to make wider and deeper changes across the whole organization over time.

FREEDOM TO FAIL

As you set out on this journey of discovery, keep in mind that not all endeavors end in straightforward success. James Dyson tested 5,271 prototypes before he built a vacuum cleaner that worked. The name WD-40 is derived from the fact that it took forty attempts to find the correct formula.[12] And Polaroid lost $200 million when it first ventured into instant movies.[13] We've been conditioned to expect one big product launch, one factory production line, and that new ideas need to be a silver bullet … a first-time success. But great discoveries usually happen in the mess of multiple attempts. Whether it be the chaotic science lab, the cluttered garage, or the paper-strewn kitchen table, many of the inventions that our lives have become predicated on started in these sorts of humble beginnings. And sometimes our discoveries can take us in an unexpected direction. Across science, technology, food, and industry, people have sought to innovate in one field and stumbled upon an alternative breakthrough. Alexander Fleming discovered penicillin while he was throwing away his experiments. As he returned to the discarded petri dishes, he found that a mold dissolving all the bacteria around it contained a powerful antibiotic. Electrical engineer John

---

[12] Sujan Patel, "8 Successful Products That Only Exist Because of Failure," *Forbes*, January 16, 2015, https://www.forbes.com/sites/sujanpatel/2015/01/16/8-successful-products-that-only-exist-because-of-failure/.

[13] Rita McGrath and Ian MacMillan, "Discovery-Driven Planning," *Harvard Business Review*, July–August 1995, https://hbr.org/1995/07/discovery-driven-planning.

Hopps invented the pacemaker while he was researching hypothermia. During his experiment using radio frequency heating to restore body temperature, he realized that if a heart stopped beating due to cooling, it could be started again by artificial stimulation. Percy Spencer invented the microwave when he noticed the chocolate bar in his pocket began to melt during his experiments with a new vacuum tube. Brothers John and Will Kellogg accidentally left a pot of boiled grain on the stove for several days. The mixture turned moldy, but the product that emerged was dry and thick. They eliminated the mold and created what we now know and enjoy as cornflakes.

The business world is often more prepared than the church world to take risks and accept failure as a means to growth. They often model the principle of scattering seeds, accepting the fact that many seeds will not germinate, and investing in whatever grows.

In releasing a bunch of inexperienced disciples to partner with him in his work, Jesus also showed he'd rather we have a go, discover for ourselves, learn from our mistakes, and come to him more aware of our weaknesses and our need for his help, than to do nothing and bury the resources and opportunities he gives us.

We have to be prepared to fail if we're going to attempt to fly.

PROTOTYPING YOUR WAY FORWARD

EQUIPPING OTHERS TO DISCOVER

Leaders will all have to learn how to fail gracefully at the edge of their competence, without pretending they know what they don't know.
BOB JOHANSEN

Life is a series of building, testing, changing, and iterating.
LAUREN MOSENTHAL

We can only live changes: we cannot think our way to humanity. Every one of us, every group, must become the model of that which we desire to create.
IVAN ILLICH

In *The Lean Startup*, Eric Ries recounts the start-up story of Zappos, the world's largest online shoe store. Zappos founder Nick Swinmurn saw a gap in the market because there was no online site with a wide selection of shoes; but rather than jumping in with a huge investment, Swinmurn started with a low-level prototype.

His hypothesis was that customers were ready and willing to buy shoes online. To test it, he began asking local shoe stores if he could take pictures of their inventory. In exchange for permission to take the pictures, he would post the pictures online and would come back to buy the shoes at full price if the customer bought them. Zappos began with a tiny, simple product.[1]

This tiny, simple product not only tested the core hypothesis, but it also tested multiple assumptions and aspects of the business plan, as well as building customer engagement. Like yeast in the dough, Swinmurn's small experiment paid off. In 2009, Zappos was acquired by Amazon for a reported $1.2 billion.[2] Not bad for an initial hypothesis, a few photos, and a scrappy prototype.

As we move through the Discover phase, we often uncover what is hiding in plain site as core beliefs, and we also unearth fresh insights. As you work with the core group in the Discover phase, you need to encourage them to look at things both from a wider perspective and in more detail. Imagine using a wide-angle lens on a camera so that you can take in the full vista and see the terrain more clearly, but then using a micro-lens so you can zero in on a butterfly sitting on a flowerhead to examine it up close. The core group may find it difficult to reconcile these two views, but without this, they risk missing the important details or misunderstanding the wider picture those details fit into.

As we've uncovered in the previous chapters, the change process is predicated on the strength of the pioneering group. If we're to harness the power of collective intelligence, and if we're going to prototype our way forward, we need to develop a strong core group of pioneers with a posture of learning and practice.

FIND THE RIGHT PEOPLE

Everett Rogers, who wrote about the diffusion of innovations, notes the importance of engaging and mobilizing the first 16 percent of the organization to create an organizational tipping point toward a new culture and practice. This

---

[1] Eric Ries, *The Lean Startup: How Constant Innovation Creates Radical Successful Businesses* (London, UK: Portfolio Penguin, 2011), 57–58.

[2] "Amazon Closes Zappos Deal, Ends Up Paying $1.2 Billion," TechCrunch.com, November 2, 2009, https://techcrunch.com/2009/11/02/amazon-closes-zappos-deal-ends-up-paying-1-2-billion/.

first 16 percent is made up of both innovators (2.5 percent) and early adopters (13.5 percent). They are key not only in the Discover phase but also in driving change across the whole organization. Rogers says, "The greatest response to change agent effort occurs when opinion leaders adopt, which usually occurs at somewhere between 3 and 16 percent adoption in most systems. The innovation will then continue to spread with little promotional effort by change agents, after a critical mass of adopters is reached."[3]

One of the organizations Movement Leaders Collective works with is Uptick, a development track within the Baptist General Association of Virginia (BGAV) that invests in high-potential, high-capacity young-adult leaders. They strategically use this 16-percent principle and craft intentional language to communicate it. John Chandler, founder of the development track, notes in his book *Uptick* that they were "looking for the 'top 3 percent' (young innovators within BGAV) as Uptick candidates. Early on, we said, 'It only takes 16 percent!' (to impact positively the overall BGAV)—and a decade later, that has proven to be true."[4] These were shorthand ways of saying that Uptick could contribute to the flourishing of a larger system by giving voice and investment to a small group of younger innovators and early adopters.

When I coach organizations, I often talk to leaders about identifying "goldfish" and "elephants." The saying goes, "An elephant never forgets," and so if an elephant in your organization tries something once and it doesn't work, *they never forget* (or at least, they *rarely* forget!). They are the ones who will rebuff ideas with reasons why they won't work or the assertion that, "We tried that once, and it was a disaster." Elephants are generally risk-averse, which means they serve as guardians for the journey at best and an anchor to halt progress at worst. They are not wired to engage or enjoy the Discover phase. Failure can be an identity statement for elephants, as they tend to hold to the narrative that, "It failed, so I am a failure, and I am never doing that again." Elephants represent the middle-to-late majority in the Diffusion of Innovations Curve. They need products and processes that have been tried and tested, so it's usually best to keep them away from the prototypes. However, it is essential to keep the elephants that occupy

---

3   Rogers, *Diffusion of Innovations*, 222–23.

4   John Chandler, *Uptick: A Blueprint for Finding and Forming the Next Generation of Pioneering Kingdom Leaders* (Cody, WY: 100 Movements Publishing, 2019), 249.

significant leadership positions in your organizational hierarchy informed of the process and progress. Elephants will need reassurance that prototypes are for information gathering and aren't the finished product.

Goldfish, on the other hand, are almost immune to the lasting effects of failure. That's why they are essential in the experimental dynamics of the Discover phase. Goldfish represent the innovators and early adopters, as the 16 percent most pioneering types on the Diffusion of Innovations Curve. They have short-term memories, so they try, fail, learn, pivot, and try again. And again. And again. They have a higher tolerance for failure, a stronger drive to experiment, and may even appear to have short-term memory loss! There is a wonderful scene in the 2014 *Lego Movie* where Batman is throwing his bat-stars at a button to open a gate. He misses, misses again, and again, and again, to the point of awkward. Finally, he strikes. He hits the button, the door opens, and he utters the words, "Yes, first time."[5] That's the reality for a goldfish.

In a new start-up, faith-driven venture, or church plant, there will likely be almost solely goldfish. Existing organizations will have both elephants and goldfish—though probably far more elephants. In the Discover phase, we primarily need goldfish. As we move into subsequent phases, we will need elephants for their ability to act as guardians, for their previous experience and learning, and for their ability to analyze what's worked and what hasn't. But in the initial phases of both Dream and Discover, we need goldfish in our core group. They supply optimism and perseverance so that risk can be embraced and many experiments can be conducted, which will create valuable learning for the whole organization. Goldfish won't need much encouragement to get involved in prototyping in the initial stages of the Discover phase. However, they will need help to refocus and reflect so that they can share intentionally with the wider organization (and influential elephants) rather than just pressing ahead.

SOCIAL GOES FIRST

As well as describing innovators and early adopters as goldfish, they can also be likened to elite runners in the marathon or special forces in an army. Everyone

---

[5] *The Lego Movie*, directed by Chris Miller and Phil Lord (2014; Burbank, CA: Warner Bros. Pictures).

will eventually need to run the race or fight the battle, but this pioneering group will push out first.

Missiologist Ralph Winter refers to these pioneers as a "sodal" group. (The majority of individuals in the organization [elephants] are described by Winter as "modal.") Pointing back to the example of the early church, Winter notes that Paul was "'sent off' not 'sent out' by the Antioch congregation. He may have reported back to it but did not take orders from it. His mission band (sodality) had all the autonomy and authority of a 'traveling congregation.'"[6] In an existing organization, the *sodality* therefore has the commissioning from the center to go, and they take responsibility to go first and further than the edges of what exists right now. Their mandate is to test what is new, experimental, and uncertain for the good of the whole. Being part of the sodal group has significant intensity and intentionality and it is therefore a high-bar invitation.

Only a small number of people in our organizations will thrive and can engage effectively in this phase, so we need to be wise and discerning about who is selected. We will come to the point when our prototypes have been modified and tested and can then be rolled out more widely to the modality. (More on this in the Design and Deploy phases.) But it's crucial to stagger the process of change, with the right people involved at each phase.

Many years ago, Anna and I felt called to move to a specific part of the city we lived in. A few other sodally minded goldfish agreed to make the move with us. As others in our church community heard about what we were doing, they too got excited about the vision and expressed a desire to join us. In the end, around fifteen people relocated with us into the area. Though every individual who came was a committed disciple of Jesus, not all of them were sodally oriented. We quickly found that what should have been a phase of pioneering goldfish being released to rapidly prototype and experiment was hindered by the needs of elephants, who naturally took things at a slower pace and became bogged down with details rather than remaining curious and open to risk and new possibilities and opportunities. On reflection, we should have moved with a smaller key group of sodal, pioneering goldfish who were free to scout out

---

6   Ralph D. Winter, "The Two Structures of God's Redemptive Mission," address given to All-Asia Mission Consultation in Seoul, Korea, August 1973, http://www.undertheiceberg.com/wp-content/uploads/2006/04/Sodality-Winter%20on%20Two%20Structures1.pdf.

the land, build relationships with those in the area, and experiment with new ways of making connections. We could have invited the elephants to move in and help establish the work at a later date. Instead, we became distracted by the needs of elephants, who were overwhelmed by the innovation and uncertainty inherent in the Discover phase.

WE NOT ME

As the pioneering core group steps out and embraces experiential learning to discover what God is doing, the goal is to gather a breadth of understanding that can only come from drawing on a team of people rather than one or two individuals. In his books *The Tipping Point* and *Outliers*, Malcolm Gladwell speaks of the principles of interconnected and interdisciplinary learning that create change, mold our heroes, and shape our reality.[7] In *Outliers*, he talks about the mosaic of relational dynamics within a community of people—as well as its mix of expertise and experiences—that coalesce to form and mature individuals who become the "heroes" of our Western culture—people such as Taylor Swift, Steve Jobs, Brené Brown, Rihanna, and Bill Gates to name but a few. It's the collective intelligence of the scene around these people that forms and unlocks the genius within them.

Brain Eno, the musician and producer, calls this "scenius." Geniuses he notes, are not individuals who pop out from nowhere. They emerge from within a dynamic context (scene) that involves others: "Scenius stands for the intelligence and the intuition of a whole cultural scene. It is the communal form of the concept of the genius. Scenius is like genius, only embedded in a scene rather than in a gene."[8] Scenius is contextual intelligence that produces a communal genius. As we say in our Movement Leaders Collective training, "The genius isn't in the room; the genius *is* the room."

The history of art, science, and sport is crammed with examples of scenius. In modern literature, there was the Bloomsbury Group in London, the Inklings

---

[7] Malcolm Gladwell, *The Tipping Point: How Little Things Can Make a Big Difference* (New York, NY: Little, Brown and Company, 2002); and *Outliers: The Story of Success* (New York, NY: Little, Brown and Company, 2008).

[8] Bruce Sterling, "Scenius, or Communal Genius," *Wired*, June 16, 2000, https://www.wired.com/2008/06/scenius-or-comm/.

in Oxford, and Algonquin Round Table in New York. In art, there was Paris in the 1920s, the lofts in Soho (NYC), and more recently, the Burning Man festival in Nevada. In science, there was the Lunar Society in England, the Manhattan Project in the US, Building 20 at Massachusetts Institute of Technology, Lockheed Martin Skunk Works in the UK, and the ever-spreading Silicon Valley.[9] Notable examples in sport include the Class of '92 with Manchester United or La Masia, and Barcelona's football academy, which produced the likes of Messi, Iniesta, and Xavi. Neil Armstrong may have uttered the quintessential mantra of scenius when he walked on the moon in 1969 and declared, "This is one small step for man, one giant leap for mankind." But Armstrong's lunar landing took years of research and multiple prototypes. NASA estimates approximately 400,000 people were involved.[10]

Our default tendency is to overlook the power of communal discernment and collective intelligence, and instead deify the solo-heroic leader. As I wrote in *Red Skies*, "We continue to default to the solo-heroic leader: the great warrior leading their troops into battle; the genius who diagnoses the problem; the secret agent who diffuses the bomb with two seconds to go; the tech entrepreneur who dominates the market."[11]

If anyone could have been a solo-heroic leader, it was Jesus. He didn't *need* the disciples for his mission; he *chose* the disciples for the mission. He worked through them and with them. Jesus didn't train the disciples on an individual basis, and he didn't supply them with a shopping list or to-do list for them to action. He brought together a random and untested group of future leaders and let them be part of something where they could learn and discover, together. They each brought their heritage, personality, and gifts and created a mosaic of communal learning that formed and shaped them.

9   For an interesting reflection about how the church should be a place of discovery, see Anthony Siegrist, "The Church Needs to Be a Place for Radical Innovation: Here's How," Missio Alliance, August 1, 2018, https://www.missioalliance.org/the-church-needs-to-be-a-place-for-radical-innovation-heres-how/.

10   Megan Keup, "9 Inspirational Teamwork Examples," Project Manager, July 2, 2019, https://www.projectmanager.com/blog/teamwork-examples.

11   Rich Robinson in L. Rowland Smith (ed), *Red Skies: 10 Essential Conversations Exploring Our Future as the Church* (Cody, WY: 100 Movements Publishing, 2022), 164.

SWIM AGAINST THE SOLO-HEROIC TIDE

If scenius is part of Jesus' model of leadership and vital in the tapestry of history, we surely must consider it imperative for the Discover phase—and ultimately for our organizational future. We need to actively swim against the tide of solo-heroic leadership and the systems that perpetuate it.

Accomplishing this begins with a communal and collaborative approach to change, leveraging the collective intelligence within the core group. It is this valuable resource that is vital as we prototype and seek to solve the adaptive challenges we face. Whether we like it or not, we live in a world that is so fast-paced, interconnected, and multi-layered that one man or woman can't digest all the information and predict the outcomes. No one person could figure out all the alternative combinations in this vast sea of information and chart a way forward with certainty. And yet this is the model we so readily default to. Our solo-heroic, personality-driven, command-and-control style leadership is ill-suited to the ever-changing world in which we live—and it is a roadblock to discovery.

Whether through the work of Creo or Movement Leaders Collective, when I talk about collective intelligence with leaders, teams, and organizations, it usually both resonates and jars. It resonates because, on a gut level, we know it's impossible for one great leader to make everything work, for one strategic plan to bring change, or for one vehicle to be effective in every context. We know our systems, organizations, hierarchies, and strategies are not the be-all-and-end-all. Most leaders are aware that they need help and insight from others. We know we need each other, and we need to be adaptable.

But it also jars. There is a juxtaposition because, although it resonates deeply with us, the notion of scenius—or collective intelligence—also runs against the grain of most of what we know, feel, read, and have experienced in leadership. It is the antithesis of our current leadership paradigm and praxis. In many conversations with leaders over many years and in varied contexts, the majority of them say, "Yes, I love the idea of collective intelligence … but … it would never work in our system." Our systems are built to create, elevate, and overload the individual leader at the top.

One church leader I have been coaching has dynamism, charisma, bright ideas, and plans to change the world for Jesus. But as we talked, he expressed how he had become tired and frustrated, and was feeling burdened. He was running hard and expecting everyone to keep up. Like a lone ranger driving the Discover phase single-handedly, everyone around him was merely taking notes. Recognizing some of his tendencies in myself, I needed to harness my own self-awareness as I coached him in overcoming those challenges. He was living in the realization that his life was not working on any level, and his spirituality, marriage, family, team, and ministry were suffering. We journeyed through the deeper reasoning, prevailing logic, and unconscious worldview that had led him to this place, as well as the brokenness, drivenness, and myth of the solo-heroic leader that the world had sold him, and he'd bought into. We spent time in prayer and reflection and discussed what needed to shift in his thinking and practice, and where his head and heart needed repentance and reorientation toward the person and practice of Jesus.

To help him move away from solo-heroic leadership tendencies, we used some practices from the Design phase (more to come in later chapters) to craft statements that would function as reminders, such as, "Move from command-and-control to question-and-answer." These statements, which he could repeat internally, would help him reposition himself as he led meetings and interacted with his staff. We created frameworks for behaviors. For example, he gave himself three "chips" he could play in every meeting—with a chip being making a comment or setting a direction—which would intentionally limit his impact in discussions, allowing others in the room to contribute and discover things for themselves more meaningfully. It also helped ensure he was only giving valuable input or opinions rather than regular advice or orders. We spent time praying for and imagining a different future for those he served and thinking through how he could help unlock more kingdom potential in others.

We still need leaders in the Discover phase, but we must utilize a new dynamic of leadership because we have created systems and structures that make our leaders experts rather than learners and the sole voice rather than one who encourages a communal discussion. Good leaders create culture rather than give directions; they ask helpful questions rather than provide answers; they get the best out of everyone rather than make themselves look good; they are the player-coach rather than the star player. We need guides rather than heroes and collective intelligence rather than the perspective of one individual.

THE DANGER OF A SINGLE STORY

To ensure you effectively harness collective intelligence, you will need to prayerfully discern who should be involved in your prototyping. If the core group driving discovery are all staff members, or all white males over the age of fifty-five, or all living in a particular part of the city, it will narrow what we unearth. If the pioneering core group is homogeneous, it will not yield true discovery but rather reinforce confirmation bias. This means as leaders, we can't just pick people who think like us or look like us. If we do that, we create a culture that reflects our strengths and shares our blind spots rather than mining the gold of a diverse group.

Different people bring different perspectives and skill sets, ask different questions, have different narratives, see different realities, and pursue different possibilities. As these differences come together, authentic discovery is a natural by-product. As community change facilitator Shabrae Jackson Krieg says in *Voices Rising,*

> When we sit down with others, whether those we are seeking to serve, or those we are serving with, there is often some previous paradigm or way of looking at the situation. There's a narrative that has been passed down. And unless we can listen to all the ideas, that narrative can be singular, and it can be harmful.[12]

This is echoed by Nigerian writer Chimamanda Ngozi Adichie in her TED talk, "The Danger of a Single Story." She says, "The single story creates stereotypes, and the problem with stereotypes is not that they are untrue, but they are incomplete. They make one story become the only story."[13] With a single story, our discovery will not be untrue, but it will be partial. To combat this, we need different mindsets (cognitive diversity) and different skill sets (competency diversity) in our core pioneering group. This diversity will allow us to collectively *see* differently (mindsets) and *do* differently (skill sets), leading to more divergent thinking and behaviors that in turn lead to a more holistic process and dynamic discovery.

---

[12] Jackson Krieg, *Voices Rising,* 391.

[13] Jackson Krieg, *Voices Rising,* footnote 47, 397.

Cognitive Diversity + Competency Diversity = Collective Intelligence
(Different Mindsets) + (Different Skill Sets) = (Dynamic Discovery)

Think about building a house, which requires multiple competencies and a degree of cognitive diversity. If we just had a group of plumbers building a house, we would trust the plumbing but probably not the foundation, the wiring, or the roof. Having an architect build the house would mean it was perfect on paper, but that may not translate to bricks and mortar. What we need is an architect, a project manager, a builder, a plumber, and a whole variety of tradespeople. Cognitive and competency diversity prevents a one-size-fits-all response, a brittle solution, or huge deficits and blind spots.

In our churches and organizations, we often have one "trade" build the whole "house"—only occasionally inviting others to give some expert advice, which leads to collective blindness (where we all miss the same thing) or collective drift (where we all lean toward the same conclusion). This can also be true of a Christian entrepreneur who depends on their own skill set as they pioneer a new venture. However, to be most effective in testing hypotheses and creating prototypes in the Discover phase, we need to include a variety of voices and perspectives.

In assessing the roots of innovation, American professor Joseph Henrich notes that,

> Once we understand the importance of collective brains, we begin to see why modern societies vary in their innovativeness. It's not the smartness of the individuals … It's the willingness and ability of large numbers of individuals at the knowledge frontier to freely interact, exchange views, disagree, learn from each other, build collaborations, trust strangers, and be wrong. Innovation does not take a genius or a village; it takes a big network of freely interacting minds.[14]

As you lead your pioneering core group, it's imperative that you create opportunities for people to offer perspectives or opinions and that you never settle for the first opinion or defer to a dominant voice. Every team member should feel the agency and have the opportunity to share their insights and questions

---

[14] Quoted in Matthew Syed, *Rebel Ideas: The Power of Diverse Thinking* (London, UK: John Murray, 2019), 266.

with the group. And the aim should always be to unearth the richness of shared learning rather than achieving a personal or political agenda.

ACTIVATING DISCOVERY IN YOUR ORGANIZATION OR VENTURE

Below are three practices that enable your core group to learn by doing and create a shared experience of what it means to discover together, as well as formulate a first prototype (or several prototypes) to test.

During this phase, you and your team will experience confusion, vulnerability, and frustration, as well as inspiration, excitement, and conviction. Take time as a team to name, reflect, and explore these emotions. For example, if the core group feels inspired, ask yourselves *why* you are feeling inspired. It may be that a core principle or truth is being revealed or there is a significant learning. Stripping back to the *why* behind these responses may lead to further insight and innovation.

Although the Discover phase can be highly energizing, it can also take a heavy toll on the innovators and early adopters so, as a leader and organization, consider how you can reward, resource, and remind leaders throughout this phase.

- **Reward = regular celebration:** This encourages and incentivizes your core group to be experimental throughout the Discover phase. If their latest failure gets laughed down, or their idea is ignored, they're unlikely to continue to push the boundaries of discovery. Seek to reward learning and progress rather than just "success."
- **Resource = intentional investment:** This includes money but also time and effort. Equip and empower your core group to continue to experiment in the Discover phase by considering where they may need funding, time away from other responsibilities, or training to release them to experiment fully.
- **Remind = continual direction:** This ensures everyone keeps moving forward, they remember that the primary aim of the Discover phase is learning, and they stay encouraged in the face of failure (because they know it provides valuable learning). Communicate through words, pictures, and stories to remind your team to keep their eyes on the prize and continue to gather valuable learning.

PRACTICE #1: CULTIVATE SCENIUS

As we explored earlier, investing in creating a culture of collective intelligence will be vital for your learning and growth as well as that of your core group in the Discover phase. So, as you gather a pioneering group that will begin to work together toward testing a hypothesis and creating a prototype, you will need to create a scenius culture. In *Collective Genius,* the authors note that, as a leader,

> The last thing you want is a team that defers to you to set a course, to be chief innovator and then simply implement your vision. ... If your goal is innovation then your role must instead be to create an environment—a setting, a context, an organization—where people are willing and able to do the hard work of innovation themselves: to collaborate, learn through trial and error, and make integrated decisions.[15]

Think about the setting, structure, and dynamics of how you collaborate, as well as the influences that shape this culture. Your core group needs to work in short, dynamic sprints with prototypes focused on problems or prizes and will interact formally and informally in both structured and spontaneous ways. There must be multiple working documents, potential prototypes, and experiments being run simultaneously, as well as a physical place or digital platform (or both) to share ideas and facilitate interaction. As leaders pour energy into prototyping, it may mean they don't have as much capacity for another role or responsibility in a different part of the organization, so they will need to be released to spend the time, effort, and energy on the prototype. The efforts these groups make do not always yield a short-term return, but the focus is on a longer-term impact that will serve the organization for years to come.

Below are some ways to develop collective intelligence within the core group.

- **Create a sense of shared purpose:** Having a shared prize or problem will lead to a growing sense of camaraderie and commitment to one

---

[15] Linda A. Hill, Greg Brandeau, Emily Truelove, Kent Lineback, *Collective Genius: The Art and Practice of Leading Innovation* (Boston, MA: Harvard Business School Publishing, 2014), 66.

another, and the shared prize or problem will become collectively owned rather than attributed to one leader.

- ○ *As a leader, think about how you can ensure—through your use of language, celebration, and framing of every interaction—that each team member is clear on why the core group exists and what it is seeking to achieve, and has emotive and strategic ownership of the discovery process and desired outcomes.*

- **Encourage generosity:** Be generous and open to others, offering gifts and skills, and recognize that other people have gifts to give you and one another. Encourage mutual giving and receiving. Freely share best practices, frontier learning, battle-won wisdom, treasures, and insights. Find correction and direction in learning from others' experiences.
  - ○ *As a leader, make sure the shared outcomes and learning of the group are more important than any one person's preference or agenda.*

- **Foster trust and mutual respect:** Encourage a sense of mutual submission and interplay, where each person is valued, and contributions are received without judgment. Define the culture through words and actions to create a camaraderie so that in the pressure of the Discover phase, each person "has the back" of the rest of the team.
  - ○ *As a leader, make sure every voice is encouraged and engaged with in team meetings and interactions, regardless of hierarchical rank or position.*

- **Make time to be together:** Take time to hear each other's stories, understand each other's strengths and weaknesses, and process together the shared purpose to uncover the different hopes of the preferred future each member has. Learn what the team can lean on each other for, and where they can depend on the strengths or insights of different team members. Understand and be aware of each other's weaknesses and deficits, which is vital for the team to bond as a stronger unit and to leverage the strengths and manage the weaknesses of each team member.
  - ○ *As a leader, make sure you create structured and spontaneous opportunities for team members to listen, interact, and learn together. This can be little and often, as well as longer, deeper times.*

- **Encourage rapid exchange of tools and techniques:** As soon as something is experienced, observed, or formulated as an idea, share it, and then dissect, critique, iterate, and improve it.
  - *As a leader, make sure you look for the platforms and possibilities for ideas to be rapidly shared, critiqued, complimented, and changed. This could be through in-person interactive sessions together or digitally via Slack, Google Drive, WhatsApp threads, and so forth.*
- **Celebrate shared success:** Ensure that when a breakthrough erupts, a record is broken, or a new reality emerges through the efforts of the core group, the success is claimed by everyone. View these as a "shared win" rather than a solo triumph. Prize the common good and communal process over individual breakthrough, position, or acclaim.
  - *As a leader, make sure you actively celebrate the communal win, as well as each individual's part and collaborative contribution.*
- **Welcome novelties:** Embrace innovation and new ideas rather than entertaining negative resistance from naysayers. Celebrate and actively encourage the renegades and mavericks who are necessary for innovation.
  - *As a leader, continue to initiate discussions about new ideas or insights, and consistently review your processes and systems for innovations and improvements.*
- **Make risk normative:** Encourage the group to applaud exploration, prototypes, and bold, innovative moves. Embrace and appreciate risk. Allow and foster friendly competition that sparks creative and collaborative breakthroughs.
  - *As a leader, celebrate effort, process, and initiative, rather than just outcome and impact, and always seek to stretch beyond the status quo.*

It takes time to build relationships, define shared purpose, and learn from one another. If we are pushing for short-term effectiveness as our primary aim, we will always pick "delivering the task" over "developing the core group." But developing the core group as a guiding coalition for the process will produce more effective results over the medium and long term, in both the quantity and quality of what the group can deliver. It's a short-term cost for a long-term gain.

PRACTICE #2: RUN A PROTOTYPE

In the Discover phase, your core group may choose to run one prototype where together you all focus your work collaboratively in a specific area to create learning and unearth core principles. The aim of the prototype is to name a hypothesis or core belief you want to test and design an experiment that will help you learn the most in this area.

As stated throughout, for an existing organizational context, you don't run a prototype on the center stage, in the spotlight, or involve everyone in the first test run. Make sure your prototype is tested "off center" so that the experimentation doesn't cause consternation to the wider organization. That way, you can minimize any collateral damage and can focus on learning from the experience. If everything goes well, you can get ready to iterate and develop for the whole organization at a later stage.

The example below focuses on a prototyping process for a church, church plant, or denominational context. Running a prototype is also essential for a faith-driven venture or nonprofit, but the context and application will be different.

- **Pick a puzzle, problem, or potential:** Choose an area identified in the Dream phase that you will focus on (solving a problem, pursuing a prize, testing a practice, or releasing potential in a place or people group).
  - ○ *Key question: What's the ONE area you're focusing on?*
  - ○ *Example: Our small groups are not missional or evangelistic (problem).*
- **Create a hypothesis:** In the area of focus, name your hypothesis for achieving change. This is the theory you will focus on and test with your prototype. If everything is a priority, nothing is a priority.
  - ○ *Key question: What's the theory for how you will best achieve the dream?*
  - ○ *Example: We believe with prayer, training, and encouragement our small groups will gain a passion for mission and more evangelistic practice.*
- **Select a group:** Bring together a small team with camaraderie and commitment. This may include all the members of the core group

who have been engaged in the change journey so far or a subset of this group. You may also need to invite some specific pioneering leaders into the process, depending on the nature of the prototype. This group now needs to harness relational dynamics, creativity, and imagination, which creates an intensity of activity and accesses diverse perspectives.

- o *Key question: Who are the most appropriate leaders to invite into the group?*
- o *Example: We will gather two staff members and three small group leaders as a core learning group.*

- **Set a time frame:** Focus the leaders and the process to create boundaries and stimulus. If there is no urgency and there are no boundaries, the creative energy is harder to unlock and channel. Be aware that if the prototyping period is too long you will lose the intensity, and if it is too short you won't gather enough data to test your hypothesis or have a clear measure of success and validated learning.
  - o *Key question: What's your specific time frame (one day, one week, one month)?*
  - o *Example: For the next three months, we will work with three small groups to unlock a passion for mission and identify opportunities to be evangelistic.*

- **Create a process:** Set the framework, boundaries, learning objectives, and desired outcomes for the prototype to keep forward momentum. The process needs to be mapped out for the group as a framework for them to follow. There's always the possibility of going "off plan," but it's important to keep learning and moving forward.
  - o *Key question: What's your framework for the process?*
  - o *Example: We will prayer walk the neighborhoods and engage in open conversations with people in the area to gather data for the three small groups. We will create one missional prototype for each small group and a plan to mobilize every member of each small group into mission.*

- **Measure progress:** Encourage the core group to gather data and metrics for learning. Create feedback loops that help the team review and then design iteratively so that they continue to improve in future phases. The scorecard reminds the core group that validated learning is the measure of success in the Discover phase and helps them plot their progress.

     ○   *Key question: What's your scorecard?*

     ○   *Example: We will measure i) how many non-Christians each group connects with, ii) how many faith-oriented conversations are had, iii) how many members of the small group are mobilized to engage with non-Christians, and iv) what opportunities and barriers the small group experienced in this process.*

- **Collate learning:** Gather the prototyping group to reflect on their learning, review progress, and ask the "why" questions. These discussions and analyses help to clarify what core principles have been unearthed, what new information has surfaced, and what hypotheses and assumptions have been verified and which ones haven't. A vital part of this process is to identify which principles are core to the organization and therefore should be shared with the next group of leaders in the Design phase.

     ○   *Key question: What have we learned?*

     ○   *Example: We will take time to review the engagement of the groups, breakthroughs in mission, and practices and language that were beneficial in helping people to become passionate about mission or in identifying opportunities to be evangelistic. This review will help us uncover principles that can be shared with other groups in the future. For example, we have learned that people are unsure how to share their faith and that training increases people's confidence significantly.*

PRACTICE #3: CREATE A DISCOVER LAB

Practice #2 focused the whole group to work on one prototype for one area. However, the aim of a Discover Lab is for the core group to be able to test multiple hypotheses and ideas by running numerous prototypes simultaneously. The stages of the Discover Lab help you be clear with the core group about your aims as you meet, gather information, run multiple prototypes, and reflect together.

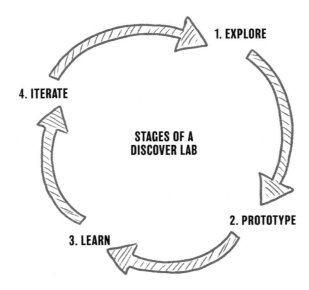

1. Explore: Read, pray, observe, and discuss the problem/s, potential/s, or prize/s with your group of pioneers (e.g., we are receiving feedback that people in our church are unsure how to share their faith, we have minimal adult baptisms and salvations, and our small groups have had the same people in them for many years). Look back, look around, investigate the area, and create a plan to gather validated data through multiple sources and experiments. Define the hypotheses you are testing (e.g., we believe that people's discipleship and faith journey is more vibrant when they embrace mission as well as community and formation) and the areas you feel it is important to learn within. ***Understand what you are testing and define what you want to learn.***

2. Prototype: The core groups build multiple 1.0 prototypes (see Practice #2 above on how to build a prototype) that test each of your numerous working hypotheses. These prototypes allow you to gather data from multiple sources and examine your assumptions (e.g., one small group will run an Alpha course; another group will do servant evangelism; one group will do welcome dinners for their neighbors; one group will train their people to be able to share their faith effectively; another will do a spiritual mapping exercise). Make sure each member of the core group knows which prototype they are working on, who they are working with, and what they are testing. ***Take the first step.***

3. Learn: Pause, gather the data from each prototype, and analyze it to unearth core principles by comparing and contrasting your findings. As the core group examines the findings, looking for trends and themes across the multiple prototypes, remember to measure progress and effort against your desired outcomes (e.g., what are the behaviors of the small groups that *are* connecting with non-Christians and that have healthy and vibrant discipleship? What was the faith journey of the last five people baptized, and what are the patterns from which we can learn? What are the behaviors of the groups that are closed and aren't connecting with non-Christians?). Consider which prototypes were effective and why, and what needs to be changed, improved, or reframed in other prototypes. Before you enter the iteration stage, ask yourselves what you learned from the tests, whether your hypothesis still stands or needs to be adapted, and how you would design and develop a stronger 2.0 prototype. *Analyze the data, ask the deeper "why" questions, and uncover key learning for the next prototype.*

4. Iterate: Create a clear and more cohesive "working theory" for the creation of your 2.0 prototype, which will aim to gather more data, more accurately test your clearer hypothesis, and give you outcomes that can validate your learning toward designing something that may be able to scale (e.g., the initial test was run in multiple forms with a low number of small groups and pioneers, so how can we include more small groups and involve leaders who are not as pioneering to support them to reimagine missional discipleship and mobilize the people in their groups to this end? How can we include the learning from the initial prototype phase in the training of the next group of leaders?). *Start to sharpen your hypothesis and build momentum toward the Design phase.*

Then Repeat: Go through the cycle intentionally again, allowing the knowledge gained to sharpen your work. This loop can be repeated numerous times with third, fourth, and ninety-fourth prototypes to gather data and obtain a well-tested hypothesis that you can now consider carrying forward into the Design phase as a working theory and use to engage the wider organization. The further the core group is into the prototyping stage, the more you begin thinking about how your learning could impact or be integrated across the whole organization. Most organizations have to wait until their 3.0 or 4.0 prototype before they have the rigor and insight to engage the early and late majority (elephants) across the wider community or organization. (See the Design and Deploy phases.)

As you and the pioneering team begin to glean insight from the Discover phase and the various prototypes you have run, you will be ready to think about how this learning will be implemented more widely across your organization. Remember, this isn't the final stage of the journey. Many people make the mistake of thinking the first prototype (or even the third or fourth) is the result they are aiming for.

The Discover phase is a means to an end, not an end in itself. Trust the process, gather the learning, and know that there's plenty more of the journey to come.

DISCOVER 101

PRIZE

Gather insight and unearth principles through experiential learning, as well as grow in clarity and conviction of God's leading.

PEOPLE

Primarily innovators and early adopters, with some organizational stakeholders.

LEADERSHIP EXPRESSION

A mature Coach who is *intentional* and *instructive*.

SHADOWSIDE

An immature Coach who creates dependent people by giving too much instruction and not enough responsibility and creates an over-reliance on the genius of the Coach.

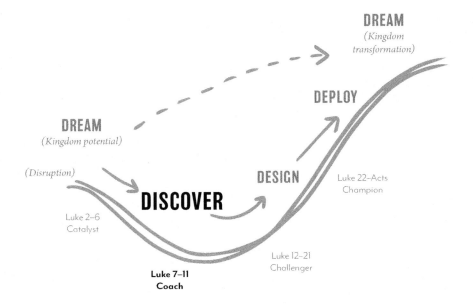

DREAM
(Kingdom transformation)

DEPLOY

DREAM
(Kingdom potential)

DESIGN

(Disruption)

Luke 22–Acts
Champion

DISCOVER

Luke 2–6
Catalyst

Luke 12–21
Challenger

Luke 7–11
Coach

SCRIPTURE: LUKE 7–11

In these chapters, Jesus is a Coach, who is *intentional* and *instructive* with the small group of disciples he is forming and transforming through experiential learning and apprenticeship. Jesus models the message while slowly but surely increasing the disciples' responsibility. Among others, a religious activist, a couple of fishermen, and a tax collector begin a journey of transformation, going from bystanders to disciples. Every interaction is a learning opportunity around key kingdom principles, and every day is a day of discovery.

The disciples are formed through experiencing Jesus' anointing by a sinful woman (Luke 7: 36–50; forgiveness, sacrifice, devotion), the women following Jesus (Luke 8:2–3; dignity), the parable of scattering seeds (Luke 8:4–15; adaptive learning, contextual awareness), encouraging them to put their "lamp" on a stand (Luke 8:16–18; boldness in incarnational witness), naming who his family was (Luke 8:19–21; relational commitment), calming the storm (Luke 8:22–25; spiritual authority), the feeding of the five thousand (Luke 9:10–17; provision), the cost of being a disciple (Luke 9:23–26; sacrifice, commitment), and looking for people of peace (Luke 10:1–16; incarnational mission). Jesus is sometimes explicit in the learning moments for the disciples, but often he is not. Through experience and explanation, they are coached in kingdom wisdom rather than spoon-fed information.

Luke 10 holds three key themes that Jesus repeatedly communicates to the disciples throughout his earthly ministry: incarnational mission with others (vv. 1–24, the sending of the Seventy-two), sacrificial service (vv. 24–37, the Good Samaritan), and personal intimacy with God (vv. 38–42, Mary and Martha).

YOUR CHANGE-AGENT JOURNEY

- Where do you need to operate as a Coach to be both intentional and instructive with those in your organization or venture?
- How can you initiate discovery through experiential learning and prototyping with a small group of pioneers?

PHASE THREE
DESIGN

/dɪˈzʌɪn/
"the way in which something is planned and made"
OR
"to intend for a particular purpose"

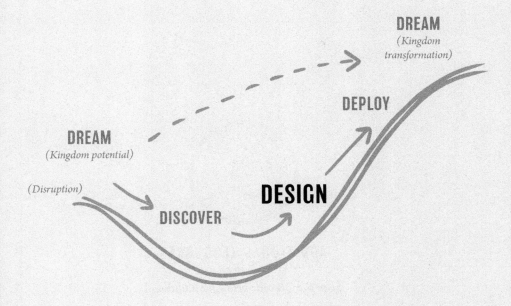

DREAM
(Kingdom transformation)

DEPLOY

DREAM
(Kingdom potential)

DESIGN

(Disruption)

DISCOVER

PROBLEM

Instead of being creative, strategic, and adaptive, the Western church often relies on a one-size-fits-all approach to every context, leading to formulaic efforts that rely on human effort and lack contextual intelligence.

We tend to rely on generic playbooks rather than partnering with God in each unique context.

PROCESS

Move from one-size-fits-all to Spirit-led, contextualized core principles.

PRIZE

Clarify core principles that can be expressed by every leader, in every context, in partnership with God.

ADDITIONAL RESOURCES

Scan the QR code below for additional resources, including videos, practices, and a toolkit to accompany the Design phase.

allchangejourney.com/resources

BEAUTY AND BLUEPRINTS

CREATED TO DESIGN

Those who make history are those who submit to the one who orchestrates it.
JOHN R. MOTT

*The nature of God is contextual and bearing witness
to [the] gospel is a contextual matter.*
ELIZABETH CONDE-FRAZIER

As for the future, your task is not to foresee it, but to enable it.
ANTOINE DE SAINT-EXUPÉRY

Did you know that an adult human being is made up of 7,000,000,000,000,00,
000,000,000,000 (seven octillion) atoms?[1] Or that the human nose can detect
about one trillion smells?[2] Or that if you laid out all the DNA molecules in your
body end to end, they would reach from the sun to the earth and back over six
hundred times?[3]

---

[1] Matthew Burke, "Mind-Blowing Facts About the Human Body," Factinate, January 27, 2017, https://www.factinate.com/things/50-interesting-facts-human-body/.

[2] Kat Long, "25 Amazing Facts About the Human Body," Mental Floss, March 19, 2019, https://www.mentalfloss.com/article/570937/facts-about-the-human-body.

[3] Anne Marie Helmenstine, "10 Interesting DNA Facts," ThoughtCo, updated January 28, 2020, https://www.thoughtco.com/interesting-dna-facts-608188.

When we look at the human body or the natural world around us, it doesn't take long to see God's hand. He has designed our world with intricacy, purpose, and beauty. The miracle of a newborn baby, the cyclical patterns of the seasons, the ebb and flow of tides, and the variety of species on our planet all point to God's incredible attention to detail.

Genesis 1:2 says that as God began to create, "the earth was formless and empty," but over the following six days, he transformed it into something of great order and beauty. Romans 1:20 tells us, "Since the creation of the world God's invisible qualities—his eternal power and divine nature—have been clearly seen." He is a God of frameworks, seasons, order, patterns … a God of design. He knits us together and, from beginning to end—from Noah, to Abraham, to the Ten Commandments, to the establishment of a royal line, to the dimensions of the temple, to Esther, to the birth, death, and resurrection of Jesus, to the commissioning of the disciples … and looking ahead to the Second Coming—God has a plan. And of course, because we are made in the image of God, we have that same ability to plan and design.

KINGDOM FRACTALS

The mesmerizing beauty of a snowflake, the perfect symmetry of a fern, or the intricate patterns of a tree branch are all examples of God's perfect creation design.

Science and mathematics have named these "fractal patterns." A fractal is a natural phenomenon or detailed pattern that repeats itself throughout a system at scale. Fractals in creation have a beautiful symmetry and recurring pattern that deeply resonates with us as humans.

Applied to the Design phase, fractals are the repeating patterns of your organizational core principles that are applied in multiple contexts. In biology, DNA is a vital component of coding and replication. It distills biological information that determines identity and behaviors, and this information is then replicated and passed on to the next generation.[4] Harvard scientists have discovered that our DNA packs itself tightly into a structure known as a "fractal globule."[5] In the same way that DNA is an identity marker in every cell in every part of your body, the central dynamic of the Design phase is to clarify core principles that, in the Deploy phase, will be embedded into every part of the organization from the smallest unit (single disciple) to the largest unit (the whole organization or venture). The New Zealand All Blacks, a dominant force in world rugby for many generations, have applied this principle by creating "an institutionalized *system* of continuous improvement … that works on the *super-structural level* (the season, and the four-year World Cup cycle), the *team level* (selection, the tapering of performance, tactical preparation, etc.), and the *individual level,* ('Things I Do Today')."[6] Within this system, the culture is based on a code of behaviors embedded into every player and across the whole playing squad and organization.

In the Design phase, we use "pilot projects" to experiment with frame-works, patterns, and rhythms that will help the whole system itself to align and multiply. (See more in "Piloting Your Way Forward," on pages 163–65). These pilots help us unlock fractal dynamics in our leaders by creating gener-ative energy across the entire system. They help leaders embody core values in their behavior as recurring patterns—rather than one-off, reactionary

---

4   "The Structure and Function of DNA," National Library of Medicine, https://www.ncbi.nlm.nih.gov/books/NBK26821/.

5   Peter Reuell, "3-D Image Shows How DNA Packs Itself into a 'Fractal Globule,'" *Harvard Gazette* in SciTechDaily, March 12, 2012, https://scitechdaily.com/3-d-image-shows-how-dna-packs-itself-into-a-fractal-globule/.

6   James Kerr, *Legacy: What the All Blacks Can Teach Us About the Business of Life* (London, UK: Constable & Robinson Ltd, 2013), 64, emphasis mine.

behaviors—which will move them and the organization toward the stated vision. Over time these repeated actions and interactions become rhythmic, regular, and natural to them and those they influence. A small core of leaders living this way will make an initial impact, but when multiple leaders across the system adopt these behaviors, the active participation of many creates a groundswell that leads to a tipping point across the whole organization or venture. This is what Jesus modeled with his disciples. He lived out core principles (kingdom DNA) and embedded them in the behaviors of his disciples, who then recreated those priorities in the life of the early church and beyond. It's like the power of the mustard seed that grows into a tree or the effect of yeast that works its way through the dough (Luke 13:18–21).

In the New Testament, Paul's apprenticeship of Timothy shows the power of embedding core principles intentionally in someone else through word and deed and then equipping them to repeat the pattern with others. In 1 Corinthians, Paul holds Timothy up as an example:

> I urge you to imitate me. For this reason I have sent to you Timothy, my son whom I love, who is faithful in the Lord. He will remind you of my way of life in Christ Jesus, which agrees with what I teach everywhere in every church.
>
> 1 CORINTHIANS 4:16–17

Paul is not merely encouraging the church to remember his *words* but to imitate Timothy's *actions* (as Timothy imitates Paul who imitates Christ). In 2 Timothy, Paul says, "The things you have heard me say in the presence of many witnesses entrust to reliable people who will also be qualified to teach others" (2 Tim. 2:2). In this example, the recurring fractal pattern that passes on kingdom DNA across multiple generations is passed from Jesus to Paul, to Timothy, to "reliable people," to "others," and beyond.

In the way of Jesus, Paul, and Timothy, leaders of the change journey must be "living examples." They need to embody the core values and actively live toward the shared purpose in ways others can see, experience, and be affected by. We often think titles, roles, and hierarchical influence bring change; however, relational influence is a far more powerful currency. When people are positively impacted by relationships and living examples, they listen, learn, and change because they want to, rather than because of a hierarchical obligation. A powerful sermon or the lifestyle of a distant, public figure can be inspiring; but deep, lasting influence comes from those with whom we have physical proximity and relational closeness. Being a living example to others will help activate participation and initiate change across your organization in a way that your emails, meetings, and rewards never will.

Many churches I have coached have sought input after a failed first attempt at implementing a change in their discipleship, leadership development, or community transformation efforts. However, what often transpires is that the behavior patterns of the core leadership haven't changed, and very few, if any, have attempted to live out what they are asking others to go and do. It is similar to the classic "do as I say, not as I do" parenting model, which, as we all know, doesn't work. If mere messaging was enough to get the job done, then the gospel would be a series of multiple Sermon on the Mount diatribes rather than Jesus embodying the message and apprenticing the disciples. Incarnation is at the heart of the gospel (John 1:14), and it's essential that we incarnate the life we are calling others to lead. Much of the early and late majority need to see evidence of the innovation in action through tried-and-tested results, as well as your team living out the values. This is the most compelling evidence and apologetic you can give them.

RHYTHMS AND RULES

Designing something effectively means that when you get to the next phase (Deploy), the core principles can be repeated as a rhythmic and recurring pattern rather than a one-off event. Spiritual mentor and leadership coach Shelly Miller says that rhythms are key to human flourishing. "Rhythms describe the art of living a life embodied with meaning and intention in the same way God creates."[7] Rhythms are also key to organizational flourishing, so, as you approach the Design phase, thinking about patterns and rhythms will be vital for ensuring the core principles are lived out as contextualized practices across the whole organization or venture, regardless of whether you are in a start-up or existing organization. If the change process is going to be truly fruitful, the design needs

---

[7] Shelly Miller, *Rhythms of Rest: Finding the Spirit of Sabbath in a Busy World* (Bloomington, MN: Bethany House Publishers, 2016), 18.

to work like a fractal pattern—something that will scale organically. Anything that is too specific may fail to apply in other places.

The practice of sabbath is an example of a key rhythm that is part of the Genesis design (Gen. 2:2–3) and is a recurring pattern of work and rest (Exod. 31:14–17)—a fractal in God's perfect design. In his book *Subversive Sabbath*, biblical professor and pastor A. J. Swoboda talks about how God has woven the rhythm of sabbath into his system for life:

> Creation was created perfectly. Everything that it needed in order to function properly was included. God created an environment perfectly suited for life to thrive. Examining the biblical account, we see that the Sabbath is an integral part of God's creation … God does not create accidentally. He creates intentionally. God made a system *for* life, not just a system *of* life. It is an intricate system with sabbath built into it. In this system, everything is dependent on something else to thrive. The system must be protected—or tragic things begin to happen.[8]

Monastic orders understand the importance of rhythms for living faithfully to God and his purposes in a communal setting. The fractal design of such communities is referred to as a "rule of life." The Northumbria Community, a contemporary monastic community in the UK, describes their rule of life as something that "serves as a framework for freedom—not as a set of rules that restrict or deny life, but as a way of living out our vocation alone and together."[9] The Order of the Mustard Seed, the monastic community at the heart of the 24-7 Prayer movement, describes their rule of life as "a set of principles and practices we build into the rhythm of our daily lives, helping us to deepen our relationship with God and to serve Him more faithfully."[10] Throughout history, Christian communities have been undergirded by a shared rule of life. However, as individuals, we also have a rule of life—even if we're not consciously aware

---

[8] A. J. Swoboda, *Subversive Sabbath: The Surprising Power of Rest in a Nonstop World* (Grand Rapids, MI: Brazos Press, 2018), 121, 123–24.

[9] "What is a Rule of Life?" Northumbria Community, accessed April 4, 2024, https://www.northumbriacommunity.org/who-we-are/our-rule-of-life/what-is-a-rule-of-life/.

[10] "Be True. Be Kind. Go," Order of the Mustard Seed, accessed April 4, 2024, https://www.orderofthemustardseed.com/.

of it. In discussing this reality, Chris Webb, a Benedictine Anglican priest, references a 2008 survey published in the scientific journal *Nature*:

> They followed the movements of over 100,000 people by anonymously tracking their cell phone signals. They found that we tend to revisit the same places, at the same times, with an astonishing (and almost monotonous) predictability. In other words, if you like cappuccinos, chances are high that you visit the same coffee shop most days, and usually at the same time in your daily routine. There is a pattern to our activities. We build structure into our days. We create family traditions and rituals. Our churches use "liturgies," even if we never write them down — we tend to follow the same order of worship week by week. Even though we often rejoice in spontaneity and excitability, the truth is we like routines; we prefer order to chaos.[11]

A communal rule of life is not an attempt to dictate people's behaviors. As Justin Whitmel Earley notes in *The Common Rule*, "a 'rule of life' is much less about obeying rules than it is about finding communal purpose."[12] In the Design phase, the clarity of a set of core principles linked to rhythmic behaviors—a rule of life—makes it possible for the big, future, amorphous dream to be an everyday reality. It enables each individual to take small, regular, and personal steps to live out the values (the DNA unearthed in Discover) and move intentionally toward the vision (the Dream).

A rule of life is expressed most healthily when it is empowered by the Holy Spirit and lived out in the context of community, which provides accountability and solidarity for the life choices we are making. Everything we design should point to Jesus and create more Christlike leaders and communities. As James K. A. Smith says, "The body of Christ should be a testimony to the kingdom that is coming, bearing witness to how the world will be otherwise. Our work and our practices should be the foretaste of that coming new kingdom."[13]

---

[11] Chris Webb, "How to Create a Rule of Life Based on the Six Streams," Renovaré, originally published January 2010, https://renovare.org/articles/rule-of-life-six-streams.

[12] Justin Whitmel Earley, *The Common Rule: Habits of Purpose for an Age of Distraction* (Downers Grove, IL: IVP, 2019), 14.

[13] Smith, *You Are What You Love*, 174.

FIRST-CENTURY DESIGN

Throughout the Gospels, we see how Jesus communicated and embodied kingdom design principles through stories and behaviors, and then embedded these in his disciples through repeatable patterns. Jesus shared a kingdom *worldview* with the disciples, created *environments* for them to experience kingdom principles, and then formed the disciples' *behaviors* so that they embodied these principles. Our Movement Leaders Collective training uses this frame of worldview (Paradigm), environments (Platform), and behaviors (Practice) to help leaders consider how their core DNA shapes their thinking, culture, structure, and efforts.

In the Gospel of Luke, Jesus shares a kingdom worldview and DNA through the stories of the waiting servants (Luke 12:35–49), the mustard seed (Luke 13:18–21), the narrow door (Luke 13:22–30), the great banquet (Luke 14:15–25), the lost sheep, the lost coin, and the lost son (Luke 15) ... and the list goes on. Effective design involves something we feel invited into—a bigger story rather than a formula or framework. But as well as telling parables and stories, Jesus also created environments and gave more specific blueprints—clear principles by which to live—meaning the kingdom DNA was embedded in the thinking and practice of the disciples through behaviors and patterns. The Lord's Prayer (Luke 11:2–4) is a simple design of prayer that Jesus gave to his twelve disciples to act upon. Similarly, the Lord's Supper (Luke 22:19) is another design pattern Jesus shared with his disciples and asked them to continue in remembrance of him. The Greatest Commandment (Mark 12:28–34) gives us a design by which to live out the Ten Commandments—we keep the first four by loving God, and we obey the last six commandments by loving our neighbor.

In biology, DNA shapes both our identity (who we are) and our activity (what we do); and kingdom DNA is the same. The Great Commission (Matt. 28:16–20) left Jesus' disciples (and us) in no doubt of our fractal mandate to make disciples of all nations. Our *identity* is as sent disciples (who we are), and our *activity* is disciple making (what we do). Over three years, Jesus' initial call to "Come, follow me" shifted to the final commission of "Go and make," as the DNA of movemental Christianity was embedded within the identity and activity of the disciples. Jesus designed multiplication and movement into the system as part of the repeating kingdom fractal of disciple-making DNA. We see contemporary mutations of this DNA expressed through institutional Christianity, where our primary *identity* is formed more by the badge and brand of our organization ("we are Baptists," "we are Presbyterians," "we are Pentecostals," "we are Free Church"). Or our primary *activity* tends toward attractional Christianity, where we invest money, time, and effort to attract consumers to come to us at our central site or service. However, instead of *institutional* Christianity ("badge and brand") or *attractional* Christianity ("come to us"), the original DNA was *movemental* Christianity ("go and make"). The challenge for us today is to recover a first-century design in a twenty-first-century context.

DEM BONES, DEM BONES …

In Ezekiel 37, God reveals his vision for spiritually reviving and resurrecting his covenant people. This passage gives us three key elements for kingdom design that we can harness to clarify, embed, and replicate our organizational DNA in the Design phase.

> [7] So I prophesied as I was commanded. And as I was prophesying, there was a noise, a rattling sound, and the bones came together, bone to bone. [8] I looked, and tendons and flesh appeared on them and skin covered them, but there was no breath in them.
>
> [9] Then he said to me, "Prophesy to the breath; prophesy, son of man, and say to it, 'This is what the Sovereign LORD says: Come, breath, from the four winds and breathe into these slain, that they may live.'" [10] So I prophesied as he commanded me, and breath entered them; they came to life and stood up on their feet—a vast army.
>
> [11] Then he said to me: "Son of man, these bones are the people of Israel. They say, 'Our bones are dried up and our hope is gone; we are cut off.'[12] Therefore prophesy and say to them: 'This is what the Sovereign LORD says: My people, I am going to open your graves and bring you up from them; I will bring you back to the land of Israel. [13] Then you, my people, will know that I am the LORD, when I open your graves and bring you up from them. [14] I will put my Spirit in you and you will live, and I will settle you in your own land. Then you will know that I the LORD have spoken, and I have done it, declares the LORD.'"

EZEKIEL 37:7–14

In this vision, the bones come together, bone by bone, to form a *Skeleton* (v. 7). Next come the tendons and the flesh: the *Skin* (v. 8). And finally comes the breath: the *Spirit* of the Lord (vv. 9–10). These three elements of Skeleton, Skin, and Spirit offer a vital framework for the Design phase.

Applying this metaphorically to the change journey, the *Skeleton* consists of kingdom principles and core values (DNA) that transcend culture and context. For example, KC Underground uses a simple framework for their micro-churches that incorporates the three elements of worship, community, and mission.[14] In their book *The Church as Movement*, JR Woodward and Dan White Jr. identify the same elements but use different language—"to live in *communion* with God, and out of the overflow of our life with him, we live into our sentness as a *community*, carrying out his *co-mission* to be a sign, foretaste and instrument of his kingdom in ever-expanding geographical areas."[15]

The *Skin* is the expression of these principles applied in different ways and contexts. Using the example of the microchurch frame above, the "community" dimension (relationship within Christian community) can be expressed in multiple ways—a meal, sharing an encouraging word with another believer, a small-group retreat, sacrificial sharing of resources, a family fun day, or babysitting each other's kids.

The *Spirit* is about designing in partnership with the Holy Spirit, with God at the heart of every initiative, informing and empowering all we do. As we design, we look for where God is at work and ask him to bring direction to our learning, to foster creativity in our contextualization, and to breathe life into our efforts and activities.

As you move through the Design phase, you will need to consider how to incorporate the kingdom fractals of Skeleton, Skin, and Spirit into your plan at every level. They will help the core values and key principles (Skeleton) unearthed in the Discover phase to be embedded and expressed in multiple different contexts across your organization (Skin), all empowered by God (Spirit). If we don't incorporate all three of these elements, we will end up constantly prototyping and trying new things and never solidify and

---

[14] See "Our Manifesto," accessed April 4, 2024, https://kcunderground.org/story.

[15] JR Woodward and Dan White Jr., *The Church as Movement: Starting and Sustaining Missional-Incarnational Communities* (Downers Grove, IL: IVP, 2016), 23, emphasis mine.

strengthen our initial attempts. Or we'll create a formulaic expression that isn't contextual. Or we'll propel ourselves forward in our own strength, ignoring what God is trying to reveal to us and building things on entirely the wrong foundations.

JESUS LIVED SKELETON, SKIN, AND SPIRIT

"Literally" is an overused word these days. My kids will *literally* start every sentence with the word "literally" to magnify the importance of what they are about to say. So, in the vernacular of my kids: Literally, Jesus was Skeleton, Skin, and Spirit. Many of us are familiar with the translation of John 1:14 in *The Message*: "The word became flesh and blood, and moved into the neighborhood." The Skeleton of God's word and truth took on humanity's Skin (literally!) and dwelt among us, as Jesus came to earth to do the work of his Father (Spirit).

Skeleton: Jesus taught and embodied key principles (e.g., prayer, formation, dependency on God, sacrificial service) in his life and leadership, which were repeated by the disciples across the Gospels and were then carried into the early church. Jesus was intentional rather than accidental in his formation of the disciples, as well as in his actions and interactions with others. He designed multiplication into the system by calling and forming his succession team (the disciples) who became leaders and went on to be movement makers.

Skin: Jesus formed his disciples in a local context rather than delivering detached theories, concepts, or classroom-based learning. He spoke with story, metaphor, and cultural references (e.g., agrarian metaphors for a farming community), allowing people to locate themselves in the story and respond in their own way. Jesus used numerous different ways to engage and welcome people, to teach, heal, and challenge, all dependent on the individual and their context. There was never a one-size-fits-all approach.

Spirit: Jesus' posture and practice showed complete dependency on God: "The Son can do nothing by himself; he can do only what he sees his Father doing, because whatever the Father does the Son also does" (John 5:19). He took time to retreat, pray, be silent, embrace solitude, and listen to the Father. He knew his mission and was not swayed by popularity or opposition. Jesus spent his whole life pursuing the prize God had called him to and instructed his disciples to wait for the Holy Spirit to come upon them before they started the next season of the work.

THE EARLY CHURCH LIVED SKELETON, SKIN, AND SPIRIT

This framework of Skeleton, Skin, and Spirit was also expressed in the early church as they extended movemental Christianity.

Skeleton: Although we often like to think of the early church as a spontaneous and unstructured movement, spreading wherever the wind blew, it also had an intentional, organizational Skeleton. There were recurring patterns of meeting together, spiritual formation, prayer, worship, teaching, inclusion, care for the poor, mission (Acts 2:24–47), and shared decision-making (Acts 15:1–21). These weren't delivered as stand-alone programs but were organic, living elements of a functioning community. Paul's letters show that there was ongoing instruction to ensure that the skeletal teachings of the gospel continued and remained faithful in all locations.

Skin: Paul's letters to the early church demonstrate cultural intelligence in these embryonic initiatives in multiple, diverse cities. The gospel was shared and embodied in different ways, applicable to the cultural context in which they found themselves. Paul was a master of contextual intelligence, navigating the Greek setting in different ways from the Jewish ones. One example of this is Paul's shift from using the language of "rabbi/disciple" to referencing the metaphor of parental relationships as the gospel crosses from a Jewish to a Greek context (e.g., 1 Cor. 4: 14–17).[16] Paul used the same Skeleton (teacher/learner in discipleship formation through knowledge transfer, apprenticeship, and immersion) but changed the Skin, as the missional context shifted.

Paul's practice of finding people of peace also illustrates his ability to contextually adapt. Whenever Paul entered a new town or city, he would normally head to the synagogue to begin preaching the gospel. But when Paul entered Philippi in Acts 16, there was no synagogue.[17] So, on the Sabbath, instead of

---

[16] Paul Beasley-Murray, "Should You Stop Using the Term 'Disciple,'" *GoodFaithMedia.org*, August 22, 2016, https://goodfaithmedia.org/should-you-stop-using-the-term-disciple-cms-23595/.

[17] "There was no synagogue there, which means that there were fewer than ten Jewish men in the city. The believers, mainly Jewish and Gentile God-fearing women, met outside the city." See "Paul's Ministry at Philippi," Ligioner.org, April 10, 1992, https://www.ligonier.org/learn/devotionals/pauls-ministry-at-philippi.

heading to the synagogue, he headed to the river where he expected to find a place of prayer. There, he found Lydia, who is described as a worshiper of God, and the Lord "opened her heart to respond to Paul's message" (v. 14). In a Jewish context, it had been effective to spread the gospel throughout the synagogues, but in this new context Paul changed his methods, and the first church planted in Europe was a house church in the home of a businesswoman.

Spirit: We see the early church's reliance on the Holy Spirit in all that they did. The early church was brought to life by the Spirit at Pentecost (Acts 2). The Spirit guided the Council at Jerusalem as they wrestled with the difficult decision of whether Gentiles should be circumcised (Acts 15:28). It was the Spirit who directed Ananias to visit Saul and lay hands on him for the recovery of his sight (Acts 9:10–19). The Spirit brought Peter to the house of Cornelius (Acts 10:9–43). Paul and his companions were blocked by the Spirit from going to Asia Minor (Acts 16:6). The early church knew the importance of seeking God's guidance and leadership in all the decisions they needed to make.

LIVING SKELETON, SKIN, AND SPIRIT TODAY

Every organization I have worked with has its own set of core principles and core values. They are often written on the wall of its lobby and on its website. Usually between three and eight key points, they can be both meaningful and meaningless at the same time. *Hospitality, prayer, mission, integrity, welcome*—all wonderful words, rich in meaning … but with the potential to mean nothing and have little or no impact. This has always been a challenge for God's people. God gave the people of Israel a fractal pattern to embody when he gave them The Ten Commandments on stone tablets (Exod. 20:1–21), but consistently living them out was another matter. We often live in an old covenant reality, where our core principles are written on walls and websites—the contemporary equivalent of the "stone tablets." Instead, we need to move to a new covenant reality, where the principles are expressed through our lifestyles and behaviors, written on the "tablets of human hearts" (2 Cor. 3:3). Hospitality, for example, is a great principle, but the practice of opening our home once a week to share a meal with someone is a recurring pattern that points to a lifestyle of hospitality.

In a team I led a few years ago, we recognized that we were strong apostolically with lots of strategy and effort, but we wanted to embrace more of the prophetic so we could be led more by what God was saying than by our master plans. As we adopted the core principle of being more prayerful, discerning, open to God, and Spirit-led, we wanted to create a repeatable behavior that helped every individual apply that value in every environment. So, we took on a simple practice of a "prayerful, prophetic pause." At the start of every meeting, we paused, prayed, listened, and then discussed what we felt God was revealing for that particular meeting. This eventually created an organizational culture of listening to the Spirit and looking for where God was at work. As new people joined the team and visitors attended, they were drawn into a culture that was expressed by an embodied behavior of prayer and listening to God.

UP THE OTHER SIDE

Until now, much of what we've been doing in our change journey is essentially unlearning and relearning, as we go down into the valley.

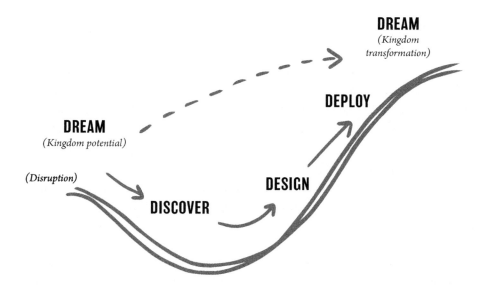

Through unlocking our kingdom imagination in the Dream phase and embarking on experiential learning in the Discover phase, we've embraced disruption and engaged with the *kairos* moments God has offered us. As we come to the Design phase, we've crossed the lowest point of the change journey and gained valuable learning and insight.

In their book *Metanoia*, Alan Hirsch and Rob Kelly describe this point in the change journey as follows:

> By this point, we have engaged with a huge amount of un/learning; we have become aware of the frailties in our current way of doing things; we have sought to examine our systems to see what hinders and what helps in terms of achieving our preferred future; and we have also looked at alternative ways of fulfilling our unique calling. This is the point of nakedness and openness to God, but this is precisely the place where God can impact us in a new way. The bottom of the curve is powerful because it is where God meets us … in the valley. Like Israel in the desert for forty years or Jesus' passion on the cross before the resurrection, this is that point … where insight into how to resolve the wicked problem is finally given. This is the turning point.[18]

Now we start to move upward out of the valley to begin to initiate and architect the future we desire to see. We move from primarily reflecting on the initial learning through prototyping toward designing a spiritual and strategic process for catalyzing change across the whole organization or venture.

DESIGN … TO 1.0 AND BEYOND!

As we embrace the Design phase, it is vital to remember God's original plan for humanity. We are designers and are created to design with others, as Adam and Eve were commissioned to do with God in the Garden of Eden. Kingdom design is not for personal gain. Nor is it about designing solo or in a vacuum. Skeleton, Skin, and Spirit give us a fractal pattern for kingdom design that allows us to unlock potential across many people and places in a way that is God-empowered and contextually relevant.

Effective design is aesthetic; it needs to be beautiful and simple. Think of the products we buy, the people we listen to, or the stories we read. If we are left cold by an encounter—whether with a person, a product, an experience, or an event—we are unlikely to engage with it again, let alone commit our time,

---

[18] Alan Hirsch with Rob Kelly, *Metanoia: How God Radically Transforms People, Churches, and Organizations From the Inside Out* (Cody, WY: 100 Movements Publishing, 2023), 113.

money, and effort to it. We are even less likely to share or recommend it to someone else. But beautiful, simple design draws us in and captures our hearts and imaginations, and we can't help but share it with others.

When our kids were younger, they always loved playing with Lego bricks. Over the years, they made, broke apart, and remade numerous different creations of their own imagination as well as those inspired by film, TV, and books. In the same way, design should be simple enough that others can engage with it, beautiful enough that they are drawn to it, and sufficiently accessible and applicable that others can create and recreate it in different contexts and cultures.

Effective design not only draws people into the story but also allows them to contribute to the narrative. If others can speak into it and shape it, then they will own it, champion it, use it, and share it.

It moves from being an idea held by a few to a journey lived out by many.

THREE IS A MAGIC NUMBER

LEARNING TO DESIGN

You've got to think about big things while you're doing small things, so that all the small things go in the right direction.
ALVIN TOFFLER

A nation's culture resides in the hearts and in the soul of its people.
MAHATMA GANDHI

The truly great companies of the 21st century will change within the context of their core ideologies while also adhering to a few timeless fundamentals.
JIM COLLINS

Buurtzorg is a Dutch healthcare provider that has intentionally disrupted the top-down, institutional model of nursing with a means of holistic care that has revolutionized community care in the Netherlands. Based on the core values of client-centered care and community-based nursing, their self-managing teams are empowered to build client-based solutions in their local context, with the support of a smart IT system and a back-office function. With over fourteen thousand employees and no centralized hierarchy or middle managers, their model has now been introduced in twenty-five countries. Their client satisfaction rates are the highest of any Dutch healthcare organization, and they have repeatedly won awards for being the best employer in the Netherlands. Buurtzorg's teams make decisions themselves, deciding how to organize their work and share responsibilities; and they continue to be entrepreneurial and innovative within their own context.[1] Speaking of the process of contextualization (Skin) across the dispersed work of Buurtzorg, founder Jos de Blok says,

> If you create these small environments where people feel ownership, you can replicate it all over the country and all over the world. It has to feel organic and logical for everybody. We said let's keep things open in terms of the support that was needed but we said that we are not going to use traditional approaches. …We will have the support that's needed, in a way that is simple, can be understood by everybody and is integrated as much as possible in the daily work of people.[2]

Blok points to the power of platform and patterns to create a strong system where learning is integrated across the whole rather than having the insight held in one component part of the system: "There are patterns in how you care for people, so you should build on these patterns, and every time you get new insights based on what you're doing, you share that knowledge. The support systems should be logical and simplified, but you should not underestimate the complexity of what's going on."[3]

The secret to Buurtzorg's success was a strong Skeleton that ensured DNA was consistent but organically and creatively expressed in multiple dispersed contexts (Skin). Its core guiding principles and flexible application enabled it to scale across the Netherlands and eventually the globe.

As Christian leaders, we are not only seeking to create a strong Skeleton in our organizations or ventures that can be embodied creatively through various expressions of Skin; we are looking to be constantly guided and led by the Spirit as well.

---

[1] "The Future Work Awards," RSA, accessed February 5, 2024, https://www.thersa.org/projects/archive/economy/future-work-awards/winners/buurtzorg; "The Buurrtzorg Model," Buurtzorg, accessed February 5, 2024, https://www.buurtzorg.com/about-us/buurtzorgmodel/.

[2] "In First Person: Jos de Blok," Executive Network, accessed March 25, 2024, https://www.shrm.org/executive-network/insights/people-strategy/first-person-jos-de-blok.

[3] "In First Person: Jos de Blok," Executive Network.

SO FAR, SO GOOD?

In the Design phase, we must distill the learning experiences from the previous phase and codify principles (Skeleton) so that many others can express them in different contexts (Skin) as they follow Jesus (Spirit). Once learning has been codified, it can be applied in multiple places by multiple people across multiple generations.

When coaching and consulting with organizations, at this stage I often remind them of where they are in the process—to reflect on how far they have come, reorientate them to where they are, and to refocus them on where they are going. Likewise, as you lead others in this process, it is important at this stage to summarize and make explicit where you have journeyed, where you are right now, and what's still to come.

- **Dream Phase: Partner with God to Unlock Kingdom Potential**
  Open your eyes and ears to God's new truth to begin to imagine a different future and unlock kingdom potential.
- **Discover Phase: Prototype to Test a Hypothesis**
  Learn and gather as much data as possible in the most efficient and effective ways to test a working hypothesis.
- **Design Phase: Pilot to Develop a Theory**
  Utilize and distill the initial learning from the prototypes to start developing a theory and build pilots to solidify your learning and create a strategic frame.
- **Deploy Phase: Process to Make Change a Reality**
  Implement the strategic frame by developing a process that can be scaled and influence the whole organization.

PILOTING YOUR WAY FORWARD

In the same way that the first prototype never fully works and requires iterations, so the design process will also be an evolving one. It cannot be static or one-dimensional. What you design initially will need to be tested, refined, and sharpened so that you develop something you are confident can be fruitfully and effectively scaled in the Deploy Phase. We do this testing by creating a pilot—"a small-scale release of a product or feature to a select group of users, aimed at collecting valuable feedback. Pilots are typically used … to test a new product or feature's usability, functionality, and desirability to mitigate risk."[4]

Whereas the prototype's orientation is simply to discover, a pilot is a more focused and robust design, with a higher orientation toward implementation. Initially in the Discover phase, we were more speculative with our prototypes, saying, "We're not sure what will work, so we'll try a few things and find out." But in the Design phase, with our more intentional pilots, we are moving toward, "We think this will work, but we need to find out with a few more people before we get everyone involved."

When an architect designs a building, he or she starts with a vision of what the building might look like (Dream). That concept is scribbled on paper or experimented with on a computer program (Discover). This process then becomes blueprints and a miniature model (Design). Those designs then become reality as the foundations are laid, the building is constructed, and the fixtures and fittings are added (Deploy). As leaders, we often dream of big buildings or argue over fixtures and fittings, but we miss the key design elements in between. Pilots help us to solidify and strengthen those elements that will be vital to the building's size, layout, and aesthetic.

In the previous phase (Discover), I referred to the work I was part of in an under-resourced community, where we identified "making a difference shoulder-to-shoulder *with* people" as a key principle. This initial learning was unearthed by a group of people who were all committed to pioneering and testing the following hypothesis: "Authentic community impact happens best through word and deed in the context of relationship." This core group proto- typed various activities, including soccer clubs, Easter egg hunts, community meals, home-based Alpha courses, movie nights, intentional dinner parties, and kids clubs. These prototypes taught us that some events were too large and some too small, that it was important not to do mission *to* the community but rather *with* the community, and that the most authentic and attractive gospel expression for a non-Christian was the everyday life and relationships of the Christians within a missional community. We solidified our learning in pilots that incorporated informal, lightweight, and low-maintenance events. These

---

4   "Product Pilot Guide for Product Managers," *userpilot*, October 9, 2023, https://userpilot.com/blog/product-pilot/.

were events that people wanted, that we did together with the community, and "added value" by making a positive difference. They focused on 1) family (kids clubs, family fun days, and movie nights) and 2) food (community meals and intentional dinner parties). To provide a good cross-section of learning, these pilots were run by different missional communities across the city—some in suburban, more affluent areas; and some in urban, more underserved areas. In this process, as a core group, we also added an additional pilot of the Passion Audit—a training resource we created that we hoped would provide a framework every missional community leader could use in their own context.

The pilots helped to refine our theories, leading to a clear strategy that helped every leader in their own context. Eventually, we were able to move into the Deploy phase with a strategic process that served every one of our missional communities with the core principles of food, family, sustainable rhythms, added-value, and working shoulder-to-shoulder. These were five skeletal principles for community impact, alongside a Passion Audit, that every leader in the Deploy phase could use with their missional communities. We were also able to share this with other churches, denominations, and organizations interested in learning how to support their leaders.

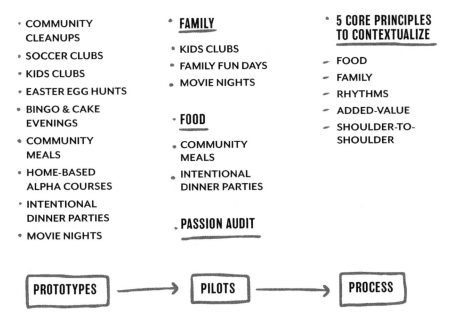

- COMMUNITY CLEANUPS
- SOCCER CLUBS
- KIDS CLUBS
- EASTER EGG HUNTS
- BINGO & CAKE EVENINGS
- COMMUNITY MEALS
- HOME-BASED ALPHA COURSES
- INTENTIONAL DINNER PARTIES
- MOVIE NIGHTS

FAMILY
- KIDS CLUBS
- FAMILY FUN DAYS
- MOVIE NIGHTS

FOOD
- COMMUNITY MEALS
- INTENTIONAL DINNER PARTIES

PASSION AUDIT

5 CORE PRINCIPLES TO CONTEXTUALIZE
- FOOD
- FAMILY
- RHYTHMS
- ADDED-VALUE
- SHOULDER-TO-SHOULDER

PROTOTYPES → PILOTS → PROCESS

FOCUS, FOCUS, FOCUS

In the Discover phase, you generally lead with a yes to try to test broadly and grow through active prototyping to gather as much data as possible. However, now, as you enter the Design phase, *no* becomes part of your vocabulary as you become more intentional about your activity rather than reacting to every opportunity. We become more strategic about where we are investing, how we are learning, and what we are building. We create fewer but more focused pilots to confirm and prove our theories before we finally allow everyone across the organization to experience the new process in the next phase.

In the previous chapter, I introduced Skeleton, Skin, and Sprit as three key elements for kingdom design that we can harness through our pilots. As you move through this phase, you will need to clarify your organizational DNA and core principles (Skeleton), create a fractal pattern for these to be embodied by every individual and group through contextualized practices (Skin), and equip everyone to look for where God is at work and partner with him in that (Spirit). Whether you are launching a new venture or renewing an existing organization, Skeleton, Skin, and Spirit offer a frame that will bring continuity, longevity, and scalability to your endeavors.

Over the last fifteen years, I have run learning communities that focus on discipleship, leadership, community, and movement. These have taken place globally, including in India, Kenya, and New Zealand.[5] Although the core principles of the training (Skeleton) were the same, the expression of the principles in each country looked very different (Skin), as we looked for where God was at work (Spirit). This meant that we didn't have a uniform model of training, regardless of context. In India, participants were wrestling with the caste system and the challenges this presented for disciple making. In Kenya, in 2020, the median age was 20.1 years, and 50 percent of Kenyans were under the age of twenty-five; so, participants were particularly processing how to disciple young people.[6] And in New Zealand, they were grappling with how to start new initiatives of disciple making within an existing denominational structure. After

---

[5] See https://catalystmovements.com.

[6] Natalie Cowling, "Demographics of Kenya—statistics & facts," December 21, 2023, https://www.statista.com/topics/7750/demographics-of-kenya/#topicOverview.

engaging in learning communities for four to six years, each team now leads its own contextualized disciple-making movements and leadership training. They have shifted from being participants to partners in the work; and Samit, Oscar, and Amy are now the movement leaders in each of the countries and are still friends and ministry partners many years later.[7]

START WITH THE END IN MIND

Skeleton, Skin, and Spirit provide a frame we use to seed and scale kingdom change across both the whole organization and each individual context. In an existing organization, these three elements help activate the participation of multiple leaders across the organization while also unlocking generative energy and creativity within specific contexts. In a new initiative, these three elements enable leadership and effort to be dispersed so that more leaders share responsibility to grow the work. We will now explore each of the three elements in more detail.

SKELETON
(Core Principles)

SPIRIT
(Holy Spirit
Partnership)

SKIN
(Contextualized
Practices)

---

[7] See https://hi72.org (India); https://www.m28network.org (Kenya); https://www.goodsoilcollective.org.nz (New Zealand).

SKELETON (CORE PRINCIPLES)

A body without a skeleton is a pile of mush: a blob. As an organization or venture, the Skeleton is your DNA, made up of your theological framework, meta-ideas, core principles, and key values. It's your non-negotiables and the essence of who you are (identity), upon which everything else is built and your behaviors are shaped (activity). As you design for change and growth in an existing organization or define your DNA at the inception point of a new venture, your Skeleton should be easily embodied, clearly communicated, and regularly replicated across the whole organization.

The Skeleton helps bring clarity, intentionality, and authority to your key principles and core values, which confirm your identity and undergird your activity. Our goal is to grow and extend that DNA and culture—*how* we do things, not just *what* we do. The further away someone in an existing organization or venture is from the center, the more important it is that they know the core principles so they can embody them at a distance in their context. When those in an organization do not have physical proximity to one another, it is only the core values and shared vision that unite them.

Having a clear Skeleton that guides the change process also helps us to avoid micro-management or command-and-control leadership styles. As the work of a venture, church, or organization grows and scales and distance increases, leaders cannot make every decision or connect with every person. A framework of core principles that aligns with the organization's culture and behaviors helps ensure healthy growth. This prepares the organization for the next stage of the journey (Deploy). Dee Hock, the mastermind behind the growth of Visa, once noted that, "To the degree that you hold purpose and principles in common among you, you can dispense with command and control. People will know how to behave in accordance with them, and they'll do it in thousands of unimaginable, creative ways."[8]

---

[8]   Peter Baumgartner, "What a lack of trust can do to a team," *Opensource.com*, July 6, 2017, https://opensource.com/open-organization/17/7/lincoln-loop-trust#.

SKIN (CONTEXTUALIZED PRACTICES)

When you pay attention to the Skin, you're paying attention to the context and actively seeking to be creative with how your principles are applied through contextualized practices in multiple settings. No two people, environments, or locations are the same. We must ask ourselves, "What will work in this place, with these people, at this time?" Talking about contextual intelligence (CQ), author and church planter Michael Adam Beck says,

> CQ comes from the Latin *contextere* which means "to weave together"; and the conjunction of two Latin words: *inter* which means "between" and *legere* which means "to choose or read." CQ is literally about "accurately reading between the lines" (the threads that intertwine to form a context). It was Yale psychologist Robert Sternberg who first popularized the term "contextual intelligence." He suggests that all intelligence is contextual. Intelligence does not develop in a vacuum or in a laboratory with standardized tests and objective answers. A genius IQ is useless if it can't be practically applied in real-world scenarios.[9]

Paying attention to context (Skin) brings beauty, creativity, and flexibility. Shortcutting the hard work of contextualization is like taking any kidney available and using it for a transplant, regardless of blood type or match.

There's flex in the kingdom design system so it can adapt, iterate, and develop over generations rather than being a formulaic playbook. This flexibility can be built into the system by the designers themselves, but it can also be fostered by those who interact with the design as they interpret, translate, and integrate the core principles to fit their specific context. Effective design allows those who are implementing it to feel a sense of ownership. There is both continuity and a sense of freedom to adapt to the context—for example, DNA being embodied in multiple small groups across a church, in multiple churches across a denomination, or in multiple teams across a faith-driven venture.

In this phase, we need to ensure our design can be applied in every place and people group.

---

[9] Michael Adam Beck in L. Rowland Smith (ed), *Red Skies*, 46.

SPIRIT (HOLY SPIRIT PARTNERSHIP)

When we consider our design, we need to remember that we want to see *kingdom* change and *kingdom* fruitfulness. As we engage with the Holy Spirit, we must continue to have Scripture as our foundation and guide, and Jesus must be our defining center for identity and activity. Only when God breathed on the skin and bones in Ezekiel 37 did they stand up and become an army. Engaging with Spirit in our design process means all our activity is God-initiated, God-infused, and God-oriented.

Embracing Spirit through prayer, Scripture, communal discernment, and engaging with the Holy Spirit helps us to better understand the insights we gained from the Discover phase. We look for where God is at work and leading us rather than operating from a human-centered strategic plan. As Cath Livesey, leader of the ministry Accessible Prophecy, says in *Holy Disruption*:

> We need the capacity to imagine a world other than the one legitimized by the dominant culture and the powers of consumerism, individualism, and so on. We need the Holy Spirit to interrupt what we think we know—to so unsettle our established paradigms that we can humbly allow something different to emerge.[10]

The Design phase is both spiritual and strategic; this means that all our DNA, ideas, and strategies are made in alignment with God and from the leading of his Spirit.

BRINGING IT ALL TOGETHER

Calibrating Skeleton, Skin, and Spirit can feel like a juggling act, and we often need a daily reminder that we are partnering with God in his work. We can easily end up working *for* God rather than walking *with* God. As leaders and organizations, we can often drift toward prioritizing one of the three elements over the other two. As we engage in the design process, we need to ask questions that take us beyond our existing learning, knowledge, and processes—and we also need to embrace different types of listening: prayerful reflection (listening to

---

[10] Cath Livesey, *Holy Disruption: Harnessing the Prophetic to Shape a More Christlike Church* (Cody, WY: 100 Movements Publishing, 2022), 126.

God), team discussions (listening to each other), and feedback loops (listening to others). All of these are vital if we want to maintain a humble learning posture and design with these three elements present. Dynamic interactions with God, each other, and other people create awareness and accountability so that in our everyday ministry and kingdom design we are shaped by God's Word and work (Spirit), we are intentional in the structure of our kingdom principles (Skeleton), and we apply these principles contextually (Skin).

CHANGING THE CONVERSATION— THE 100 MOVEMENTS PUBLISHING JOURNEY

Returning to our 100 Movements Publishing example, when the initiative reached the Design phase, it had a good catalog of books and a faculty of authors, so the team began to work on its Skeleton—defining the criteria for accepting manuscripts and becoming more discerning about what books they agreed to publish. They began to build systems and processes that were repeatable, creating templates on Google Drive and Asana, and forming repeatable patterns and practices that could scale. One key design element was the simple and sticky tagline of "Changing the Conversation"—a memorable phrase that succinctly communicates the dream.

100MP also took on partnership projects with other organizations. The 100MP Skeleton of editorial and production processes was expressed in the branded products of other organizations (Skin). They also began to subsidize projects with key authors who were more diverse in either topic or ethnicity—those who didn't have a platform or a business model that would sell thousands of books but had a key message to be shared with the church.

The team also focused on intentionally listening to the Holy Spirit as they reviewed manuscripts so that they weren't only making decisions based on the caliber of the author or the quality of the manuscript but also on the conviction of the Spirit. They sought dependence on God for both resource provision and the editorial process.

After launching six years ago, the publishing ministry is now on the edge of the Deploy phase. Due to the nature of the publishing industry and of starting a new initiative, the change journey has been quite prolonged. Sometimes change takes six months. Sometimes it takes six years. However long it takes, we should always ask questions of ourselves and our circumstances. We should seek to learn from what has happened and what is happening to strengthen us as we look ahead and move forward.

THE WEAKEST LINK

In both the everyday activity of your organization, as well as the kingdom design process itself, you will likely be naturally strong in one dynamic—Skeleton, Skin, or Spirit; naturally middling in another; and weakest in a third. And, like the proverbial chain, you will only be as strong as the weakest link. Because the three dynamics function as an interdependent system, we not only lose the value of our weakest element, but we also miss out on the synergy present when all three combine. In modern leadership circles, the focus is often on "playing to your strengths," but we must also be attentive to our weaknesses and the interplay between the three dynamics.

In addition to identifying our weaker dynamic, we must also be aware that it is easy to drift toward one of these three elements or forget one of them. Most of us don't set out to minimize Skeleton, Skin, or Spirit. (There's no board meeting to vote God out; no conscious decision to only employ one strategy over the others.) Often, though, we unintentionally end up with a lack in one of the areas through numerous small and seemingly minor decisions. We focus on the big areas of concern and respond accordingly, whereas we are more likely to miss the more mundane decisions as they creep past us, and we unconsciously drift off course.

Below are examples of what can happen when one of the three design elements is missing, whether your context is a faith-driven venture, micro-church, church, nonprofit, or denomination. In the Design phase, as you think about the organization itself and creating first pilots and then a frame that can be replicated in multiple contexts, allow God to nudge you to a place of self-awareness so that you can integrate all three into your kingdom design.

SKELETON AS THE WEAKEST LINK—*FREE-FOR-ALL* (LACKS INTENTIONALITY)

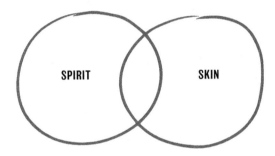

When there's a weak or absent Skeleton, it's often because a leader or team has an aversion to strategy or structures. In the absence of a clear skeletal framework, which helps us to codify kingdom principles, growth is often limited to one generation, one leader, one team, or one context.

A lack of framework creates either a *bottleneck* or *anarchy*.

A *bottleneck* is formed because leaders at the heart of the work can't identify the principles behind what's worked in the Discover phase and are therefore unable to codify and communicate these principles (Design) to be able to train others or scale their intuition or instinct (Deploy). The work may grow, but it's dependent on a few leaders, and it will only be actioned by those close enough to the center to imitate the expression. If those in the wider organization aren't able to understand the principles, the change process will not translate into their context. Leaders further away from the center don't understand *why* they're doing what they're doing; or they might have a completely different interpretation of a new initiative because there's no codification to help them to understand it or to compare it with previous means of operating.

Without a framework, opinions, politics, charisma, and choice rule the day, leading to *anarchy*. People interpret and embody what they want, so there is no cohesion, no shared purpose, and no strategic architecture. There is energy—in a hundred directions—but it's diffuse. At its worst, a weak Skeleton can lead to division and confusion, with everyone pursuing their own ends in their own ways.

SKIN AS THE WEAKEST LINK—*FORMULAIC* (LACKS CONTEXTUALIZATION)

Without healthy Skin, the core beliefs and values aren't adapted to new situations or environments, and in our Design phase, we end up with either a theoretical, abstract plan or a singular solution that jars with the context.

A lack of contextualization leads to *empire* or *franchise*.

Much of the European ecclesiology exported by missionaries to Africa and Asia is a prime example of the *empire* model, where a dominant culture is exported into another. My friends in India once sent me a photo of a local ordination service with a procession of bagpipes—a tradition that continues to this day because of the Scottish missionaries who first took the gospel to that part of the world. It's a design that lacks cultural awareness, importing the whole package and paraphernalia from another context rather than discerning and distilling the *principles* and then expressing them in contextualized *practices*.

A *franchise* happens when a strong skeleton ends up as a rigid structure with no flexibility or consideration of the context. For example, in the business world, Starbucks has been successful in many locations across the world; but in New Zealand and Australia—where individuals generally appreciate a more unique, high-caliber coffee experience—Starbucks failed.[11] In Christian ministry, it's what happens when a church leader lifts a discipleship plan from a leadership conference and immediately tries to implement it across their whole system, or when a Christian entrepreneur takes another business's strategy and runs it verbatim. We apply someone else's answers to specific contextual questions. People are left confused, disillusioned, or feel controlled as a solution is forced upon them, and the Skeleton becomes a straitjacket rather than a supporting framework.

In 1991, John Major, the newly appointed British prime minister, wrote a five-page letter to the outgoing prime minister, Margaret Thatcher, explaining why he was abolishing her flagship "poll tax." He described the tax as "unfair, uncollectable, indefensible." The design flaws in the communication, clarity, equity, and collection of the tax itself, had all contributed to its downfall. The team that had designed the poll tax comprised a small group of white men, all from the upper echelons of society, who had reported that working as a group together was an enjoyable and invigorating experience, leading them to be confident in their vision and strategy. It was a clear example of how the narrow demographics of this working party meant the design process was flawed from the beginning. Their lived experience was a far cry from the context for which they were designing, and they worked in isolation from the real world, without robust feedback or the influence of a diverse perspective. As a group, they had little concept of the difficulties local councils would face in trying to collect the tax where there was a high number of rental properties, with occupants regularly moving around. They didn't consider the potential impact for those on low incomes, nor had they experienced what it meant to live close to the

---

YB Editor, "How Starbucks failed in Australia," *Yellowbees*, May 11, 2023, https://www.yellowbees.com.my/how-starbucks-failed-in-australia.

poverty line. They also failed to think through the implications that many would avoid registering to vote, simply so that they could circumvent paying the tax.[12]

If we are designing with people who look and think like us, then we are designing in a narrow framework and will subsequently produce a niche solution. For instance, a group of men would struggle to design a leadership development program for women; a group of Europeans would struggle to design a community engagement program for Africans; and a group of millennials would struggle to design an app for those over seventy. Doing the hard work of contextualization forces us out of our natural preferences. As humans, we are creatures of comfort, so we must make ourselves aware of the strong pull to uniformity and familiarity, and counter this by intentionally engaging with the Holy Spirit, the context, and with those who are different from us as we design.

SPIRIT AS THE WEAKEST LINK—*FORCED* (LACKS DEPENDENCY)

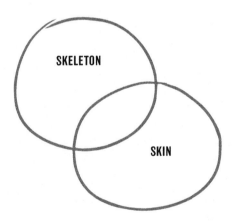

When we minimize the Spirit in the Design phase, we have a set of universal, kingdom principles (Skeleton) that can be contextualized in many places (Skin), but they are simply human ideas. Without the Spirit, we take God's playbook but drop him from the team. We deify ourselves, place our competency at the center, and our efforts look remarkably similar to that of the world's.

---

[12]   See Syed, *Rebel Ideas*, 47–52.

A lack of dependency simply leaves us with *systems* or *striving*.

Leaders take the latest management or business principles, pulling content or frameworks off the shelf or out of a book, and implement them as a *system,* without engaging in prayer or reference to Scripture. In a church led this way, neither Christians nor non-Christians experience any of the mystery or otherness of God. Instead, they encounter human effort, management systems, and words without power. The culture is defined by *striving*, and the driving force behind the work is human ideas, expressed in human strength. If we can run the church as an organization and operation without Jesus, then we have become what Bonhoeffer referred to as "Christless Christianity."[13]

This is exactly what the Pharisees did. They placed themselves and their efforts at the center of the story, designing religious architecture that resulted in human effort, rules, and regulations, and created cultural customs that lacked relationship with, or holy reverence for, God. As gatekeepers to a religious system, they prevented their community from living a dynamic, kingdom-oriented life with God.[14]

Partnership with the Spirit in our design process is vital because we will, by human nature, always seat ourselves on the throne of our lives, making the work about our effort, our agenda, our acclaim, and our initiative. To help overcome this, it's important to engage with God through rhythms of prayer, silence, and solitude, as well as forming deep and meaningful relationships with those who can support us, challenge us with different perspectives, and to whom we can be accountable. If decisions aren't submitted to God and others, we will end up hurting ourselves and those we love and lead, as well as our organizations.

KNOW THYSELF

As well as identifying our weaknesses, it is equally important to identify our strongest element and understand how this can become the dominant or sole element of our design. This is why pilots are essential; they challenge us to develop a three-dimensional process where otherwise—naturally or instinctively—we would only have one or two of the three elements.

---

[13] Dietrich Bonhoeffer, *The Cost of Discipleship* (New York, NY: Touchstone, 1995), 59.

[14] See, for example Matt. 12:1–14 and Matt. 23.

If we are dominant in Skeleton (core principles), who we are and what we design may feel cold, brittle, formulaic, analytical, theologically militant, and human-driven, with a danger that it has a mono-message or a one-size-fits-all franchise approach.

When Skin (contextualized practices) is dominant, with the emphasis solely on context, who we are and what we design may lack intentionality and cohesion or may become niche, individualistic, dispersed, or theologically compromised, and can struggle to scale healthily.

If Spirit (Holy Spirit partnership) is dominant, who we are and what we design may lack intentionality, contextualization, accountability, and a frame to scale. It may also be theologically immature and contextually weak. Such designs can become personality-driven around an individual leader's spiritual gifting or the spirituality of a small community. At worst, this misemphasis can lead us to use "thus sayeth the Lord" in abusive and harmful ways.

Overcoming the tendency to overlook our weakest element or overemphasize our strongest element helps us to harness the synergy of all three, allowing us to create an intentional, contextual, God-empowered work.

	Skeleton	Skin	Spirit
Key Element	Core principles	Contextualized practices	Holy Spirit partnership
Healthy Expression	Intentional not instinctive	Contextual not chaotic	God-empowered not human effort
Defining Ethos	Clarity and intentionality on core beliefs, principles, and values expressed across the whole	Engaging and embracing the culture and context	Looking and listening for where God is at work and joining him there
Reduced Expression	**Formulaic:** An organizational playbook without regard for context or nuance	**Free-for-all:** Multiple agendas with no guiding principles or accountability framework	**Forced:** Human effort that relies on good ideas and management systems for our own gain

The core community Jesus formed over three intense years sparked the early church and cascaded into a global movement by embedding and embodying kingdom/movemental DNA in multiple generations and places. We need that same intensity and intentionality to architect a framework and roadmap that can be shared across the whole organization and to many generations, so change can permeate everything from the smallest unit to the largest, in every corner of our culture and structure.

FRAMING THE FUTURE

EQUIPPING OTHERS TO DESIGN

*There is immense power when a group of people with similar
interests get together to work towards the same goals.*
IDOWU KOYENIKAN

*The world doesn't change one person at a time. It changes as
networks of relationships form among people who discover they
share a common cause and a vision of what's possible.*
MARGARET WHEATLEY AND DEBORAH FRIEZE

Just because it's common sense doesn't mean it's common practice.
GILBERT ENOKA

Your baby takes their first steps, your best friend gets married, you visit the
Grand Canyon, your partner receives an award. If you're over forty, you're
probably posting it on Facebook; if you're in your thirties, it's on Instagram;
and if you're younger, you'll be stitching it on TikTok—all within seconds of
creating the video. By the time you read this book, no doubt there will be at least
one more platform to add to the collection.

Not so long ago, those of an older generation might have called it a "Kodak
moment." Instead of taking out their smartphones, they'd be fumbling with a

camera case, fiddling with the dials, posing the shot, and waiting days for the film to be developed—hoping at least one picture was worth keeping. For years, Kodak held the dominant market share of the photography industry. Established in the late nineteenth century, Kodak spent nearly one hundred years as the leading manufacturer of cameras and film.[1] Their advertisements encouraged customers to "Take a Kodak with you" and "Kodak, as you go," selling a new way for ordinary people to capture the memories of their lives.[2] But despite its dominance in the industry, Kodak famously filed for bankruptcy in 2012, just as everyday photography was booming in the digital age and the word "selfie" was entering the dictionary.

LEARNING FROM KODAK

We might assume Kodak simply missed the opportunity for digital innovation, that a competitor got there first with the technology, and their demise was part of the tough world of business. But, in fact, Kodak was the first to make the discovery! When Kodak electrical engineer Steve Sasson invented the technology for digital photography in 1975, you'd think Kodak would have jumped at the chance to utilize it and drive the industry forward. Instead, in Sasson's words, they told him, "That's cute—but don't tell anyone about it."[3] Kodak executives were fully aware from their own research in the '80s that digital technology would take over film and paper printing in the next ten to twenty years. They even invested in the technology, becoming the first company to invent a mega-pixel camera. But, despite all the information and resource available to them, they refused to pivot their business toward digital. They made the initial discovery but faltered in the Design phase. What they had in their hands in the present distracted them from what they could take hold of in the future. Their competitor, Fujifilm, adopted the technology—with Sony, Canon, and Nikon quickly following—all shifting toward digital.

---

[1] Michael Zhang, "A Brief History of Kodak: The Rise and Fall of a Camera Giant," PetaPixel, June 14, 2018, https://petapixel.com/2018/06/14/a-brief-history-of-kodak-the-camera-giants-rise-and-fall/.

[2] Gus Lubin, "These Are The Gorgeous Kodak Ads That Made Photography Popular," *Business Insider*, January 19, 2012, https://www.businessinsider.com/these-were-the-gorgeous-kodak-ads-that-made-photography-popular-2012-1.

[3] Chunka Mui, "How Kodak Failed," *Forbes*, January 18, 2012, https://www.forbes.com/sites/chunkamui/2012/01/18/how-kodak-failed/.

Although Kodak continued to invest in digital, they were unable to accept that it would take over their existing methods of print—the area that formed the core of their profitable business. While competitors were investing in the digital industry, Kodak invested more in fighting to protect their existing film and paper business. Their initial success led to their eventual defeat. The defense of the old led to the downfall of the entire company. By the time they realized their mistake, it was too late.

There's a lot we can learn from stories like Kodak's. It takes courage to embrace change across the whole when it risks our modes of operating that have historically brought success and have shaped the identity of our organization. It's hard to make a change when it threatens the areas where we are winning or things that are seemingly working well. As Niccolò Machiavelli says in *The Prince*,

> There is nothing more difficult to take in hand, more perilous to conduct, or more uncertain in its success, than to take the lead in the introduction of a new order of things, because the innovator has for enemies all those who have done well under the old conditions, and lukewarm defenders in those who may do well under the new. This coolness arises partly from fear of the opponents, who have the laws on their side, and partly from the incredulity of men, who do not readily believe in new things until they have long experience of them.[4]

We can embrace the disruption, pursue a dream, and discover something new, but we will never realize the potential of whole-scale change if we're unwilling to let go of our previous successes. As Professor Kamal Munir, pro-vice-chancellor of Cambridge Judge Business School, noted when interviewed about Kodak's demise: "Whenever I ask why a certain company that has fallen on hard times is doing badly, I always start by asking why it was successful in the first place. That is where the answer lies."[5] Similarly, it often happens that the next move of God is most opposed by those who were at the heart of the last.

Instead of waiting too long to adapt, another danger is that leaders move on too quickly to the next innovation without the hard work required to

---

4 Niccolò Machiavelli, *The Prince* (Toronto, Canada: HarperTorch Classics, 2015), epub edition, 43.

5 "The rise and fall of Kodak's moment," University of Cambridge, March 14, 2012, https://www.cam.ac.uk/research/news/the-rise-and-fall-of-kodaks-moment.

make changes to the design. When this happens, new ideas never reach their full potential. It takes discipline and effort to create a prototype in the first place. But it also requires discipline and effort to refine a first prototype from the Discover phase to make it a pilot in the Design phase, which then has the potential to influence the many in the Deploy phase. Rather than pushing through the design process, many of us either give up on a prototype entirely (if it's seemingly failed), or we move full steam ahead, expecting everyone around us to intuitively grasp hold of our idea and implement it in their context ... while we move on to our next great idea with numerous prototypes in our wake. If we take the time to slow down and pay attention to what is happening, we might just see our ideas effect the change they are capable of.

The Design phase is particularly challenging for pioneers who love to move to the next frontier. Natural innovators will need to embrace the discipline required to push through this phase. Thinking back to Awareness (hear) and Application (obey) (see pages 18–20 and appendix one), the *Instinct* leader (high Application/low Awareness) will have a big vision (Dream) and activate lots of prototypes (*instinctive* Discover). However, this leader will need the discipline to strengthen and solidify the learning from those prototypes to create pilots and frameworks (Design) to develop something that can scale (Deploy). The *Concept* leader (low Application/high Awareness) will share hypothesis after hypothesis (Dream) and create the philosophical frame for many pilots (*conceptual* Design). However, the danger for this leader is that the blueprints will remain conceptual and are never tried and tested, so there will be assumptions, ideas, and possibilities, but nothing is ever built (Deploy).

ADDING MORE PEOPLE INTO THE MIX

So far, the core group driving the process has been made up of mostly innovators and early adopters (goldfish) and, if you are part of an existing organization, a few key organizational stakeholders who are most likely to be the early majority (elephants). Through the previous phase, this core group has gathered all the learning from experimentation and multiple prototypes and now will begin to test that learning more intentionally through specific pilots. This piloting process clarifies and solidifies the design of a frame (Skeleton) and begins to embody this as a living example and proof of concept in multiple contexts

(Skin) empowered by God (Spirit) to prepare to engage a wider audience in the Deploy phase.

Although the pilots in the Design phase will still mainly be the domain of the innovators and early adopters, this pioneering group needs to mix up the gene pool by bringing in some more organizational stakeholders or trusted advisors. If you are sparking change in an existing organization, rather than a new venture, you will also need some leaders from the early majority. This will strengthen the design work by engaging a broader audience with differing perspectives. If a group of pioneers simply design in a vacuum, they will produce a pioneering solution that will only work for a small percentage of the whole. (Remember the poll tax group in the previous chapter.) Engaging a larger number of leaders here can draw in those with relational sway and who are in organizational positions to start influencing a larger percentage of the whole organization. This process takes time and, although slightly more public, is not yet front and center for the organization.

The combination of the existing pioneering group and a new engagement with organizational stakeholders and the early majority can sometimes mix as ineffectively as oil and water! There will be many perspectives within the group (different appreciation of risk, different levels of imagination, and different priorities), and the responsibility of the leader is to manage this well, uniting everyone around the collaborative work of design. This is vital in an existing organization if the design is to influence many, or for a pioneering venture to move from a "scrappy start-up" to a stronger and more mature organization capable of scaling.

ACTIVATING DESIGN IN YOUR ORGANIZATION OR VENTURE

The Design phase is the hinge point, where the process moves from few to many and from potential to actualized. This phase is full of potential, as initial learning is clarified and condensed into a framework that can be shared more widely and more leaders are invited into the process. It's the time when the work of a few begins to reap a reward, moving us closer to the tipping point—"the one dramatic moment … when everything can change all at once," which Malcolm Gladwell says is essential for culture change.[6]

---

[6]   Gladwell, *The Tipping Point*, 9.

In order to see holistic, broad, and lasting change, we must clarify our key learnings from the Discover phase by asking ourselves these questions:

- What worked, and what didn't?
- Why did it work, or why did it fail?
- What has God revealed to us in and through the process?
- What has biblical and organizational resonance?
- What specific contexts were fruitful and why?
- What was a universal principle that would work anywhere versus a contextual reality that worked in one particular setting?
- Where was there a recurring pattern (that we saw repeat itself over numerous experiments) rather than a one-off occurrence? If there was a recurring pattern, what was the core principle that was repeated?
- What were the non-negotiables when the prototype succeeded? How do we test these non-negotiables to validate our assumptions?
- What is the framework that can be repeated? How do we test this framework to validate our assumptions?
- What did we learn that would have the most significant and far-reaching impact on the whole organization?

These questions will help us to effectively identify the truth that has been discovered in the previous phase, which can be solidified and sharpened in the Design phase, and then deployed in the next phase.

Below are two practices for each of Skeleton, Skin, and Spirit that will enable your core group to design holistically. These practices will inform the creation of more specific pilots that will provide the learning you need to clarify the organizational processes that many will eventually engage with. This work will form a solid foundation and strategic framework on which you can build for the next phase.

SKELETON PRACTICES (INTENTIONALITY)

When my children were old enough to have their own set of house keys, I made several copies. But, to our frustration, some of the copied keys didn't work. A copy of a copy of a copy gradually begins to differ from the original. The copied key will usually fit into the lock, but it might not turn it to open the door. In organizations, when we make a copy of a copy—whether it is a core value, training process, or ministry structure—there's often a drift away from the original intent because the message has been lost or diluted in some way as it is passed on. The further away from the leadership team or core community, the more intentional we must be in instilling and embedding core principles across our culture. A strong Skeleton ensures this.

Practice #1 (Skeleton)—Intentional or Accidental?

Matthew Wride, president at DecisionWise, shares how one of his colleagues once turned up to a new job without wearing a tie: "As he looked around, he quickly noticed that nearly every man was wearing a tie. So, what did [he] wear the next day? A necktie. He tacitly perceived the culture and then adapted his behavior accordingly. This organization had a 'tie' culture even though it was not expressly established in the dress code."[7] Culture exists, whether we like it or not. The question is whether we are intentional or accidental about the culture we foster in our teams, groups, communities, and across our organization as a whole. Culture is the set of natural behaviors that people embody as the expression of core values. Angela Duckworth, in her book *Grit*, notes that,

> Culture has the power to shape our identity. Over time, and under the right circumstances, the norms and values of the group to which we belong become our own. We internalize them. We carry them with us. *The ways we do things around here, and why* eventually becomes *The way I do things and why*.[8]

Regardless of what is written on your organization's website, policy documents, or what the leadership team says, your culture can only be known by observing the actions and priorities of people in your organization. Your culture is expressed by

7 Matthew Wride, "Culture Unveiled: 8 Principles for Defining and Measuring Organizational Culture," DecisionWise, accessed March 27, 2024, https://decision-wise.com/resources/articles/culture-unveiled-8-principles-for-defining-and-measuring-organizational-culture/.

8 Angela Duckworth, *Grit: Why Passion and Resilience are the Secrets to Success* (London, UK: Vermillion, 2017), 247.

- unspoken values (what you naturally celebrate, invest in, and defend);
- unconscious behaviors (how people instinctively act without thinking); and
- unidentified influence (what automatically happens when the leader isn't around).

A good way to become aware of your culture is to consider what someone would say your values were if they

- spent a week with your team;
- saw your team's schedule;
- reviewed your organizational budget;
- listened in on your team's conversations;
- read the last hundred emails you and your team sent; or
- saw who is on your core team and who your key leaders are.

The following practices will help your organization shift from being passive, accidental, and implicit, to purposeful, intentional, and explicit—both in your everyday activity and in your kingdom design.

- **Speak out unspoken values**—vision and values should be clear, compelling, and communicated regularly and explicitly in many contexts and many engaging forms.
  - ○ Frequently use key terms and phrases so they become part of everyone's vocabulary.
  - ○ Actively and regularly celebrate and reward (via testimony, public celebration, promotion, increased responsibility) when the values are embodied.
  - ○ Visually communicate values across the website, materials, gatherings, and communications.
- **Make unconscious behaviors conscious**—awareness, ownership, intentionality, and participation in practices need to become part of everyone's experience across the organization.
  - ○ Encourage leaders across the organization to audit their own behaviors so they can assess strengths and weaknesses, which can then be addressed with additional training, apprenticeship, and resources.

o Create training environments and equipping processes so that anyone across the organization can begin to live out the core principles.

o Offer opportunities and environments for people to experience the core values embodied in a healthy way, to help individuals move from theory to testimony in their understanding of core values and healthy culture.

- **Acknowledge unidentified influence**—positive leadership influence and other positive relational influences need to be highlighted, owned, and celebrated; and negative influences challenged, changed, and ceased.

  o Give places of greatest relational and organizational influence to the leaders who embody organizational values.

  o Offer intentional training in areas of unhelpful or unhealthy behaviors that contradict your core values to equip leaders to embody desired practices.

  o Invest in the people and places of greatest relational and positional influence across the organization to ensure the core values are embodied and celebrated in these places.

Practice #2 (Skeleton)—Dial Back to Conscious Competence

Some great sportspeople become great coaches. Others don't. The difference is primarily whether they can dial back to conscious competence. Great coaches recognize it takes focus, intentionality, and perseverance to move from their unconscious competence ("I'm world-class at what I do, but I don't always know how to explain it to others") back toward becoming consciously competent ("I'm great at what I do, I know why, and I can share that with others to help them become better"). Many of us have skills in which we are unconsciously competent—driving a car, making a coffee, leading a meeting—but we do these things without really thinking about the skills we are using. Only when we focus on conscious competence can we codify our learning from the Discover phase and subsequently create pathways for many to learn and apply these principles. In the Design phase, we are consciously creating a frame and process to pass on our values or skills, which allows others to apply these principles in their own context (versus them simply being a niche idea adopted by a few pioneers).

To enable each leader within the core group to dial back to conscious competence and codify the communal core learning from the Discover phase will require the following:

- **Slow down.** If you move too fast as a leader or core group, you operate and design in your instinct. Slowing down gives you a chance to reflect on what you're doing and why you're doing it.
- **Allow others to ask you questions.** This will pull out the instinctive frameworks, metrics, principles, and processes unearthed from the Discover phase as you harness scenius and unlock cognitive and competency diversity, both of which strengthen the design process.
- **Write it down.** This will force the core group to externalize and clarify the principles and processes that have become natural to them so that they can be simplified and codified for others as part of the design process.

SKIN PRACTICES (CONTEXTUALIZATION)

In the previous phase, we were in a season of learning that unearthed our core principles, taking them from intuitive to overt and intentional. In the Design phase, as we take our core principles (Skeleton) and think about how these will be embodied and practiced across the whole of our organization, it's important to consider diverse perspectives that help us understand the impact this will have in many different contexts (Skin) and with many different people. Without this consideration, we will be formulaic, and our efforts to grow and scale will have inconsistent results.

Practice #3 (Skin)—Know Your Context

When our kids were babies, we had access to a wealth of parenting resources, with all sorts of techniques for feeding, sleep patterns, and bonding. We could have read all the books in the world, but none of their authors knew the individual needs and circumstances of our children. Just like every baby, every people group or place your leaders are seeking to be and bring good news to is unique.

One useful resource to help leaders apply core principles in their context is the Passion Audit. (This tool was mentioned in the previous chapter as an example of a pilot.) The Passion Audit allows every leader to look for what God is doing (Spirit) and adapt core principles into their own context (Skin). When I have trained missional community leaders, I've used the Passion Audit below to help leaders or a group to unlock their passions for their context, as well as reflect on the context itself. The audit provides a frame to help leaders to listen to what's said and not said, as well as to observe behaviors and identify heroes, causes, and concerns in their context.

- **What is God saying?**
  - Are there any prophetic words or Scriptures?
  - As you pray, what does God reveal of his heart for the people or place?
  - Where are you moved with compassion?

- **What are your heart's desires?**
  - What are you passionate about, and what excites you (e.g., kids, young people, family, environment)?
  - What would the "kingdom come" look like here?
  - How do the passions of the context align with your God-given passions?

- **What is your holy discontent?**
  - What grieves or saddens you about the context?
  - What's bad news in the context (e.g., kids on street corners, litter, graffiti, abuse, family breakup)?
  - Within the core group, what do you all see or perceive as the lack, deficit, or pain of the context?

- **What are the opportunities?**
  - Where are the places of peace—of grace, influence, and invitation?

- ○ Who are the people of peace?
- ○ What do people celebrate, engage with, invest in, and gather around in the context?

- **What are the needs?**
  - ○ Where could you be a blessing and good news to the context?
  - ○ What is missing that would bring life to the context?
  - ○ What intentional rhythms or patterns would the community engage with?

Practice #4 (Skin)—Five Perspectives

One of the key resources we use within Movement Leaders Collective and Creo as we coach leaders and organizations is APEST dynamics (apostolic, prophetic, evangelistic, shepherding, and teaching), based on the apostle Paul's fivefold teaching in Ephesians 4 and built out by Alan Hirsch in his books *The Permanent Revolution* and *5Q*.[9] We believe we cannot be the kind of mature church envisioned in Ephesians 4:12–16 without the full ministry mode of APEST. Jesus was the perfect model of each of the fivefold functions, and as we consider how we design for our organizations, we can use this framework to create a Jesus-centered design process, maximizing the diversity of perspectives and wisdom contained within our organization.

In the Design phase, as we are seeking to scale the learning from the Discover phase across the whole organization and into many places and people into the next phase, each of the fivefold functions offers a different perspective and stimulus, enabling a fully synthesized process of change.

- The apostle focuses on strategy, impact, and growth.
- The prophet champions values, integrity, and justice.
- The evangelist prioritizes mission, inclusion, and mobilization.

[9] See Alan Hirsch and Tim Catchim, *The Permanent Revolution: Apostolic Imagination and Practice for the 21st Century Church* (San Francisco, CA: Jossey-Bass, 2012) and Alan Hirsch, *5Q: Reactivating the Original Intelligence and Capacity of the Body of Christ* (Atlanta, GA: 100 Movements Publishing, 2017). See also https://5qcentral.com.

- The shepherd emphasizes community, depth, and relationships.
- The teacher values ethos, integration, and instruction.

As we think about any context (Skin), whether it be a missional context, a small group, a team, or a department, we want those with each of the fivefold giftings to bring their unique perspective to the design process. Below are the primary questions each of these would be concerned with:

- **Apostolic—what's the prize?** Looking for the places of desire, hope, and value that can move the context forward and toward something better.
  - ○ *Key Questions*: What's the framework and strategy for us to be most effective in our mission? Where and what are the leverage points within the context? What's the new form or frontier we are being called toward that will create the most kingdom impact?
- **Prophetic—where's the pain?** Looking for the places of deficit, injustice, marginalization, and existentialism.
  - ○ *Key Questions*: Where is the sense of God's word and direction? Who are the forgotten and marginalized in the context, and where are their places of injustice? What are the deep questions the community is asking? Where are we not living with integrity in line with our values?
- **Evangelistic—what's the possibility?** Looking for places of connection, celebration, passion, existing relational networks, and opportunities to be and bring good news.
  - ○ *Key Questions*: Who are the connectors within the context? Where are the places and what are the causes people gather around, get excited by, and want to participate in? Who are the influencers within the community? How can we effectively communicate good news in this context?
- **Shepherding—who are the people?** Looking for places of isolation, relational need, and opportunities to create community and make connections.
  - ○ *Key Questions*: Where are people isolated? What are the relational,

social, and emotional needs of people within the context, and where does the context itself need greater relational depth and unity? What are the barriers to relational connection and depth?

- **Teaching—where's the potential?** Looking for places of growth in learning, apprenticeship, and formation.
  - ○ *Key Questions*: What are the topics, areas, and elements where people need better theological understanding, and where do they need to grow in competency? What are people trying to learn, improve, or understand? Where does the context need better systems, processes, and integration to more easily and fully express its potential?

As an example of using APEST perspectives in the design process, below is how 100 Movements Publishing has begun to clarify what they are trying to accomplish, how they can maintain a Christlike focus in their efforts, and how they can be aligned with their vision of sparking the imagination of the church for movemental Christianity and calling the church back to being a Jesus-centered people movement.

- **Apostolic**—Books that change the conversation and have an impact and influence.
- **Prophetic**—Books that represent diverse voices and cover topics that call the church to greater faithfulness.
- **Evangelistic**—Books to equip people to share their faith contextually, confidently, and faithfully.
- **Shepherding**—Books to edify and encourage leaders, communities, and the church.
- **Teaching**—Books that have a rigorous theological reflection process and spark kingdom imagination.

Seeking each of these five perspectives will enable you to design well for the whole organization. Start by having one-on-one conversations and creating forums where you gather those from each of the five functions—ideally inviting those with leadership positions and those who have a good perspective on the experiences of others within the organization. Consider how you facilitate interconnected dialogue rather than just one leader's idea or one dominant APEST dynamic. Organizations and communities that celebrate every voice rather than allowing a few charismatic characters to dominate will be more likely to create a healthy kingdom design process—it allows everyone to feel seen and invited to play their part.[10]

Although including all five APEST perspectives is essential in the Design phase, continued engagement with all five is vital if we are to see kingdom transformation of the organization on an ongoing basis. If we're not using the perspectives and giftings of all parts of the body, we miss something of Jesus' full power and redemption in our world. Consider who is missing from the key conversations and decision-making as you implement change and engage with the design process. As you move beyond the Design phase, consider how you can ensure all perspectives are integral to the leadership and development of your organization, and how you can actively value the strengths each of the APEST giftings contribute. You may need to address gaps in leadership or pivot toward certain giftings for their strengths at particular times.

SPIRIT PRACTICES (DEPENDENCY)

There is no checklist or module for equipping leaders to engage with the Spirit in the Design phase. But we must learn how to be aligned with God and his purposes so that, as our work grows and develops, it is Spirit-led and Spirit-empowered, as well as being biblically grounded and Jesus-focused.

Practice #5 (Spirit)—Learn to Perceive

In Isaiah 43, the author relays God's words, "See, I am doing a new thing! Now it springs up" (v. 19). In the Design phase, part of embracing the Spirit is asking God to help us to see. We choose to humble ourselves, our senses, and what we can see with our own eyes and ask God to reveal in beautiful Technicolor what we can only see in black and white. This is a prayerful and prophetic process where we ask God for his revelation while being grounded in Scripture. We have data from the Discover phase from our prototypes, and now as we pilot in the

---

[10] For help identifying APEST in your leaders, go to https://5qcentral.com.

Design phase, we have a clearer sense of strategy and insight, but in prayer, we are asking God to show us where *he* is at work rather than us telling him what *we* are working on. The great missionary Hudson Taylor said it this way: "I used to ask God to help me. Then I asked if I might help him. I ended up by asking God to do His work through me."[11] We need open hearts and minds, soft eyes, a childlike faith, and an inquisitive spirit to look for where God is at work in what we've discovered and where we find ourselves.

As we look ahead—not just with our intellectual and strategic plans—we need to look for the direction God might be leading us, which may be different from the one we had planned. In Luke 4, the crowd wanted Jesus to stay in their village, but Jesus knew he needed to leave for another place to proclaim the good news (vv. 42–44). The disciples were heading with Jesus to Jairus's house when Jesus stopped for the hemorrhaging women who touched his cloak (Mark 5:21–43). The disciples tried to keep the children away from Jesus, but Jesus welcomed them in and used them as a picture of faith (Mark 10:13–16). Jesus was open to the Father's guidance, revelation, and direction; and if he was, we should be too. As we listen to God together, we may communally sense a deep conviction for us to engage in a particular activity or move in a particular direction.

The second half of Isaiah 43:19 concludes with God saying, "Do you not perceive it?" There is a new thing bubbling up that can be *seen* (with our eyes), but God is asking whether we can *perceive* it (with our mind/ imagination). We need to open ourselves to the threads, themes, and truths God might be revealing that are beyond our own intellect, knowledge, and perspective; and we need to equip all our leaders in the Design phase to be able to do the same.

When we engage with the Spirit in the design process, it becomes a spiritual journey, not just a strategic process (Skeleton) or a sociological engagement (Skin). God leads, and we should follow. In prayer, he may highlight to us a particular leader or place that the organization should engage with or invest in. (Remember, the Bible contains a who's who of unlikely suspects God chooses to work in and through.)

---

[11] "Quotes by Hudson Taylor," Grace Quotes, accessed April 3, 2024, https://gracequotes.org/author-quote/hudson-taylor/.

The exercise below helps inform your design process by identifying where God is at work and joining him. It can be used by an individual leader, a leadership team, or a community.

- Draw a mind map of all the threads and themes you perceive God may be weaving together. This may include Scriptures, questions, pictures, passions, problems, people, comments from others, and prophetic words.
- Ask in prayer and through communal discussion what God is revealing that pulls together all the fragments of people, projects, places, and possibilities.
- As you identify what God is saying and where he is at work in your context, ask yourself/yourselves how you should respond to partner with him.

Practice #6 (Spirit)—Look for God's Favor

As we explored in the Discover phase, the parable of the sower illustrates four different soils that yield four different results—one with no return; two with meager, short-lived returns; and one multiplying crops of thirty, sixty, and a hundred times (Mark 4:1–20). Unlike the factory production line, every soil does not produce the same return. Jesus loved and valued everyone equally, but he didn't invest his time, energy, and effort equally. He had a core of three (Peter, James, and John), a team of twelve, and a group of seventy-two whom he engaged with more intentionally than the crowds. He invested in the few for the benefit of the many.

As Jesus sent his disciples out in Luke 9:1–10 and Luke 10:1–24, he told them to enter a house and discern if it was a house of peace. And if it was, he told them to "stay there" (Luke 10:7). He didn't say, "Knock on as many doors as possible" or, "Bring them back to me." He didn't say, "Stay and argue with them until they relent and let you in." He said, "Look for the place where peace is present and resides, root yourself and stay there, and be served by them" (paraphrase mine). These were the places and people that Jesus knew would yield the greatest kingdom return. And Jesus told his disciples that if they didn't find a person or a house of peace, they were to keep moving and keep looking.

In the Design phase, we need to create a framework that helps leaders look for and discern places of peace, good soil, and the possibility of a high kingdom return. If we learn anything from Jesus here, we must learn that he did not always look in the obvious places or the places where the world looked for leaders, opportunity, and investment. He was led by his Father's voice, and as we make decisions on leaders, investments, and directions, we need to communally listen to and be led by the Spirit to look for the places and people of peace. Again, this exercise can work for an individual leader, a leadership team, or a community.

- Reflect on the good soil (Mark 4:8) in your context (people and places of peace). What would a 30-, 60-, 100-fold gospel return look like?
- Reflect on the other soils in the context.
  - Where is the path where the seeds are eaten up (Mark 4:4)?
  - Where is the rocky soil where the seeds wither (Mark 4:5–6)?
  - Where is the soil where thorns grow alongside the seed and choke the plants (Mark 4:7)?
- As you recognize the good soil and people and places of peace, what does it look like to "go and stay" there?

The validated learning from our pilots in the Design phase allows us to create a strategic framework that has clear, core principles (Skeleton); that can be creatively expressed through contextualized practices (Skin) in multiple places and people; and that are all informed by and aligned with God's leading (Spirit). This provides a synergy and clarity that allows us to move beyond the smaller group involved in the Design phase and to begin to invite and engage the whole organization or venture in a staged engagement process (Deploy).

This means the work goes from the few to the many, from the edge to the center, and truly allows the vision for the preferred future (Dream) and the learning from the initial prototypes (Discover) to be embedded across the whole organization.

DESIGN 101

PRIZE
Clarify core principles that can be expressed by every leader, in every context, in partnership with God.

PEOPLE
The core group of innovators and early adopters, with some organizational stakeholders, now widens to engage more organizational stakeholders and a wider section of leaders from across the organization.

LEADERSHIP EXPRESSION
A mature Challenger who *restates* and *reveals*.

SHADOWSIDE
An immature Challenger creates discouraged people by constantly naming the deficit, critiquing the system, and pushing toward the future too hard or harshly.

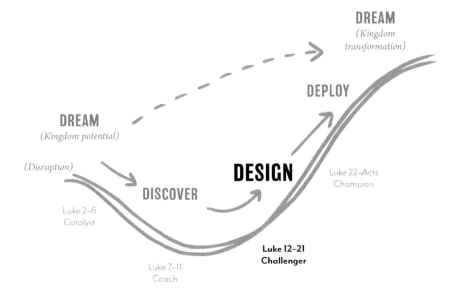

SCRIPTURE: LUKE 12–21

In these chapters, Jesus is a Challenger who *restates* the vision and *reveals* the priorities for the disciples. Luke 12 begins with Jesus warning his disciples about various issues, including what is spoken in private being spoken in public (vv. 2–3), future persecution (v. 11), greed and arrogance (v. 15), and that there will be division (vv. 49–53). He also gives encouragements that architect the kingdom design of how he wants his disciples to live, telling them not to worry (vv. 22–31), that God is pleased to give them the kingdom (v. 31), and that where their treasure is, there their heart will be also (v. 34). Jesus refocuses and repurposes the conversation to reveal a future, a world, and a God that is much greater than their current understanding.

Jesus unpacks his kingdom design and core principles through the various parables, exhortations, and interactions of the middle chapters of Luke (13–18), including the mustard seed, narrow door, great banquet, lost sheep, lost coin, lost son, shrewd manager, and persistent widow. As well as these parables, he speaks of the coming kingdom, details the circumstances of his death, and challenges his disciples to deny themselves and take up their cross daily (Luke 9:23).

As Jesus enters Jerusalem (Luke 19–21), we see him acting as a cultural guardian and strategic architect for a future movement, as he enables the disciples to intellectually and experientially grasp the ethos of the kingdom. He is preparing his disciples for the next phase of their journey and designing the church of Acts and beyond.

YOUR CHANGE-AGENT JOURNEY

- Where do you need to operate as a Challenger to restate and reveal the vision to multiply core principles into multiple contexts?
- How can you strengthen the design by building pilots to test the theories you are forming?

66

*Effective design not only draws
people into the story but also
allows them to contribute to the
narrative.*

99

PHASE FOUR
DEPLOY

/dɪˈplɔɪ/

"to mobilize something or someone, especially in order to achieve a particular effect"

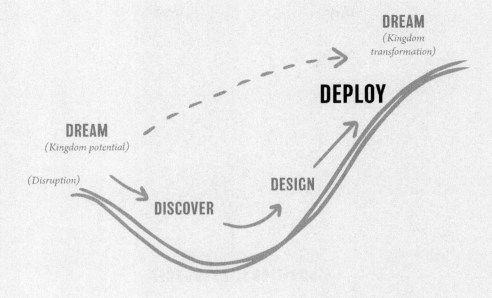

PROBLEM

Instead of being a people movement that multiplies and scales, the Western church is often a centrally managed and staff-driven institution that seeks to maintain its survival instead of embracing its commissioning.

We tend to produce consumers, manage volunteers, and organize gatherings rather than actively forming and mobilizing disciples to fulfill the Great Commission.

PROCESS

Move from a centrally driven institution to a generative people movement.

PRIZE

Catalyze deep and lasting kingdom transformation that sustains and scales to multiple generations.

ADDITIONAL RESOURCES

Scan the QR code below for additional resources, including videos, practices, and a toolkit to accompany the Deploy phase.

allchangejourney.com/resources

A PEOPLE MOVEMENT
AND A MOVING PEOPLE

CREATED TO DEPLOY

The most difficult thing is the decision to act. The rest is merely tenacity.
AMELIA EARHART

*There are essential differences between an institution and a movement:
The one is conservative, the other progressive; the one is more or less
passive yielding to influences from the outside, the other is active in
influencing rather than being influenced; the one looks to the past, the
other to the future. In addition, the one is anxious, the other is prepared
to take risks; the one guards boundaries, the other crosses them.*
H. R. NIEBUHR

*If you want to build a ship, don't drum up people to collect
wood and don't assign them tasks and work, but rather teach
them to long for the endless immensity of the sea.*
ANTOINE DE SAINT EXUPÉRY

Two churches have profoundly impacted the North American church
in the last forty years: Willow Creek Community Church (Chicago),
and Saddleback Church (California). Pioneering and validating a

seeker-sensitive, church-growth approach to ministry, their influence has both spread and reinforced an attractional form of church that is found in much of the West and even beyond.[1] In North American culture, where, until fairly recently, many people had a Christian heritage or at least an awareness of the Christian faith,[2] these methods and vehicles worked to attract, engage, and organize existing Christians as well as those who had lapsed from their faith.

One undesirable consequence of this attractional model has been the rise in "consumer Christians"—individuals who equate the Christian life with attending a weekend service rather than participating in the Great Commission in their everyday lives. In 2007, Willow Creek surveyed their members to determine the effectiveness of their own church programs and found that "increasing levels of participation in these sets of activities [church programs] does NOT predict whether someone's becoming more of a disciple of Christ. It does NOT predict whether they love God more or they love people more."[3] As Alan Hirsch says in *The Forgotten Ways*, "Almost all expressions of church in the West are implicitly vulnerable to nondiscipleship, professionalized ministry, spiritual passivity, and consumerism. The problem is rooted in the profoundly nonmissional assumptions of the system itself."[4] This expression of church has seeped into our thinking about Christian ministry in its various forms. Movements are the archetypal form of Christianity and need to be recovered today to impact the future. Whether you are a church planter, Christian entrepreneur, or a leader of a nonprofit, church, or denomination, unlocking the kingdom potential of movement dynamics is a vital pursuit.

---

[1]   "How Saddleback Church Connected and Inspired Parishioners Across the Globe," EXTexting; "How Willow Creek is Leading Evangelicals by Learning From the Business World," *Fast Company*; McKnight, "The Legacy of Willow Creek 3," *Jesus Creed*; Lee, "Rick Warren Mastered the Formula for Suburban Church Growth."

[2]   See "Modeling the Future of Religion in America, How U.S. religious composition has changed in recent decades," Pew Research Center, September 13, 2022, https://www.pewresearch.org/religion/2022/09/13/how-u-s-religious-composition-has-changed-in-recent-decades/.

[3]   Chuck Warnock, "Willow Creek Study Says Church Programs Don't Work," ChuchWarnock.com, October 24, 2007, https://chuckwarnockblog.wordpress.com/2007/10/24/willow-creek-study-says-church-programs-dont-make-better-disciples/.

[4]   Alan Hirsch, *The Forgotten Ways: Reactivating Apostolic Movements*, 2nd Edition (Grand Rapids, MI: Baker, 2016), 35.

The Deploy phase is about mobilization, reproduction, and multiplication in the way of Jesus—with every person across our organization taking part in the vision and values that have been unearthed in the previous phases. The primary aim is to have multiple leaders who understand and embody the organization's DNA and core values (Skeleton), are empowered and equipped to partner with God (Spirit) and can contextualize these core principles in their life and leadership (Skin). This is not just about the *quantity* of people mobilized or the amount of activity they engage in, but the *quality* of their discipleship, leadership, and kingdom impact.

MOVEMENTS CHANGE THINGS!

In August 2018, a Swedish fifteen-year-old decided to skip school and sit outside her country's Parliament, demanding urgent action on the climate crisis. Greta Thunberg vowed to strike every Friday until Swedish policies complied with the 2015 Paris Climate Agreement. Her actions drew global attention, and shortly after her first school strike, hundreds of thousands of young people across the world joined her. The strikes ended after 251 days, but the organization she inspired, #FridaysforFuture, now has fourteen million people involved in 7,500 cities on all continents.[5] Thunberg sparked a global movement of young people actively campaigning for changes to government policy and raising public awareness of climate change across the world—referred to by commentators as "the Greta effect."[6]

Today, many in the West, particularly young adults, are skeptical and distrustful of institutions and are more likely to be drawn to movements— either social movements (which seek social changes for a more just society) or social networks (which have little hierarchy or organization but a lot of

5   Remy Tumin, "Greta Thunberg Ends Her School Strikes After 251 Days," *The New York Times*, June 10, 2023, https://www.nytimes.com/2023/06/10/world/europe/greta-thunberg-graduates-activism.html; see https://fridaysforfuture.org/.

6   "Greta Thunberg," Wikipedia, accessed April 3, 2024, https://en.m.wikipedia.org/wiki/Greta_Thunberg; "How one Swedish teenager inspired a global movement for climate change," Greenhouse, accessed April 3, 2024, https://greenhouse.agency/blog/greta-thunberg; "Greta Thunberg: Who is the climate activist and what has she achieved?" *BBC News*, January 30, 2024, https://www.bbc.co.uk/news/world-europe-49918719#.

informal, shared passion). The founder of Spirit & Truth, Matt Reynolds, notes,

> People are fundamentally longing for something more than mildly religious entertainment and self-help. They are yearning to be a part of something bigger than themselves. They want their lives to count for something. I think this is evidenced by the way various cultural movements like Black Lives Matter have gained dramatic appeal among younger generations. It is no coincidence that the majority of the places where Christianity is growing also happen to be places where choosing Jesus requires real sacrifice. Costly discipleship is the essence of Jesus' way. When Jesus left the earth, he did not have a big church, but he did have women and men who were willing to die for his vision.[7]

Movements have an exponential, dynamic, scalable energy and are adaptive and innovative. Beyond the campaign initiated by Thunberg, consider the impact of movements sparked over the centuries by Alexander the Great, Charles and John Wesley, William Wilberforce, William J. Seymour, Mahatma Gandhi, Martin Luther King Jr., Nelson Mandela, Mother Teresa, and Steve Jobs, to name but a few.

Although these individuals might have been catalytic in sparking or scaling movements, for something to truly move from a *moment* of change to become a *movement* of change, it must be owned and pursued by many people, in many different places, and in many ways. This is the work of the Deploy phase. The cause takes on a life of its own, and each disciple is activated to embody and pursue the purpose themselves. For example, every person who owns a car can become an Uber driver; every person with a bedroom can become an Airbnb host; every owner of a smartphone can become a YouTuber; and every person who witnesses or is the victim of sexual harassment or abuse can speak up with #MeToo.

In general, movements can be defined as:

A group of people who actively participate toward a shared purpose, in a relationally bound DNA-based organism that has generative energy and grows to multiple generations.

---

7   Reynolds, "The Death Rattle of Consumer Christianity."

In the same way, in the Deploy phase, we want our organizations and ventures to unlock organic, generative energy rather than only being defined by organizational structures or efforts. In their book *Brave Cities*, Taylor McCall and Hugh Halter talk about shifting away from centralized structures that depend on individuals:

> Decentralization is defined as the transfer of control of an activity or an organization from the few to the many. For centuries, the form, functions, priesthood, and polity of the church have been centralized around a few people or in one place. We've got to flip this model on its head. ... Leadership should happen from the bottom rather than the top and be circular rather than hierarchical. And the most gifted leaders and the most magnetic spaces must look to empower others and expand outward. As we decentralize, kingdom movements become less and less dependent on single leaders or single visions. What becomes natural is a culture of going out as opposed to inviting in; a culture of innovation instead of stagnation; a culture of interconnected creative works instead of franchised carbon copies; a culture of adversity and risk instead of safety and security. It's virtually impossible to stop a decentralized movement. The target is constantly moving to the point where there is no target.[8]

This is what it means to create Jesus movements and unlock the power of movemental Christianity in and through our ventures, churches, denominations, and organizations. Adapting the earlier general definition of movements, a *Jesus* movement can be defined as:

> *Disciples who actively participate in a shared kingdom purpose, in a relationally bound DNA-based organism (embodying the Greatest Commandment) that has generative energy and grows to multiple generations (fulfilling the Great Commission).*

Movement Leaders Collective exists to serve and support leaders who have chosen to pursue exponential/movemental growth. We have committed to a long-term relational and strategic focus on one hundred movement-ready organizations and one thousand movement-ready leaders, serving them through

---

[8] McCall and Halter, *Brave Cities*, 60.

peer community, collaborative learning, and catalytic training. Our defining dream—and the driver for our Deploy phase—is to give new life to the "church as movement" by deeply embedding six movemental capacities (mDNA) into the life and leadership of catalytic organizations and leaders. The six elements of mDNA are key aspects of movemental Christianity expressed and embodied in Jesus movements.[9] For a short summary of mDNA, see appendix two: "mDNA: The Six Essential Elements of Jesus Movements" or visit www.themxplatform. com/startthejourney.

Organizations that MLC partners with—such as Kansas City Underground, Redeemer City to City, Tampa Underground, Recruits, and Fusion[10]—are all seeking to more intentionally release their generative and organic energy to become Jesus movements. Their efforts toward embodying the Greatest Commandment and fulfilling the Great Commission drive them to expand into multiple contexts with a network of leaders incarnating the organization's values and animating their vision in a myriad of expressions, environments, and contexts. We see this same drive among the entrepreneurs participating in Creo, who are starting and scaling social-impact ventures, nonprofits, and faith-driven businesses to see social, spiritual, and systemic impact.

AS OLD AS TIME

The story of God's people has always been about deployment—about a people movement and a moving people. It was a people movement before a denomination or institutional reality and a story before a statement of faith … and it has always been marked by a call to multiply. Part of God's original mandate to humankind in Genesis 1:28 was to "Be fruitful and increase in number." In the Great Commission, Jesus calls us to multiplication—this time to multiply disciples: "Go and make disciples of all nations, baptizing them in the name of the Father and of the Son and of the Holy Spirit" (Matt. 28:19). And again, in Jesus' last words before his ascension, he calls his disciples to multiply through geographical expansion: "You will be my

---

9   For a comprehensive exploration of mDNA, see Hirsch, *The Forgotten Ways*.

10 See https://kcunderground.org, https://redeemercitytocity.com, https://www.tampaunderground.com, https://www.recruits.be, https://www.fusionmovement.org.

witnesses in Jerusalem, and in all Judea and Samaria, and to the ends of the earth" (Acts 1:8).

Jesus called ordinary people to join him, and the church he founded was a missionary movement. If the church had not functioned as a movement and failed to take the Great Commission seriously, there would have been no church then or today.

As leaders and organizations, we need to recapture and reimagine ourselves as part of the Jesus movement and to have the drive for our organization, venture, or community to play its part in the grand plan. As we look back to the first-century design and look forward to our twenty-first-century context, we need to examine our status quo and ask ourselves how we can create a collaborative, dynamic, authentic, generative, and innovative community that reflects more of the Jesus movement of the first century than the consumer movement of the twenty-first.

These dynamics are key, regardless of whether you lead a microchurch, church, faith-driven venture, nonprofit, or denomination. Speaking of the generative, organic nature of movement dynamics within a faith-driven organization, Timothy Keller says,

> A church or organization with movement dynamics has spiritual spontaneity; it constantly generates new ideas, leaders, and initiatives within and across itself—not solely from the top or from a command center outside of itself. ... A church or organization that is highly institutionalized, however, is structured so that individuals cannot offer ideas and propose projects unless asked or given permission. A church with movement dynamics ... generates ideas, leaders, and initiatives from the grassroots. Ideas come less from formal strategic meetings, and more from off-line conversations among friends. Since the motivation for the work is not so much about compensation and self-interest as about a shared willingness to sacrifice for the infectious vision, such churches naturally create friendships among members and staff. These friendships become mini-engines powering the church, along with the more formal, organized meetings and events.[11]

---

[11] Timothy Keller, *Serving a Movement: Doing Balanced, Gospel-Centered Ministry in Your City* (Grands Rapid, MI: Zondervan, 2016), 211.

The generative dynamics, adaptive nature, and innovative energy of the early church give us helpful instruction as leaders in a modern-day context. As we deploy not only the innovators and early adopters (the pioneers) but seek to mobilize many across the wider community and organization, we need to think about *how* we deploy. We don't just want to get busier with more people doing more things; we want to cultivate *health* as well as growth—including, among other things, growing a vibrant spirituality, active missional discipleship, and contextualized forms of engagement. The vision and values that have been established in the earlier phases need to move further out across your venture or organization in concentric circles, embodied by an ever-increasing number of leaders and members rather than simply adding more activities, environments, or vehicles.

ADDITION TO MULTIPLICATION TO MOVEMENT

The shift from simply leading a ministry or organization to unlocking movement dynamics happens when, following the pattern of Jesus, the influence and impact go beyond one person, team, or entity. This is the threshold between a one-generational Deploy phase (ministry) and a multiplying Deploy phase (movement); the point when the DNA (Skeleton) reoccurs across multiple contexts and in different contextualized practices (Skin), empowered by God (Spirit), in multiple generations, all held together with a sense of commitment to the relationships within the team and its cause.

Although we're moving our organization or venture toward becoming movemental in nature, this takes time. We need to expect an organizational lag and come to terms with the fact that the short-term costs might be higher. There may also be a seemingly slower pace of growth as we prioritize fully embedding something new across the whole. As a leader, there will be fewer short-term results on our existing one-generation scorecard. If we measured Jesus' effectiveness in making disciples after three years, we wouldn't have the same perspective as we would after three decades or three centuries.

Simple mathematics helps us to understand the power of exponential growth rather than short-term efforts through addition. This growth could be, for example, in the context of forming and making disciples, apprenticing leaders, multiplying groups, or missional impact.

Generation	Addition	Multiplication	Exponential
1	$1 + 1 = 2$	$1 \times 1 = 1$	$1^1 = 1$
2	$2 + 2 = 4$	$2 \times 2 = 4$	$2^2 = 4$ (2x2)
3	$3 + 3 = 6$	$3 \times 3 = 9$	$3^3 = 27$ (3x3x3)
4	$4 + 4 = 8$	$4 \times 4 = 16$	$4^4 = 256$ (4x4x4x4)
5	$5 + 5 = 10$	$5 \times 5 = 25$	$5^5 = 3,125$ (5x5x5x5x5)
6	$6 + 6 = 12$	$6 \times 6 = 36$	$6^6 = 46,656$ (6x6x6x6x6x6)

In this illustration, addition represents simply using the same model or a centralized energy to add people to the crowd. This is the modus operandi of many churches and faith-driven organizations, though some begin to imagine what multiplication might look like. As you can see from the table above, in the first generation, addition wins. The effort to add a few people to the crowd or a new product or process and make short-term gains beats out the longer, deeper process of multiplication. In the second generation (if we make it that far), it's a tied game. However, as we start to unlock the power of multiplication, in the third generation of change, we are 50 percent better off. By the fourth generation, the multiplication column has double the quantity (and often higher quality); the fifth generation is 2.5 times better off; and by the sixth generation, we have tripled the impact. Multiplication efforts have a long-term pay-off if we orient toward generational growth rather than short-term addition.

However, if we truly unlock movement dynamics in the Deploy phase, then we need to look to the column of exponential (movemental) growth. This is when the whole system multiplies itself in many contexts and forms and is self-generating and self-replicating. Instead of a small group of leaders multiplying themselves within the system, the system has the generative energy to multiply itself. Think of the generative energy of the #MeToo movement, the civil rights movement, or the early church.

If we apply this to an example that occurs annually for some churches—say, a Christmas carol service—it might look like this:

- **Addition:** *Let's publicize our carol service and hopefully attract non-Christians to it.*

- **Multiplication:** *Let's try and mobilize all our people to invite non-Christians to our carol service.*
- **Exponential (movemental):** *Let's empower and encourage multiple, more informal lightweight and low-maintenance contextual expressions of missional engagement (e.g., many people/communities inviting non-Christians in their relational network to their own Christmas parties, bonfires on the beach, door-to-door caroling, dinner parties, and Christmas walks), as well as leveraging the strengths of a centrally run carol service.*

In his three years of ministry, Jesus sometimes attracted the crowd (an example of addition), but his primary strategy was to form the embryo of a movement. He gathered a core community (his three, twelve, and seventy-two), who actively participated in shared values and practices (the Greatest Commandment), and a common cause, positioning the work for movemental growth (the Great Commission). From these meager beginnings, a global movement was sparked, and we are part of that Deploy phase that continues to extend to this day. We see the core community, communal values and practices, and common cause initiated by Jesus (Skeleton), repeated and reanimated on the pages of Acts and beyond into multiple contexts (Skin), empowered by the Holy Spirit (Spirit).

To initiate the Deploy phase effectively and experience exponential growth, whether as an existing organization or a new venture, we must understand movement dynamics. If we rely on hierarchical position, organization controls, or a centrally driven process, our Deploy phase will only be a one-generational effort. We can only be in one place at one time, and even if we spend the entirety of our weeks seeking to be everywhere with everyone across our organizations, we will fail, burn out, or blow up … or all three! Management guru Peter Drucker says that,

> No organization can depend on genius; the supply is always scarce and unreliable. It is the test of an organization to make ordinary human beings perform better than they seem capable of, to bring out whatever strength there is in its members, and to use each [person's] strength to help all the others perform. The purpose of an organization is to enable common [people] to do uncommon things.[12]

---

[12] Peter F. Drucker, *Management* (London, UK: William Heinemann Ltd., 1974), 209.

Though it often seems easier to do all the work ourselves, in the Deploy phase it becomes even more important that we lead with people and through people. Without this, the dream will start, but it won't scale.

IF IT LOOKS LIKE A DUCK AND QUACKS LIKE A DUCK ...

Let's return to the earlier definition of movement and apply it specifically to Jesus movements to help us appreciate why and how these dynamics are vital in the Deploy phase. Without these elements, the only levers for change will be organizational power or hierarchical function, which are ultimately impotent for lasting, deep, and far-reaching change. However, when these movemental elements are present, they unlock potential and allow growth to happen at the edges while maintaining cohesion as the change process is embodied by every individual across the whole organization.

Jesus movements form when a group of disciples

- actively participate
- toward a shared kingdom purpose
- in a relationally bound
- DNA-based organism
- that has generative energy
- and grows to multiple generations.

ACTIVE PARTICIPATION (FULL MOBILIZATION)

Jesus movements activate every disciple in the system to contribute to the cause.

Active participation is key to the Deploy phase because we want to engage everyone in the system rather than just the small guiding group that has been involved in the earlier phases. Every person needs to feel invited in and validated, and that their participation makes a difference. The gifts, skills, and perspectives of everyone across the organization or venture are identified, welcomed, and utilized.

In the Deploy phase, we move from:

- passive Christians to active disciples
- few to many

- consumers to participants
- duty to discretionary effort
- organizational responsibility to personal skills and gifts
- professionally driven to all-play.

A SHARED KINGDOM PURPOSE (CLEAR AND COMPELLING VISION)

Jesus movements have a kingdom narrative and a Jesus-centered cause that propels people forward and pulls them together.

The raw material of a shared purpose will have been uncovered in the Dream phase, honed in the Discover phase, and tested in the Design phase. In the Deploy phase, this vision must become a defining identity and a communal purpose for many rather than solely a driver for a small group within the organization or venture. The Jesus-centered dream needs to be large enough for everyone to find themselves in it, as well as being a cause or prize to rally around that is so great that no one can do it on their own or without God.

In the Deploy phase, we move from:

- conceptual to clear
- functional to compelling
- organizational edicts to a kingdom narrative
- to-do lists to a God-sized dream
- "someone else's agenda" to "I can see myself in this."

RELATIONALLY BOUND (COMMITTED COMMUNITY AND NETWORK EFFECT)

Jesus movements display a camaraderie and a commitment to one another that creates an active, attractive, and adventurous community.

Camaraderie among the small group of pioneers will have been formed within the Discover phase, and a commitment to each other and the cause will have been solidified in the Design phase. As the small guiding coalition comes into the Deploy phase, the group that is already committed to each other must transmit the culture, as the work and interactions develop across the organization. As part of the core group, they must continue to be a dynamic, living example for others, creating an attractive and adventurous community for people to be part of. The group's sense of shared values should unite and frame relationships and move them beyond the superficial. When change is adopted across the organization or venture through relational influence—rather than because it is someone else's idea or agenda or an organizational pursuit—it becomes truly movemental. It becomes the personal story and journey of each individual who internalizes the vision and desire for change, and then explores and embodies this alongside others.

In the Deploy phase, we move from:

- passive individuals to comrades in arms
- leadership role to relational influence
- self-benefit to communal win
- functional interaction to healthy, family dynamics
- transactional exchange to collaborative relationships.

DNA-BASED ORGANISM (CORE VALUES AND STRATEGIC FRAMEWORK)

Jesus movements have an agreed-upon set of kingdom values and DNA—the organizing beliefs and principles that inform and shape every action and interaction.

Our core organization principles (DNA) were uncovered initially in the Discover phase, when we shifted our values from intuitive and internal to intentional and external. Exploring those values brought cohesion and clarity to the DNA and helped us determine which principles were most important. Those identified core values shape our worldview, form our strategic framework, and inform our investments, decisions, and activities. This DNA is embedded in communal behaviors that create a culture across the organization or venture. It is this Skeleton that allows every disciple to healthily express the creativity and freedom of the Deploy phase in even more contexts (Skin).

In the Deploy phase, we move from:

- personal preference to organizational values
- intuitive to intentional
- policy- and procedure-driven to values- and DNA-based
- plug-and-play vehicles to contextual application.

GENERATIVE ENERGY (ORIENTATION TOWARD INNOVATION AND ADAPTIVE LEADERSHIP)

Jesus movements have dynamic energy, empower innovation, and are self-generating and self-replicating.

In the Dream and Discover phases, innovation happened on the edge; but as we enter the Deploy phase, we need to bring the learning from the earlier phases into the ethos and energy of our organizations. This requires a paradigm shift in how existing organizations think about growth and development. This is easier in more entrepreneurial initiatives but harder with legacy institutions, which tend to have more entrenched mindsets. It can no longer be the case that much of the organization is focused on the delivery, management, and sustaining of tried-and-tested vehicles and processes in the present. Rather, we need to unlock generative energy and diverse perspectives that create new forms and frontiers and infuse new life into existing vehicles, groups, and environments. We must help every person in the organization or venture to engage in their context in an authentic and incarnational way.

In order for this to happen, there needs to be an intentional process of distributing decision-making powers across the whole organization or venture. This allows pioneering and experimentation to develop in many contexts and continues to allow the whole organization to harness this generative energy and frontier learning.

In the Deploy phase, we move from:

- survival and maintenance to adaption and innovation
- management to leadership
- center/edge divide to synergies across the system
- existing models and vehicles to new forms and frontiers.

GROWTH TO MULTIPLE GENERATIONS (ETHOS OF DISTRIBUTION AND SCALE)

Jesus movements cultivate paradigms, platforms, principles, and practices that embrace the challenge of pursuing generational growth and adapt to different circumstances and cultures.

Here we bring everything from the Dream, Discover, and Design phases together—the DNA is simple and sticky, the expression of that DNA is scalable, and the generational growth of the organization or venture becomes sustainable. The vision becomes communal, the learning from the Discover phase becomes embedded across the whole, and the frame from the Design phase is expressed in multiple contexts. The cumulative effect is a Deploy phase that has an organic expression of both health and growth over many generations.

There is, however, a sacrificial nature to the Deploy phase. When a young adult leaves the family home—or a team member is released into their own, new initiative—there is often a sense of loss. But, as a seed goes to the ground and dies (John 12:24), there is the potential for a great harvest. The young adult or the team member can go into another context and pour all that you have invested in them into the lives of others. To release people this way, we need to prioritize the kingdom and the name of Jesus rather than our ministry or our reputation.

In Ben Witherington's commentary, *The Acts of the Apostles*, he says that, "The suffering and even death of disciples, like their Master, doesn't lead to the squelching of the Jesus movement; it leads to its success and expansion."[13] We may not experience such extreme persecution, but we have to embrace the cost of the Deploy phase going beyond ourselves, knowing that this will ultimately bear exponentially more kingdom fruit than our own individual efforts.

For the Deploy phase to work over multiple generations, we need a future-oriented investment plan (money, time, and effort) and structural platform (training, infrastructure, communication) rather than a present-day management process. We need to invest in the development of potential and emerging leaders and missional opportunities, not just our current ones. Orientating toward scale means looking down the line at the third or fourth-generation expression and asking whether our system could cope with an exponential increase rather than just whether it is functioning well at present.

In the Deploy phase, we move from:

- a one-generational scorecard to a multi-generational perspective
- growth by addition to exponential growth

---

[13] Ben Witherington III, *The Acts of the Apostles: A Socio-Rhetorical Commentary* (Grand Rapids, MI: William B Eerdmans Publishing Co, 2001), 228.

- the dream of a few to a mobilized majority
- a narrow set of vehicles to a broad expression of contextualized practices.

CHANGING THE CONVERSATION— THE 100 MOVEMENTS PUBLISHING JOURNEY

As 100 Movements Publishing seeks to engage with the Deploy phase, the core team is seeking to intentionally champion and resource first-time authors, authors of color, and female authors. Within the Design phase, these particular areas were identified as the focus for additional effort and investment; and so, in the Deploy phase, there has been increased input, resource investment, and coaching for these groups.

The goal is to continue to produce high-caliber books and grow 100MP's platform so that the awareness and impact of their work can increase and serve the church more effectively. There is also a structural component to their Deploy phase, so there is now a clearer website, an automated submission process, and a link for purchasing bulk copies of 100MP books. The core team has been expanded at every level—developmental editors, marketing consultants, editorial assistants, and theological advisors—so there's a more robust, experienced, and diverse team to steward the growth. In the Deploy phase, "the fruit of your work grows on other people's trees"[14] and so 100MP is also working with other organizations to help them identify and publish diverse voices within their own networks.

BACK TO THE FUTURE

Successful businesses today focus on research and development, emerging markets, cultural shifts, and prototyping as important aspects of growth. The balance of keeping existing customers as well as gaining new customers, then, becomes an invisible tightrope for companies. As the Western church, it

---

[14] Management guru Peter Drucker once said this to the Christian philanthropist Bob Buford; see Brady Pyle, "Drucker and Me: What a Texas Entrepreneur Learned From the Father of Modern Management," Outofthisworldleadership.com, accessed April 3, 2024, https://www.outofthisworldleadership.com/blog-posts/drucker-me-what-a-texas-entrepreneur-learned-from-the-father-of-modern-management/.

seems we spend far too much time trying to keep our *customers* (yes, emphasis intended) happy and engaged, in an attempt to hold on to what is already a small and decreasing pool. Archbishop William Temple (1881–1944) famously said, "The Church exists primarily for the sake of those who are still outside it."[15] That was the mindset of the early church, as the movement spread into Jerusalem, Judea, Samaria, and the ends of the earth. The church isn't intended to be a social club or membership organization that exists solely for its current members, but instead is a living body called to communicate, demonstrate, and extend God's kingdom transformation in a broken world.

The essence of the Deploy phase is to move past survival, maintenance, and introspection and instead to look beyond ourselves to the future God is calling us to and to mobilize every person to play their part. It's all change—in us, and through all of us, together.

---

[15] See Susan Ratcliffe, ed., *Oxford Essential Quotations* (Oxford, England: Oxford University Press, 2016); excerpted at https://www.oxfordreference.com/display/10.1093/acref/9780191826719.001. 0001/q-oro-ed4-00010671.

MASTERING THE RUBIK'S CUBE

LEARNING TO DEPLOY

Visions for change are more compelling when they include visions of continuity. Although our strategy might evolve, our identity will endure.
ADAM GRANT

I have learned over the years that when one's mind is made up, this diminishes fear: knowing what must be done does away with fear.
ROSA PARKS

We can't predict the future, but we can invent it.
ALAN KAY

In 1974, Hungarian inventor, architect, and professor of architecture Ernő Rubik invented the Rubik's Cube. It became an instant hit and still remains one of the world's most popular puzzles. The Rubik's Cube became a craze in the 1980s, has a cult following of "Cubers," and has spawned international communities in which competitors can astonishingly solve the puzzle in under five seconds.[1]

---

[1] "How Smart do you have to be to solve a Rubik's Cube?" MEL, accessed April 3, 2024, https://melmagazine.com/en-us/story/are-you-smart-if-you-can-solve-a-rubiks-cube; "A Look Back on Erno Rubik, the Mind Behind the Rubik's Cube," Puzzlecrate, February 17, 2023, https://puzzlcrate.com/who-invented-the-rubiks-cube/.

In our family, one of our children loved the 3D Rubik's Cube whereas another preferred the 2D challenge of jigsaws. If you've ever done a jigsaw puzzle, the usual method is to start by finding the corner pieces, then lay the four edges, and finally try to fill in the middle part, using colors, shapes, and the overall image to help complete the picture. If only leading organizational change in the Deploy phase were as straightforward as a 2D jigsaw! A much more realistic analogy for leading change through the Deploy phase is the 3D Rubik's Cube.

THE RUBIK'S CUBE OF DEPLOY: ENVIRONMENTS, RELATIONSHIPS, AND HABITS

Regardless of whether we are leading a start-up, faith-driven venture, or an existing church, network, or denomination, the Deploy phase is a 3D challenge. We often spend time trying to get the tiles on our Rubik's Cube to match, and we may even have had a fleeting moment of success when one of the faces is complete—but that moment of elation is quickly replaced by deep frustration when, as we turn over the cube and move tiles on another side, multicolored chaos appears on the side we just completed.

As a leader, how many times have we fixed one situation, only to realize it has dislodged something else in our system that now needs addressing? Or we manage to set the priorities for the next quarter or the strategy for the next year, but in doing so we create stress in the finance department or a challenge as to how to communicate the changes to participants, clients, or congregants. The Deploy phase takes us beyond our ability to control, manage, be in every decision, or connect with every leader; so, if we approach Deploy as a 2D jigsaw, we will quickly become frustrated, exhausted, or demoralized.

In the Deploy phase, we need to embrace the Rubik's Cube puzzle—leveraging the strength of *both/and environments*, unlocking the power of *relational spaces*, and instilling *transformative habits*—all of which are key to discipling your organization.

LEVERAGING THE STRENGTH OF BOTH/AND ENVIRONMENTS

To create movemental growth in this phase, we will need to shift away from our natural default either-or thinking. For example, we might view ourselves as *either* introverted or extroverted; either spontaneous *or* structured; *either* a "people-person" *or* "task-focused." In *Strong and Weak*, Andy Crouch observes that the Christian world has its own either-or categories: "Is the mission of the church evangelism and proclamation *or* is it justice and demonstration? Are we supposed to be conservative *or* radical, contemplative *or* active, set apart from the world *or* engaged in the world?"[2] This list goes on.

I have often observed an amicable conversation turn sour in the Deploy phase, as one "side" campaigns against another, and it degenerates into an "us versus them" standoff. If we introduce our "new" idea or way of working in the Deploy phase to the wider organization, it almost automatically is perceived as something pitted against the "old." Unintentionally, we can create an environment where people feel forced to choose an either-or. We can throw the proverbial baby out with the bathwater, and the Deploy phase becomes about either "becoming a new organization" *or* "protecting our heritage." Whether an existing organization or a pioneering venture, disagreements can revolve around countless issues: whether to invest in younger leaders who have future potential *or* rely on more experienced and reliable leaders; choosing to invest resources in planting new expressions *or* renovating what exists; gaining an inside perspective *or* accessing an outside voice; the debate on the intentionality of the Skeleton *or* the creativity and contextualization of the Skin. Many organizations and ventures also develop a "silo mentality," which reinforces an either-or approach; departments compete against one another, entrenched in their own specialties and agendas and squabbling over resources, priority, or focus.

Dee Hock, founder and CEO of VISA, coined the term "chaordic" in describing the company's organizing principles and how they can be embedded across multiple expressions and entities.[3] The word refers to the interaction between *chaos* and *order*—a dynamic combination of freedom and discipline, where the structured and spontaneous coexist and synergize. When managed well, this creates dynamism and growth and a both/and reality. *Order*

---

[2]   Crouch, *Strong and Weak*, 13.

[3]   Dee Hock, *One from Many: VISA and the Rise of Chaordic Organization* (Oakland, CA: Berrett-Koehler Publishers, 2005).

is represented by Skeleton and *chaos* by Skin. Generally, innovators and early adopters will tend toward dynamic chaos, and your early and late majority will tend toward reliable order; but we need to harness the both/and chaordic principle in the Deploy phase if we are to see change impact the whole of our organization.

For an existing organization, one of the challenges in the Deploy phase is that the late majority can feel as though the change being introduced is part of a quest to prove one way is the best. When the late majority feel they need to defend their position, guard the heritage of the existing organization, and protect the status quo, the pioneering and embryonic change efforts from the Discover and Design phase will be in grave danger of crashing to a sudden stop. Because the late majority tend to work in facts, proof, and sensory details, the conversation can very quickly focus on issues such as how this year's budget is being spent, scheduling activities for the next six months, or other short-term concerns.

Our default to either-or is sometimes an attempt to create mental shortcuts to save our brains time and energy. When something has looked the same way for so long, it's hard to imagine anything different. This can explain the resistance to change that we may face as we roll out our innovations. If we are to design a fruitful future for our organizations, teams, and leaders, we need to embrace the tension of both/and, and foster environments that express it healthily. Giles Hutchins and Laura Storm note in *Regenerative Leadership* that "having 'no tension' in a system signifies no aliveness, no learning, no evolution."[4] Harnessing both/and is not about caving in to compromise but rather it is about thinking in terms of continuums. Andy Crouch says we need an approach that "presses us to see the surprising connections between two things we thought we had to choose between—and perhaps even to discover that having the fullness of one requires that we have the fullness of the other."[5] In *Impact Networks*, David Ehrlichman describes this reality as "dynamic tensions: 'dynamic' because they are always in flux, 'tensions' to signify a relationship between ideas or

---

[4] Giles Hutchins and Laura Storm, *Regenerative Leadership: The DNA of Life-Affirming 21ˢᵗ Century Organizations* (Tunbridge Wells, UK: Wordzworth, 2019), 72.

[5] Crouch, *Strong and Weak*, 14.

qualities with seemingly conflicting demands or implications. If managed effectively, these tensions, also known as polarities, can be a powerful source of energy."[6]

We need to reorient our thinking without overcorrecting. We need to find ways to lead well into the new world without completely throwing out the old. As we embrace the positive tension and unlock the power of AND in our various environments, those three letters open a world of possibilities, health, and maturity for us individually and for our teams.

Below are some examples of how both/and thinking can be applied in the Deploy phase, which are applicable if you are sparking change within an existing organization or seeking to solidify and scale the work of a pioneering venture.

Create Momentum *and* Invest in the Team

A healthy team with a strong culture will outperform a group of superstars every time. The caliber, competency, and commitment of your leaders in the Deploy phase are huge factors in the viability of the change process and will affect the long-term health and growth of the organization. If we are not developing Christlike leaders and creating healthy teams, we will have short-term results in the Deploy phase that will not last beyond one generation—or results that come with unhealthy interactions and ultimately undermine any result achieved. We need to intentionally invest money, time, and effort in those we lead, so the first and future generations of the Deploy phase have high levels of health as well as growth. If we push the organizational culture, structure, or leaders too hard, we risk explosion or implosion. When riding a bike, if we peddle too fast, we can run out of energy or go so fast that we hit a bump and go flying over the handlebars. However, if we ride too slowly, the lack of momentum means we feel every bump and eventually wobble and fall off. We need to ride at the proper speed, so our organizations don't stall or crash.

---

6   Ehrlichman, *Impact Networks*, 71.

	JUST Create Momentum	JUST Invest in the Team	BOTH Create Momentum AND Invest in the Team
Priority	The next frontier or new forms	Relational harmony, internal communication, and empowering team members	Accomplishing tasks to generate forward momentum *and* developing team members to maximize their potential and contribution
Value Measurement	Effectiveness, activity production, and results	Team relationships, interactions, and realizing team members' potential	Strategically spreading the investment of team members between momentum in the short term and development for the longer term
Energy Focus	Delivery of tasks	Formation and retention of existing team members	Developing character and competency; focusing on camaraderie, learning, and celebration of progress toward hitting targets and developing strategy

Build the Center *and* Explore the Edge

Center/edge dynamics are an unavoidable reality in organizations—whether that is relational (a core community and wider crowd) or structural (a head office and regional teams). It's similar to the human body, which has a heart at its center and hands and feet at its extremities. When you are cold and your body is threatened, it automatically shuts down and redirects all heat energy to its core. The body will sacrifice fingers or toes (edge) if required to keep the heat in the key organs (center). But without fingers and toes, the core could not and would not be able to move, engage, and explore the world in the same way.

Either the center or the edge will take priority in your organization. Often, the center is represented by a "head office" or the core leadership within the heart of the organization, and the edge is expressed by pioneering work on the frontlines.

You may know of very centralized entities (such as the Kremlin, where all phone lines were routed through Moscow;[7] or a spider that will die if you cut off its legs) or very decentralized entities (Al-Qaeda as a network of autonomous cells,[8] or a starfish, which can recreate itself from a detached leg because all its DNA is held in every part). The reality is that every edge needs some center, and every center needs some edge. In *The Starfish and the Spider*, authors Ori Brafman and Rod Beckstrom relate the story of CEO Deborah Alvarez-Rodriguez, who came into a hierarchical organization and sought to engage the edge and initiate chaos to maximize the both/and dynamic. She explains, "We needed to get people into a conversation and get them to be innovative and creative. People in positions of power needed to understand that great ideas come from people who are closest to the ideas." Brafman and Beckstrom go on to say that "Deborah formed cross-functional brainstorming teams with about twelve members representing all levels of the company. Management had the final say, but it incorporated 95 percent of all suggestions made."[9] As we move toward change, it can seem easier in the short term to default to either the center *or* the edge as the sole expression, but in doing so, we will miss out on the dynamism of including both.

	JUST Build the Center	JUST Explore the Edge	BOTH Build the Center AND Explore the Edge
Priority	Allocation and oversight of money, time, and effort is defined by a central team or office/headquarters	Money, time, and effort are invested in pioneering initiatives on the edge of the organization	Money, time, and effort are strategically spread between the center and the edge, as reflected in investments, budget, staffing, priorities, and attention

7   Ori Brafman and Rod A. Beckstrom, *The Starfish and the Spider: The Unstoppable Power of Leaderless Organizations* (New York, NY: Penguin Group, 2006), 52.

8   Brafman and Beckstrom, *The Starfish and the Spider*, 140–42.

9   Brafman and Beckstrom, *The Starfish and the Spider*, 131.

	JUST Build the Center	**JUST Explore the Edge**	**BOTH Build the Center AND Explore the Edge**
Value Measurement	Central infrastructure, efficiency, systems, processes, and oversight	Risk, innovation, and ingenuity	Innovation coupled with intentionality; creativity coupled with cohesion; and learning that is integrated and dispersed across the whole
Energy Focus	Personal care, policy and procedure, communications, and training	The margins, experiments, new initiatives, and innovation	Pioneering into new territory and consolidating existing ground

Although we may begin the change journey with energy, dynamism, uncertainty, and a healthy dose of chaos and creativity, as we move into the Deploy phase, we may drift back toward oversight and control, which in turn produces hierarchies and management structures. Pioneering and purpose can quickly be replaced by policies and procedures. As we introduce the change across our organization or venture and seek to become movemental in the Deploy phase, we must continue to foster a mindset and create environments of both/and.

UNLOCKING THE POWER OF RELATIONAL SPACES

In the Deploy phase, we must also harness the power of different relational spaces, considering how we can use each of them strategically. Sociologist Edward T. Hall names four different relational spaces, which he refers to as intimate (2–3 people), personal (4–14 people), social (15–50 people), and public (50+ people).[10]

Each of these relational spaces is ruled by different dynamics, with each space being able to deliver different opportunities for communicating and engaging with the change process. In *The Church as Movement*, JR Woodward and Dan White Jr. name the gift of each of the four relational spaces, noting that

---

[10] Joseph Myers, *The Search to Belong: Rethinking Intimacy, Community and Small groups* (Grand Rapids, MI: Zondervan, 2033), 22–24.

the public space gives visibility, social space creates availability, personal space offers accountability, and intimate space provides vulnerability.[11] We see these different relational dynamics in the Gospels, as Alan and Debra Hirsch note in their book *Untamed*,

> The Gospels speak of faith communities varying from twelve to one hundred twenty, and make explicit reference to a number of women who traveled with Jesus. It seems that the community of Christ was not as simple as thirteen guys roaming the countryside. There was a rich intersection of relationships, with some nearer the center and others farther away, but all were openly invited to join the kingdom-building enterprise.[12]

In the life and ministry of Jesus, we see him engage in each of these spaces. The public space is represented by the crowds, the social space is the Seventy-two, the personal space is the Twelve, and the intimate space is the Three (Peter, James, and John).

In *The Tipping Point*, Malcolm Gladwell refers to the eighteenth-century Methodist movement, as it grew from twenty thousand to ninety thousand followers in the US within five or six years. John Wesley, the founder of the Methodist movement, understood the power of the different relational spaces to catalyze movement dynamics:

> Wesley would travel around England and North America delivering open-air sermons to thousands of people. But he didn't just preach. He also stayed long enough in each town to form the most enthusiastic of his converts into religious societies, which in turn he subdivided into smaller classes of a dozen or so people. Converts were required to attend weekly meetings and to adhere to a strict code of conduct.[13]

In the same way as Jesus and Wesley, we can harness these spaces in the Deploy phase in our organization or venture.

---

[11] Woodward and White, *The Church as Movement*, 155–60.

[12] Alan Hirsch and Debra Hirsch, *Untamed: Reactivating a Missional Form of Discipleship* (Grand Rapids, MI: Baker, 2010), 154.

[13] Gladwell, *The Tipping Point*, 172.

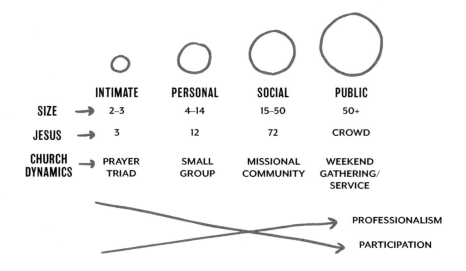

		INTIMATE	PERSONAL	SOCIAL	PUBLIC
SIZE	➜	2–3	4–14	15–50	50+
JESUS	➜	3	12	72	CROWD
CHURCH DYNAMICS	➜	PRAYER TRIAD	SMALL GROUP	MISSIONAL COMMUNITY	WEEKEND GATHERING/ SERVICE

PROFESSIONALISM

PARTICIPATION

Public Space (50+ people)

In the church sphere, public space is seen in the Sunday gathering; but the dynamic of public space isn't just about preaching or a presentation at a meeting—it can also be felt in organization-wide emails, memos from human relations, videos sent across the whole network, webinars, or monthly newsletters. In the Deploy phase, the public space allows organizations and ventures to express truth, story, inspiration, and challenge both online and in-person to many across the whole organization. We need to express the value, vision, and vehicles of change and our preferred future and next steps everyone can engage in. The size of the public space means communication is usually one-directional rather than discursive and, when in a gathered context, will reflect a higher degree of management, excellence, or organization.

Social Space (15–50 people)

The social space often operates similarly to an extended family. This is the household (*oikos*) dynamic of the early church, which comprised both blood and non-blood relationships, and where commerce and community coalesced.

In the contemporary missional church, this space is often expressed as a microchurch or missional community, where a group unites around a communal missional cause. In many more traditional churches, this space is absent, with more emphasis placed on the public (Sunday service) and personal (small group Bible study) spaces.

Social-space communities have a shared purpose (dream) and shared rhythms (fractals). They have the flexibility to subdivide into smaller groups at points (personal space) and may also periodically attend the services and gatherings of the wider church (public space). Larger than the intimate and personal spaces but smaller than the public space, this space is "large enough to dare and small enough to care." This means that it allows its members to know each other well enough to care for one another's needs, but there is enough critical mass and dynamism to engage with a shared purpose to see a collective impact. The social-space size is often very accessible to non-Christians.

This relational space is effective for encouraging the necessary relational influence that happens across the Diffusion of Innovations Curve because it enables pioneers and early adopters to interact with those who are early and late majority. It also allows people to experience change in a safe and known environment. Leaders can share new practices and provide opportunities for those further along the curve to test them out—giving them the slower approach they need to get used to change. It also allows for experimentation in mission and contextualization of core principles, which is a key aspect of the Deploy phase.

In the Deploy Phase, you might use social-space dynamics to gather a group of leaders for interactive training or to host stakeholders for a dinner. In a larger public-space gathering, it can be effective to break into social-space groupings to encourage discussion and interaction.

Personal Space (4–14)

The smaller number of people in this space leads to greater transparency, proximity, and permission to speak more honestly with one another. Personal space is often expressed as a traditional small group or Bible study group, a service team for a church ministry, or a work team or department within an organization or venture.

In personal space, there is both the opportunity to embody change practices more intentionally but also to interact more deeply about the emotions, uncertainties, and opportunities of the change process itself. There is often richer dialogue and greater interaction around the vision and stimulus for change, how people are experiencing this process, and how they might want to engage with it. This space is more about the feedback and conversation with those taking part, rather than disseminating information or edicts from the core leadership team. It can also provide greater accountability for each member to play their part in stepping out into the change process rather than simply talking about it.

In the Deploy phase, this space can be particularly useful. It allows for conversations with key individuals who need more help processing the change. This space can also be used to unlock potential—you can train and equip every small group or team across your organization or venture to embody the core principles in their context. Leaders in the guiding coalition can effectively use this environment to engage with and mobilize five to fifteen early majority leaders.

Intimate Space (2–3 people)

Intimate space is where we share emotions, experiences, and perspectives with the smallest number of people in the most transparent way. This cannot be forced, rushed, or engineered—as every relationship can only grow at the speed of trust—so these smallest units of intimate space are precious and should be nurtured and guarded. Ideally, every missional community, microchurch, or team has patterns of intimate space, not just to solve problems or to resolve conflict or for a particular project, but to foster deeper relationships.

In the Deploy phase, we leverage intimate space with two to three other leaders to encourage, challenge, and hold them to account to follow through on the process they have committed to. In the journey of change, rewiring an existing mindset and resetting behaviors, decisions, priorities, and investments, requires the continued presence of others. Opportunities in this space include instituting prayer triads for each of your leaders, building a buddy system for accountability, or encouraging each leader to create their own support network.

INSTILLING TRANSFORMATIVE HABITS

In the Design phase, we said that our core principles would need to be repeated as rhythmic and recurring patterns. Such patterns ("rules of life") are reinforced through *habits*—lived out individually and communally. These communal practices and habits mean we can disciple the whole organization or venture in embodying our core principles. Our organizational core principles (Skeleton) come to life in these multiple, contextualized practices (Skin).

Much has been written in recent years about the importance of habits.[14] In his book *The Power of Habit*, Charles Duhigg writes that "when a habit emerges, the brain stops fully participating in decision-making … the pattern will unfold automatically."[15]

There are three stages that help us and our leaders live a lifestyle where we automatically and unconsciously express the core principles together.

- **Discipline: *intentionally* doing the right thing.** In this stage, we make intentional decisions to express a value, principle, or priority. For example, we *choose* to forgive a colleague, save money, close the fridge and walk away, read Scripture and pray before doing anything else, or put our trainers on and go for a run. Whether we like it or not, feel like it or not, regardless of circumstances, we make a disciplined decision to do the right thing. Effort is required to make sure the decision happens.

  … which over time leads to …

- **Habit: *usually* doing the right thing.** This is the stage where the right decisions are made regularly but with some occasional bumps and blips. The gap between a missed decision and the next right decision narrows. Most of the time we live out what we desire, and when we don't, we quickly bounce back into routine and intentionality. Most of the time we make good decisions about our diet, we have a regular pattern of exercise, our quiet time happens most mornings, and we're able to forgive, communicate, and encourage in most interactions and recover quickly when we miss a beat.

  … which over time leads to …

---

[14]   See for example, Charles Duhigg, *The Power of Habit: Why We Do What We Do and How to Change* (London, UK: Random House Books, 2013) and Whitmel Earley, *The Common Rule*.

[15]   Duhigg, *The Power of Habit*, 20.

- **Lifestyle: *naturally* doing the right thing.** This is where our habits become a natural, normative, subconscious, and default pattern. Our decisions and reactions become instinctive rather than intentional thought processes. (When you get in a car, for example, you don't think about "mirror, signal, maneuver"; you just drive.) So, at this stage, what might have been an intentional decision about quiet time every morning becomes a natural rhythm that automatically repeats as a lifestyle. Here, our diet, decisions, interactions or whatever we'd set out to take on as a discipline becomes embedded in our thinking and action and becomes automatic.

Through perseverance and prayer, encouraging every individual in your organization to engage with this process enables them to take on the communal and contextual expression of the Skeleton (rule of life) discerned in the Design phase. Doing this in community creates accountability for these habits to become a natural lifestyle. John Wesley understood the importance of communal formation. As Gladwell notes in *The Tipping Point*, "Wesley realized that if you wanted to bring about a fundamental change in people's belief and behavior, a change that would persist and serve as an example to others, you need to create a community around them, where those new beliefs could be practiced and expressed and nurtured."[16]

This same Discipline>Habit>Lifestyle pattern can be used as a formation process to develop the character and competency of a leader or a group. By engaging in this process, individuals and small pockets of relationships (teams, communities, groups) are gradually being transformed across the whole organization, and the power of the Deploy phase can create a virtuous circle and holistic change.

---

[16] Gladwell, *The Tipping Point*, 173.

Initiating habits enables us to create muscle memory that becomes a natural lifestyle for ourselves, our community, and so, by default, our organization. The more we engage in these practices, the deeper the change will go across and through our community or team, and across the organization, as we reconstruct and relearn.

Since it is unrealistic to think you can have one-on-one interactions with everyone you lead in the Deploy phase, it is helpful to use tools to formalize fractal patterns of behavior (habits) and to ensure alignment with the stated organizational Skeleton. Canadian philosopher Marshall McLuhan reputedly said, "We shape our tools and thereafter our tools shape us." For example, consider how much the iPhone—as a tool of communication, interaction, and media—has shaped the way we live in the last decade. It has affected our relationships, discipleship, parenting, banking, education, holidays, spending, and faith journey.

When I was in my early twenties, my local church used a simple tool to foster discipleship behaviors. Based on a triangle shape, it helped every disciple form habits to connect with God (Up), connect with the Christian community (In), and connect with the world (Out). Later, as we moved to Edinburgh, our local church contextualized this simple triangle tool for the Celtic traditions in the Scottish context, expressing it as Cave (relationship with God), Table (fellowship with Christians), and Road (journey into and engagement with the world). The tool gave every leader and group (team, microchurch, or missional community) a rubric to analyze current behaviors and uncover their strengths and weaknesses in both character and competency in these dimensions. Like any great tool, this framework was simple and sticky enough that everyone could remember, understand, and apply it. At any given moment and in any situation, any leader across any part of the organization had a frame and shared language they could use for self-analysis, spiritual reflection, and strategic realignment. There was cohesion and order as the frame was the same for every leader and community, but also chaos and creativity in the contextualized expression of this frame in many different contexts and circumstances—the chaordic dynamics of Skeleton and Skin.

Effective tools synthesize complicated information into an accessible and actionable form and give people what they need to instill transformative habits and get the job done in their everyday world. In the Deploy phase, it's vital to have a few key tools and disciplines that every leader understands and applies. Over time, these actions and interactions become rhythmic, regular, and natural to them and those they influence. Having one or two leaders doing this is a win, but when multiple leaders are living this way, it creates a groundswell across the whole organization. In the Deploy phase, we want the core values and communal practices to be embedded, embodied, and extended by every leader across the whole, and recurring fractal patterns and the regular use of tools help to bring this engagement and cohesion.

BEWARE OF FALSE SUMMITS

If you've ever hiked in the hills, you probably know what it means to experience a false summit. You climb until you think you're reaching the peak, only to get to the "top" and see the real summit further in the distance. On our all-change journey, there's a danger we will experience a false summit, and think we've already made it, but there's still a way to go. In the previous phase, we ran intentional pilots and created a frame for the whole organization, and now we may be starting to see some initial success from our innovators and early adopters, with the early majority showing signs of interest and slowly but surely coming on board. At this stage, it can be easy to think that our design for change will automatically be accepted across the whole of our organization; but that assessment may be premature.

Much of the success of instigating change and scaling growth across both an existing organization and a pioneering venture has to do with whether we treat the organization as a static or living entity. In earlier chapters, we talked about the difference between a "factory" and a "field" approach. If we view change as a linear, mechanical, production-line process (factory), we will falter and fail in the Deploy phase. Instead, we need to approach this phase more like a farmer tending to crops in an organic, dynamic, and adaptive manner (field). If we think back to the image of the valley of dry bones from Ezekiel 37, and the dynamics of Skeleton, Skin, and Spirit coming together, we're reminded of the many interplays that exist between elements across an organization that help it to function more like a living organism than a static one.

We have to leverage the power of both/and environments, relational spaces, and transformative habits for us to master the Rubik's Cube of the Deploy phase and unleash the power of movemental dynamics.

TO INFINITY AND BEYOND

EQUIPPING OTHERS TO DEPLOY

*Ideas do not succeed in history by virtue of their truth but by
virtue of their relationship to specific social processes.*
PETER BERGER

*The future depends entirely on what each of us does every
day: a movement is only people moving.*
GLORIA STEINEM

*I define a leader as anyone who takes responsibility for finding the potential
in people and processes, and who has the courage to develop that potential.*
BRENÉ BROWN

In 2004, a small group of workers pitched a new idea to Steve Jobs, the founder
of Apple. They proposed to convert the successful iPod into an iPhone, but Jobs
was vehemently against it, saying, "That is the dumbest idea I've ever heard." He
was worried about ruining Apple's thriving iPod business with another product,
but he was also concerned about turning Apple into a phone company rather
than a computer company. Jobs hated cell phone companies, and publicly and
privately said he would never make a phone. Yet this group of Apple engineers
continued to research and develop the technology. More importantly, they

continued to work on convincing Jobs by using what Adam Grant refers to in *Think Again* as a "vision of continuity."[1] Their narrative to Jobs was that they weren't trying to turn Apple into a phone company—Apple would remain a computer company—but they were just adding a phone as an extra product. Grant notes that, "Visions for change are more compelling when they include visions of continuity. Although our strategy might evolve, our identity will endure."[2] As the conversation continued over the next six months, Jobs finally became curious enough to allow experimentation to continue. The engineers convinced him that they could preserve Apple's DNA. Just a few years later, the iPhone accounted for half of Apple's revenue.[3] The iPhone represented a dramatic leap in rethinking the smartphone and has globally revolutionized humanity's engagement with technology. But it was an idea that almost didn't get past the prototype phase.

EVERYONE GETS TO PLAY

If even a world-leading pioneer and innovator like Steve Jobs needed convincing over several months, we will need to enter the Deploy phase with a sober appraisal of the work involved to persuade a late-majority leader to change the way they have always done things and embrace something new.

Up until now, we've mainly been working with the innovators and early adopters, along with a few from the early majority. However, as we enter the Deploy phase and aim for our existing organization or new venture to function more like a movement, it's time to engage the early and late majority more intentionally.

Most of those involved in the core group until now will have been pioneers and therefore likely to be intuitive, imaginative, and intentional. However, as we enter the Deploy phase and welcome a broader range of groups along the Diffusion of Innovations Curve, a different type of leader comes into play. And so, the game plan needs to change. This can feel challenging for a variety of reasons.

---

[1] Grant, *Think Again*, 31.

[2] Grant, *Think Again*, 31.

[3] Grant, *Think Again*, 30–31.

Your role as a change agent makes it most likely that you are an innovator or early adopter, so you might have difficulty identifying with those on a different part of the curve. Each of these groups speaks a different language and sees the world differently—so crossing this chasm can sometimes feel like speaking French to a German! However, as you engage the early and late majority, it's vital that you learn a new language—that you know the customs of their world and that you understand that their response to change is unlikely to be your natural response. You need to harness your ability to see their perspective and empathize graciously with their experience of change.

As you developed a core group as a guiding coalition to go through the phases of Dream, Discover, and Design, you probably spent a lot of time getting used to the idea of this change. But for those you are just bringing into this journey, this is brand new. And, to them, anything "new" is scary. They haven't been in the hours of meetings or heard the tens, if not hundreds, of ideas that have been thrashed around, discarded, tried, revised, and so on. They haven't seen your process, so it's harder for them to understand and trust the idea of the change you're implementing. They are more likely to assume something will go wrong or not turn out well, and therefore want to mitigate against risk or rebel against change. This is a time for leading with grace, care, and communicating in a patient but purposeful way. But it's also a time to allow others to take the baton because it's unlikely that you are suited to leading the late majority into this new change. Those in your team and other stakeholders will be better equipped. You need to find people who act as bridges, translators, and guides for each group. Identify those within your early adopters who are "forward-facing" pioneers, who will continue to move the organization toward new frontiers. Most importantly, however, you need to identify your "backward-facing" pioneers who can act as bridges and connectors with the early majority. These "backward-facing" individuals are the guides who will bring the next group along on the journey and can function as translators to a group that speaks a different language. They are essential to maintaining the relational thread and bridge between groups. That relational influence is the key to seeing change implemented across the whole and for your organization to become movemental in its approach to change.

To help set realistic expectations, remember that each group naturally *connects* with the group on either side of them on the innovations curve, and will *influence* those to their right. Innovators can therefore communicate effectively with and influence the early adopters; and, closer to the middle of the curve, the early majority can connect with and understand the groups on either side of them (early adopters and late majority) but will struggle to connect, understand, or have meaningful interaction with an innovator. We can't just tell our organization to adopt change and assume everyone will automatically do what we say. We can't have a message that only speaks to one group or simply put everyone in one room or training program and assume they will all come out on the same page. If you want movemental change, you need to allow influence to work across all the groups rather than just hope the innovators will be able to bring everyone on the journey. Allowing each group to influence the next means they will filter out any language that the group besides them might not understand and will explain and model practices in a way that engages this group. They can also reframe and restate the process in such a way that the late majority can follow and feel invited to participate.

It's useful to remind ourselves of the caterpillar approach here, introduced in chapter two.

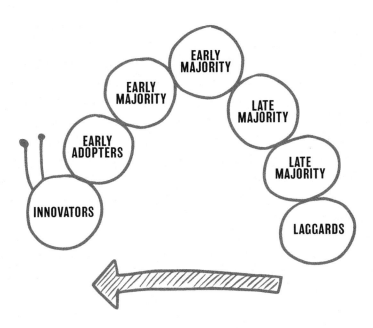

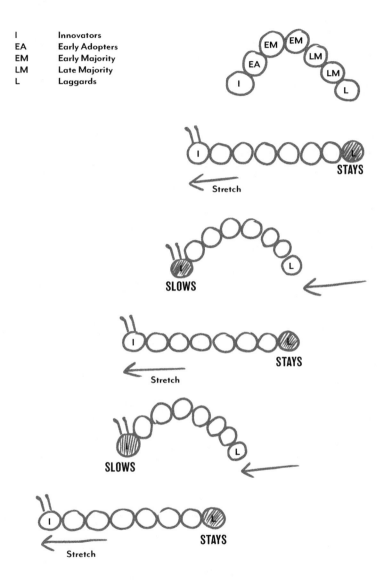

As you have been creating prototypes in the Discover phase and pilots in the Design phase, the "head" of the caterpillar (the innovators and early adopters) has stretched out forward while the rear of the caterpillar (the early and late majority) has remained in the same place. This season of stretching forward cannot last forever or it will stress the body of the caterpillar, and the component parts will start to pull apart. The innovators and early adopters must pause and allow the back end the chance to catch up. Over time, the rest of the organization catches up, as the majority slowly but surely begin to move forward. The back of the caterpillar (the early majority, late majority, and laggards) must come closer to the head of the body (innovators and early adopters) before the front can make another push forward. In this coming together of the whole, the early and late majority spend more time with the innovators and early adopters. Everyone can experience and see the reality of the change that is being gradually introduced. This provides the early and late majority with the necessary input to comprehend and embrace the change, while also allowing them to take smaller, incremental steps forward. Then the front of the caterpillar is released to move forward again for the next phase of growth.

This concertina process helps to take everyone on the journey, creating enough stimuli and generative energy in the system without stressing it (or groups within it) more than it can bear. The caterpillar process is vital for the stages of change in an existing organization, but the principle of stretching forward and then consolidating ground is equally valid for the growth cycle of a new venture.

One of the best examples of this process being undertaken effectively is from a church in the UK that I coached over many years. They commissioned the innovators and early adopters to experiment and explore, with the accountability of reporting back and the responsibility of pulling others forward. They engaged the early majority by storyboarding the change process, holding stakeholder dinners with fifteen people at each. Key leaders within the early and late majority were identified and brought on board as advocates who could speak the language of the late majority; and they wrote a white paper and a ten-year plan for the late majority to create a slow and steady, low-risk, high-detail roadmap for those most resistant to change.

Too many change processes fail in the Deploy phase by allowing the head of the caterpillar (the innovators and pioneers) to continue to push out and overextend the whole; or by asking the head to engage every part of the caterpillar (so innovators and early adopters are asked to influence groups that they cannot communicate with or have no influence over); or by asking the back-end of the caterpillar (late majority) to go out front, and the process stalls before it even starts as this group rejects risk and has little imagination for anything new or different.

SPARK CHANGE AND SCALE EFFECTIVELY

In the Deploy phase, disseminating a change process beyond one leader and the small guiding coalition needs careful spiritual and strategic implementation. Failure to do so can cause the organization to become fractured and confused. We will need to consider what *training dynamics* are required in order to develop leaders, as well as the *communication techniques* that will help us to express vision, invitation, and expectations. In this phase, we need to empower people to live the story themselves and find their place and play their part. This will mean the process ceases to be centrally driven or an organizational priority, but instead multiple people embody the core principles and pursue the shared dream in multiple places and multiple ways. Good training dynamics and effective communication techniques help the guiding coalition create a platform and process that can spark change across the organization or venture but also to scale growth effectively. Learning to leverage these areas will help everyone to navigate the Deploy phase more effectively and mobilize everyone to play an active part.

TRAINING DYNAMICS

The training pathway Jesus took the disciples on through the Gospels moved them from bystanders to disciples, from disciples to leaders, and ultimately from leaders to movement makers. At every step of the way, Jesus deepened the relationship and increased their responsibility. However, rather than looking to the training pathway of Jesus, we often default to Western educational philosophy. This methodology relies heavily on the transfer of information, usually in a classroom-style delivery that leverages one type of training (a program) or one environment (an event). This can lead to a sanitized, conceptual, and untested transfer of knowledge without ever allowing the learner to wrestle with the content and concepts themselves. It also doesn't allow any sense of trial, test, or internalizing through personal practice of what they have heard. If this was the methodology of Jesus, the disciples would have been taken out of context for three years to be trained in a classroom environment, and then launched back in as church planters—full of head knowledge but with no real-time learning, practitioner experience, or the communitas[4] needed to do all that is recorded in the book of Acts. If mere knowledge transfer was enough, then the Gospels would focus on numerous Sermon on the Mount experiences, with Jesus gathering the crowds and communicating his ideas, hoping that they would walk off the mountainside and put them into practice.

Liz Wiseman, in her book *Multipliers*, talks about how effective learning happens in real-time through real-time implications and experiences:

> Nature teaches best. When we let nature take its course and allow people to experience the natural consequences of their actions, they learn most rapidly and most profoundly. When we protect people from experiencing the natural ramifications of their actions, we stunt their learning. Real intelligence gets developed through experimentation and trial and error.[5]

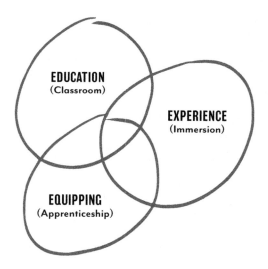

---

4 Communitas is the community that is formed from embarking on a share cause, risk, and adventure. It's therefore not normally experienced in a classroom environment! See more at https://www.themxplatform.com/startthejourney.

5 Liz Wiseman, *Multipliers: How the Best Leaders Make Everyone Smarter* (New York, NY: Harper Collins, 2010), 189.

To create a holistic formation and leadership training process and to follow the way Jesus formed, trained, and commissioned leaders, we need to strike a synergistic balance between *Experience, Equipping,* and *Education.* This is similar to the process that Jesus initiated with his disciples of Modeling and Explaining (Experience), Imitating and Embodying (Equipping), and Reflecting and Questioning (Education) (see pages 106–108). The task now is to use this frame with leaders across the wider organization.

Experience (Immersion)

To activate people to lead within their context in the Deploy phase, their learning needs to be personal, first-hand, and sensory. As we form leaders, we must consider what we want people to see and feel, and what environments and examples will allow them to gain direct experience of the core principles we want them to engage with. This is not about throwing people in at the deep end; rather, in the way of Jesus, it's about giving people the opportunity to watch, interact, observe, feel, and engage in real-time an environment or sphere in which someone else is leading. Jesus said, "Come … and you will see" (John 1:39), then moved to "Come, follow me" (Matt. 4:19), before he ended with "Go and make" (Matt. 28:19). All were active and demanded a dynamic engagement. "Come and see" involved being part of the environment Jesus created and looking, listening, and dialoguing with him. "Come, follow me" was an invitation to an experiential and immersive environment, which allowed the disciples to learn in real time. "Go and make" was the invitation and opportunity to embody, extend, and multiply in others all that Jesus had invested in them. Jesus didn't say "Come, study me," "Come, listen to me," or "Come, reflect on me." Following him was, and still is, an active learning journey. Instead of forming the disciples by a module, course, program, or textbook, Jesus trained them in context—on the road, around the table, at the campfire, and on the mountainside.

Equipping (Apprenticeship)

Equipping involves apprenticing people through intentional and active formation pathways that assist them in gaining skills, competencies, and practitioner wisdom, while simultaneously increasing their level of leadership responsibility. As we form leaders in the Deploy phase, we transition from a smaller core group to a larger number and so need to embrace the challenge of offering a first-hand apprenticeship experience that is framed and developed by a leader who is a little further down the road.

The larger the number of leaders to engage, the greater the temptation to go for a large-batch, one-size-fits-all, mass engagement strategy for leadership development. However, let's remember that Jesus didn't use a mountainside-to-mountainside strategy of mass communication. Instead, he invested in a smaller but ever-increasing number of leaders and equipped them by gradually giving them more responsibility until they were ultimately given full authority in the Great Commission.

The disciples began by watching what Jesus did, then they actively helped him, followed by participating and being coached by Jesus, to eventually taking responsibility, empowered by the Holy Spirit. The integration of skills-based learning and apprenticeship pathways will lead to leadership health and generational growth.

Feedback loops are essential in apprenticeship. People need permission to ask questions and dialogue as they process their experiences. This is especially important when working with younger leaders who live amid constant social media interaction and engagement. Offering a once-a-year review and the occasional personal development session will therefore be alien to their everyday experience. In their book *New Power*, Henry Timms and Jeremy Heimans emphasize the importance of feedback to the younger generation because, "for the most, their lives are punctuated (perhaps even defined) by the validation and engagement of others. Every text, every image, every post is a call designed for a response."[6] They note that,

> Research from the Young Entrepreneur Council shows that 80 percent of millennials would prefer to get feedback in "real time," and a 2014 Millennial Impact Report showed that "more than half (53%) of respondents said having

---

6 Jeremy Heimans and Henry Timms, *New Power: How It's Changing the 21ˢᵗ Century—and Why You Need to Know* (New York, NY: Doubleday, 2018), 225.

their passions and talents recognized and addressed is their top reason for remaining at their current company."[7]

It's therefore essential to create processes where leaders take on responsibility and learn by doing, followed by debriefing and learning through evaluation and discussion. Apprenticeship can also be effective in coworking, where the apprentice works alongside the more experienced leader on a specific project, giving the apprentice the opportunity to see the "rabbi" in action up close, ask questions, and be formed and equipped to grow in perspective, competencies, and confidence.

Education (Classroom)

Education includes teaching the core concepts, principles, theology, and tactics that every leader needs to know as they are deployed. This often forms the majority, if not all, of an organization's training process; and although it's important, it can often be ineffective as it front-loads information before the learner fully understands its relevance or realizes they need it. As we reflect on the training dynamics of Jesus, we see that he often offered a discursive debrief *after* the event rather than a preemptive monologue *before* the experience.

Jesus used story, conversation, and questions as he educated his disciples, pulling them into their own exploration and deepening their understanding as they grappled with the truth. Jesus is recorded as asking 307 questions in the Gospels and answers only three of the 183 questions he's asked.[8] He implanted in his disciples the core messages of the gospel in every interaction, and he educated them through demonstration, smaller group discussion, questions, and communal dialogue. The aim was not the transfer of information or a greater intellect; the end goal was that the information he passed on would become truths that the learners embodied, shared with others, and would spark a movement that extended beyond Jesus' time on earth. Returning to the principles highlighted in chapter two, education in the way of Jesus should call people to both Awareness *and* Application, to both hearing *and* obeying. This is

---

[7]   Heimans and Timms, *New Power*, 225.

[8]   Paul Woolley, "Questions Jesus Asked | The Power of the Question," LICC, accessed April 3, 2024, https://licc.org.uk/resources/questions-jesus-asked-the-power-of-the-question/.

important to understand and apply in the Deploy phase. People need to wrestle so that core principles and learning become their own truth rather than the organizational edict.

Dividing Up the Pie

It's easy to assume that the three elements of Experience, Equipping, and Education comprise equal slices of the training pie. However, if we follow the model of Jesus in the Gospels, it's closer to approximately 70 percent Experience, 20 percent Equipping, and 10 percent Education.

These 70/20/10 dynamics are supported by the results of a 1996 survey of 200 executives, which concluded that effective learning occurs 70 percent from challenging assignments (Experience), 20 percent from developmental relationships (Equipping), and 10 percent from coursework and training (Education).[9] There is now even a 702010 Institute, which has built leadership training, learning development, and management consultancy around the philosophy and practice of these countercultural learning dynamics.[10]

To activate and mobilize people well in the Deploy phase, we must properly balance Experience, Equipping, and Education in our training. Leaders need more than just ideas and instruction; they need an investment and intentional formation that helps them to live and lead well in their own context.

Use the simple checklist below to reflect on your organization's current training environments and dynamics. These will help you to discern where you need to move toward a more holistic training process that activates every person in your organization.

- What is our current balance of Experience, Equipping, and Education?
- What would a healthier balance look like?
- What two or three changes could we make in the short or medium term to shift the balance and dynamics of our training?
- Where can we create pilots that demonstrate this shift in our training dynamics?

---

[9] "70/20/10 model (learning and development)," Wikipedia, accessed April 3, 2024, https://en.m.wikipedia.org/wiki/70/20/10_model_(learning_and_development).

[10] See https://702010institute.com.

Experience (Immersion)
- **Status Quo:** Currently, how much of our training involves an experience where people can learn by touching, tasting, feeling, and seeing firsthand what we want them to grasp?
- **Aspiration:** We will create environments that give every leader firsthand experiences, so that they learn through observation, absorption, and embodied practices.

Equipping (Apprenticeship)
- **Status Quo:** Currently, how much of our training involves on-the-job equipping and training?
- **Aspiration:** We will create pathways that will enable every leader to grow in the skills, aptitudes, and competencies that will help them learn through apprenticeship, so that they can ultimately take leadership responsibility.

Education (Classroom)
- **Status Quo:** Currently, how much of our training involves teaching concepts, information, or techniques?
- **Aspiration:** We will create interactions that will enable every leader to deepen their understanding of the core concepts, theology, and tactics, so they are formed in discursive and interactive environments.

COMMUNICATION TECHNIQUES

In the Deploy phase, because new people are coming into the conversation, we cannot assume any prior knowledge or understanding of insider language. The early and late majority are not only newer to the process; they also have different worldviews, vocabulary, and drivers. The guiding coalition will need to reflect on the following questions to prepare for engaging everyone.

- Where do we need to simplify language or expectations for the new audience?

- How can we communicate the vision and invitation to participate with narrative, testimony, and in the relevant language of the organization?
- How can we encourage the early or late majority in their engagement?
- What narrative will inspire as many people as possible to engage and embody the Skeleton in a genuine and impactful contextual expression (Skin) in partnership with God (Spirit)?

In a world of fake news, relationship breakdowns, and culture wars, the importance of effective and authentic communication couldn't be more evident. *What* we communicate—and, perhaps more importantly, *how* we communicate—is vital if we are to make participation in the change process as accessible as possible to every member of our organization. Remember, this isn't just about getting people on board; it is about helping every person contribute their part to the ongoing movement of change. It's telling a story that they can find their place in and are energized to play their part in—alongside others. Today's best marketers understand this better than most. In *Network Power*, David John Seel Jr., asserts that we need to communicate through stories, metaphors, and pictures. He says these "serve as the frame through which we see everything else. We have to win the frame before arguing the facts."[11]

In the same way that we would adapt our communication for a listener in everyday life, based on age, ability, and culture, we need to think about how the core principles and organization's DNA we considered in the Design phase can be communicated in a variety of ways, reminding everyone who they are, where they're going, and how they are going to engage with the journey. These core principles must be verbalized often, practiced repeatedly, and celebrated regularly. They need to be embodied and demonstrated by the leadership and expressed by the wider culture of the organization so that they are tangibly seen and understood beyond words in a vision statement or catchphrases on a PowerPoint.

When thinking about verbal communication, it's important to consider a variety of methods that will impact your listeners. Good communication employs three techniques: Storytelling, Science, and Statistics.

Storytelling is a narrative-based communication method that highlights

---

[11] David John Seel Jr., *Network Power: The Science of Making a Difference* (Chester, CA: Whithorn Press, 2021), 14.

the vision, values, and DNA that are part of a bigger story, giving individuals a plotline they can write themselves into. This communication sparks in people the imagination of what is possible.

Science is a theory-based communication method that focuses more on the ideas we are testing, an experiment we're engaging in, or a hypothesis we have. It invites people to join in with the search for a different future, validating the collective findings along the way. This communication allows people to embrace an experimental reality.

Statistics is an information-based communication method that deals with facts and figures. It presents a problem, the associated data, and a formula that people can take as tangible evidence of the need for change and the cost of not changing. This communication helps people engage with the reality of the situation.

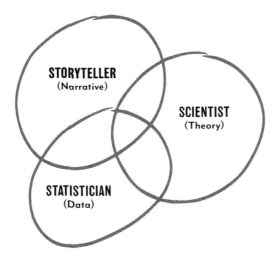

Each of us will have a natural communication style we lean toward, but communication is what people *hear*, not just what we *say*, so we need to consider the audience we are with. We need to think about the frames through which people see the world. If we are a natural Storyteller, and we are sharing a narrative and vision with a room that is primarily Statistics-driven (e.g., a visionary pastor talking to a board) or a Science-driven leader speaking to a mixed group of listeners, then we will need to adapt our natural communication style to fit the audience. At times we will need to incorporate all three dynamics. Cognitive linguist and philosopher George Lakoff says, "To be accepted, the truth must fit people's frames. If the facts do not fit the frame, the frame stays and the facts bounce off."[12]

In the Deploy phase, it is vital to devise and use a shared language for where we are going, why we are moving in that direction, how we will get there, and what key elements of behavior, culture, and strategy everyone in the organization or venture is seeking to embody.

ACTIVATING DEPLOY IN YOUR ORGANIZATION OR VENTURE

In the previous chapter, we explored the importance of both/and dynamics, relational spaces, and transformative habits. We will need to harness all of these in the Deploy phase. This phase pulls together our exploratory learning from the prototypes of the Discover phase and our intentional piloting from the Design phase, both of which contribute to the creation of strategies and processes that we implement with the majority of our leaders in the Deploy phase.

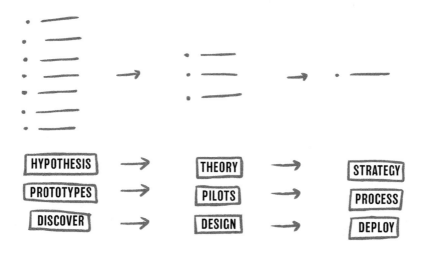

---

12   George Lakoff, *Don't Think of an Elephant! Know Your Values and Frame the Debate* (Chelsea, VT: Chelsea Green Publisher, 2014), 17.

In this journey of change, we need to remain clear, look ahead, tell the story, and continue to focus on how we are pursuing the initial, overarching dream as we move through the Deploy phase. However, we still need to embrace flexibility, creativity, and innovation in the way that we get there.

Although there is one overarching organizational dream, this phase sparks micro-expressions of the dream in the multiple leaders and contexts involved. There can be both beautiful continuity (everyone has a macro shared purpose) and creative contextualization (everyone can develop a micro-expression of the shared purpose). For example, the church we are part of in Edinburgh has a macro shared purpose of Loving Edinburgh, Being Family, and Following Jesus; but this macro dream is expressed in the multiple micro-dreams of the various missional communities scattered across the city.

In the Deploy phase, we need to function as learners rather than lecturers, explorers rather than experts, and micro-investors rather than recipients of resources from some macro-pipeline. Futurist Bob Johansen writes in *The New Leadership Literacies* that we need to look to the future ("look long") and then work backward, being flexible in our actions:

> The reason you look long is to develop the perspective necessary to come up with a good plan of action, a way forward, expressed with clarity and ideally as a story. The big lesson is to be very clear [about] where you're going, but very flexible [in] how you get there. Action should animate you. That's the basic discipline of looking backward from the future—but still acting now.[13]

Because we are in an age of era-defining disruption, we need to trade in our textbooks and tried-and-tested models for a new phrasebook, guidebook, and playbook.

A *phrasebook* gives you key terms for a new language; a *guidebook* highlights key pathways, practices, and training processes; and a *playbook* gives you tactics and strategies for action.

---

[13] Johansen, *New Leadership Literacies*, 22.

PRACTICE #1: CREATE A NEW PHRASEBOOK

Creating a new phrasebook involves translating the vision, concepts, and Skeleton into language that your organization will understand and can apply and easily share with others.

Your phrasebook will include images, phrases, terms, and metaphors that capture the imagination and make the core principles simple and sticky for your everyday leaders. For example, an organization I coached worked on the following frame for its three core values, so that each of them could be embodied by every leader, every team, and every individual:

- Statement—one word
- Symbol—one image/icon
- Tagline—one sentence
- Step—one practice

The pioneering group that has journeyed through the Dream, Discover, and Design phases needs to tell the story of the purpose and possibility of a movement in a way that resonates with the organization and invites everyone to participate in this great adventure. Your messaging needs continuity—using terms, words, phrases, and images that are already familiar to your organization. People are more inclined to accept new ideas in familiar terms. The language and narrative in the phrasebook clarify meanings and enable you to communicate core concepts and principles in a way that is accessible and engaging.

Discuss the questions below with your core team as you consider how you will create a new phrasebook.

- How do we tell a story that reminds people of who they are as disciples (biblical resonance), who we are as an organization (organizational heritage), how this pulls us toward where we are going (preferred future), and where we want everyone in our organization to go (personal embodiment of vision and values)?
- How do we communicate the change journey in a way that is visual and verbal (stories, images, heroes, icons, terms, practices) and

that captivates the imagination, offers an invitation to engage, and encourages people toward embodiment, all in an engaging, simple, and familiar way?

- What terminology and iconography should we use to communicate our organizational frameworks, expectations, and priorities to help people remember, understand, and embody the core components of the change process?

- Who are our heroes and why are we celebrating them? What narrative is being communicated through them? Are our heroes embodying our vision and values?

Practice #2: Create a New Guidebook

Creating a new guidebook is about developing an organizational map to help leaders navigate new terrain. The guidebook will include pathways, practices, and training processes that both help leaders feel they are supported and that they have the necessary frame around them to attempt something new. It will orient them to some key marker posts as they step into new territory. We must draw a new map as we explore new terrain rather than following the well-worn paths of old.

New leaders engaging in the Deploy phase will need more help navigating the new terrain (metaphorically teaching them to use a compass and training them in frontier skills), as well as practical training in new behaviors and leadership competencies. We will need to act as sherpas and guides for the many others who will join the journey at this stage and give them enough fixed points to get started, but not so many that they don't take responsibility for making the climb themselves. This will embolden early and late majority leaders to action, despite their aversion to risk or new endeavors, and even help the laggards to slowly move forward.

Discuss the questions below with your core team to help consider how you will create a new guidebook.

- How do we give our leaders clear marker posts, measures, and expectations for faithfulness, focus, and fruitfulness?

- How do we help our leaders become clear on their contextualized expression of the Skeleton and embodying the dream for their group?
- How can we give our leaders a strategic framework to focus their attention on the future while growing them in their ability to be flexible as to how they get there?
- How can we communicate and celebrate the journey (progression, obedience, and momentum) rather than merely outcomes (goals, finish lines, and completed projects)?
- How can we communicate some short-, medium-, and long-term progress markers?

Practice #3: Create a New Playbook

Creating a new playbook is about developing a toolkit and framework that outlines core principles and key strategies to support your leaders in their journey of contextualization. It is not an instruction manual for a singular vehicle, or a one-size-fits-all production line. The playbook gives your leaders new tactics and strategies for action.

Those in the early and late majority will need a more personal touch in implementing the playbook and more support in contextualization than the groups involved in earlier phases of the change journey. We must prepare our leaders for a new reality where, even with a playbook, they will have to embrace iterative learning and make "game-time decisions."

Discuss the questions below with your core team to help consider how you will create a new playbook.

- What tools and frames will our leaders need for the variety of situations they will face?
- What competencies do our leaders need to navigate the new requirements in the Deploy phase, and how might we use Experience, Equipping, and Education techniques to aid them in their leadership?
- How do our leaders grow in the competency of creating a relational engagement and apprenticeship process/pathway of passing on DNA in their own context?

- How does our playbook reflect our best practices from across the organization?
- What frameworks do our leaders need to be more strategic with their money, time, and effort?

GOING BEYOND WHAT'S POSSIBLE

As we progress through the Deploy phase, maintaining the relational connection points will be vital; but the larger the geographical area, the higher the numbers of leaders involved, or the more dispersed and digital the reality is, the harder it gets. General Stanley McChrystal, who headed up the Joint Special Operations Task Force in Iraq, talks about how to maintain relational connections as more people enter the context:

> On a single team, every individual needs to know every other individual in order to build trust, and they need to maintain comprehensive awareness at all times in order to maintain common purpose—easy with a group of twenty-five, doable with a group of fifty, tricky above one hundred, and definitely impossible across a task force of seven thousand. But on a team of teams, every *individual* does not have to have a relationship with every other individual; instead, the relationships between the constituent *teams* need to resemble those between individuals on a given team.... We didn't need every member of the task force to know everyone else; we just needed everyone to know someone on every team.[14]

As many leaders engage with the Deploy phase, and the change goes from a few to many, we need to work hard at maintaining the relational bonds. At least one person from each of the groups or teams needs to have a connection to other groups and to the leadership team and structures in your organization or venture. This creates a relational network and virtuous circle that provides encouragement, accountability, solidarity, and challenge to each group that is trying to embrace the Deploy phase and embody the change in their context. McChrystal's "team of teams" created a relational web that allowed multiple

---

[14] McChrystal, *Team of Teams*, 128–29.

experts and disciplines to be held together in a shape-shifting organization rather than getting disconnected or becoming a brittle structure that limits growth and new life.

In the Deploy phase, we must create a relational web of leaders that is robust, flexible, and adaptable and that can grow and multiply to many places, people, and generations. We need to take on the organizational Rubik's Cube, open ourselves to new innovations, and unlock the power of movemental Christianity in and through those we lead.

DEPLOY 101

PRIZE
Catalyze deep and lasting kingdom transformation that sustains and scales to multiple generations.

PEOPLE
The core group of innovators, early adopters, and some organizational stakeholders now work with the majority of leaders across the whole organization or venture.

LEADERSHIP EXPRESSION
A Champion who *resources* and *releases*.

SHADOWSIDE
An immature Champion creates disempowered people by giving permission without provision, too much freedom without frameworks, and too much yes without any no.

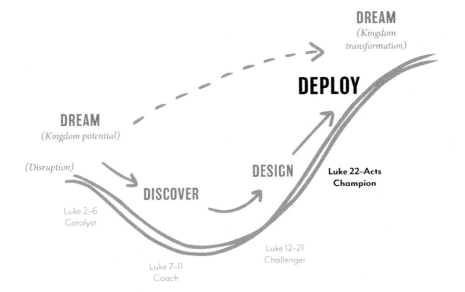

SCRIPTURE: LUKE 22-24; ACTS 1-2 AND BEYOND

In the final chapters of Luke's Gospel, Jesus is a Champion who *resources* the disciples and *releases* them as movement makers. In his death, the Champion embraces "defeat" for others to see victory. Jesus chooses the narrowest and hardest path to model to others the road ahead. Those he chose, invested in, formed, equipped, and empowered were the same ones who betrayed him (Luke 22:1–6), bickered over who was the most important (Luke 22:24–27), slept in the Garden of Gethsemane (Luke 22:45–46), and denied him three times (Luke 22:54–62). Throughout Luke's Gospel, the disciples have been apprenticed but still don't have all the answers. However, it is now time for them to take responsibility, step up, and step out.

The disciples' preparation and then propulsion into a new phase is seen in the final chapters of Luke in the Last Supper (Luke 22:7–39), the Garden of Gethsemane (Luke 22:39–46), the cross (Luke 23:26–49), the resurrection (Luke 24:1–12), the Emmaus Road encounter (Luke 24:13–32), the ascension (Luke 24:50–53; Acts 1:1–11) and into the early chapters of Acts with the coming of the Holy Spirit at Pentecost (Acts 2:1–13).

Jesus the Champion focuses on long-term influence rather than short-term impact. The release of the Holy Spirit to his disciples acts as a catalyst for the next season of growth in the early church movement. Jesus used his one generation on earth to invest in those who would take the message to multiple generations. The Champion becomes the seed that goes to the ground to produce a great harvest. Death brings new life. As we read the epistles and beyond, we see a Jesus movement that sparks and continues to scale.

YOUR CHANGE-AGENT JOURNEY

- Where do you need to operate as a Champion to resource and release the majority of leaders in your organization or venture to play their part?
- How can you most effectively deploy leaders by empowering them to reproduce and multiply the core principles in partnership with God and others in multiple contexts?

THE WAY OF THE WISE
WINDS UPWARD

FINAL WORDS

All the forces in the world are not so powerful as an idea whose time has come.
VICTOR HUGO

It's not the mountain ahead that will wear you out. It's the pebble in your shoe.
MUHAMMAD ALI

The journey of a thousand miles begins with one step.
LAO TZU

In 334 BC, Alexander the Great began his invasion of the Persian Empire. Legend has it that, upon arriving on Persian shores, Alexander commanded his officers to burn their boats—committing himself and his troops to the cause. It was a true *do-or-die* moment.[1] It is estimated that the Persian army consisted of some 250,000 soldiers, whereas Alexander's only totaled 50,000.[2] Despite

---

[1]   "The Counteroffer: A lesson from history 'Burn the Boats!'," Morgan, September 15, 2017, https://www. morganconsulting.com.au/news/the-counteroffer-a-lesson-from-history-burn-the-boats-/51814.

[2]   Dave Roos, "How Alexander the Great Conquered the Persian Empire," History, August 23, 2023, https:// www.history.com/news/alexander-the-great-defeat-persian-empire.

these odds, Alexander's campaign famously succeeded, bestowing him with his "Great" title. This "burn the boats" principle was later encapsulated in Sun Tzu's book *Art of War*, which encouraged military strategists to burn boats and destroy bridges behind their armies as they progressed, communicating to their soldiers that retreat was not an option.

Sometimes not going back is the key to success.

As you navigate your change journey, there will be times when going back to former ways will seem like a better option. When there was dust in the mouths and on the feet of the people of Israel, the cucumbers of Egypt sounded far more appealing than the milk and honey of the Promised Land (Num. 11:5). We can often glorify and find comfort in our past, and slowly and insidiously allow it to become Plan A again.

Earlier in the book we looked at Simon Peter who uttered five words to Jesus: "But because you say so." He subsequently left his boat to embark on his great adventure with Jesus (Luke 5:1–11). However, in John 21:3, still living in the shadow of the shame of his denial of Jesus and the disappointment of his Lord's death, he utters another crucial set of five words: "I'm going out to fish." He's going back to what he knows, back to where it all started, back to what he's good at. The fisherman who became a fisher of people returns to his boat and nets. Full circle.

As kingdom change agents, we will have multiple threshold moments where we can go back or press on—become a fisher of people or go back to fishing.

It's the same challenge Abraham faced when God called him to lead his family; the same challenge the Israelites faced as they stared at the Red Sea ahead of them; the same challenge Esther faced when deciding whether to speak up or keep quiet. We will have similar moments as shepherds leading through the valley, and we'll have to choose whether we press on and take people up the other side or go back to the place we started from. When setbacks come, the impulse is often to stop, hide, or shrink back rather than to step into new territory. Will we move forward to new terrain, or will we go back to what we know?

As leaders and organizations, there will always be mental and emotional "opt-out clauses." In moments of pressure or opposition, we tend to look for the easy option, return to a past solution, or cling to a security blanket. When the going gets tough, we can default back to reliance on a founder's charisma, the scorecard of weekend service attendance, the desire for approval, a tried-and-tested vehicle, or a particular goal. We have to be aware of where we might be tempted to go back to "fishing" and instead orient ourselves toward Christ and what he is calling us to over the long term.

When the price of change seemingly becomes too much—when those in our organization grumble, the process becomes hard, or we don't see instant results—we will have to hold our nerve and trust God for his breakthrough. Change efforts often only become overtly fruitful in a second, third, or fourth generation, and so an organization's short-term scorecard can exert a strong pull back to the perceived safety and comfort of the old and the known.

If we applied a one-generation scorecard to Jesus hanging on the cross on Good Friday after three years of ministry, deserted by his small band of disciples and with the crowds dispersed, we may conclude that his ministry was only a short season of fruitfulness, catalyzed by a single charismatic leader. Yet Jesus' victory and the fruit of movemental Christianity only became truly apparent in the days, months, years, and generations that followed.

CHANGE YOUR SCORECARD

Whether we will continue through the change journey or revert to our existing paradigms and practices is partly determined by how we measure success. It's human nature for people to want to know if they are "doing the right thing," and if they are "doing it right."

As we said earlier in the book, every organization has a scorecard—a measure of output and progress—whether it's implicit or explicit. For example, the established church tracks weekend attendance and other activity-based metrics; so, if we move toward a missional and micro approach—away from gathered and attractional—the metrics of "success" will need to change. When our existing programs have less momentum because people are being drawn away to new initiatives, it's easy to panic and think that the change process has been detrimental to the organization. If we judge our efforts using metrics related to previous methods and mindsets, the stakeholders of the church usually deem the experiment a failure—attendance may have decreased at Sunday services, fewer non-Christians might be coming into the building, and there might not be many success stories to broadcast. This is the point where many churches return to the old paradigms, systems, and practices, believing that the new way of doing things didn't work.

If our organizational metrics are primarily focused on quick results or public wins, our initial efforts will seem disappointing. If, however, we are seeking kingdom transformation, we need to reimagine how we define success and how we measure progress and achievement in light of that. Whether we are a start-up, nonprofit, denomination, church plant, or microchurch, our organizational scorecard needs to operate as a framework; and it will need to provide metrics that influence who people want to become as well as what we want them to pursue. So, whether we are just starting out or redefining an existing scorecard, we should ask the following.

- What are we measuring as activity, progress, and output?
- What and who are we celebrating?
- What are we communicating as normal behaviors for everyone?
- Where are we investing our money, time, and effort?

If the scorecard of our organization focuses on numbers, delivery, and short-term impact, then we will effectively create a social contract for our leaders that rewards and incentivizes immediate results and short-term addition. I've seen pioneering leaders lose their jobs or influence because they fail on the one-generation, quantity-focused, short-term scorecards that the organizations that employed them continue to use.

Although pioneering a new initiative or venture is hard work, it offers the opportunity to create a new scorecard. So, as you build a new scorecard (whether from scratch or pivoting an existing one), ask yourself the following questions.

- How can we reengineer and reimagine our metrics and measure the embodiment of our vision and values and the expression of our strategy?
- How can we create a scorecard for the whole organization—as well as for each team, group, and individual leader—that aligns with our core principles?
- How can we celebrate faithfulness, obedience, experimentation, and innovation?
- How can we link our scorecard to behaviors and actions rather than just beliefs and words?

We'll also need to consider how we can set clear goals along the way that help us to achieve the ultimate goal we are aiming for. Celebrating small steps in and through the valley, rather than just looking at how far we have still to go, will enable leaders to stay the course. Bill Parcells, the successful NFL coach whose team won the Super Bowl twice, intentionally created a culture where small successes drove his team toward larger goals and a bigger picture. In an article published in *Harvard Business Review*, he said:

> In training camp, therefore, we don't focus on the ultimate goal—getting to the Super Bowl. *We establish a clear set of goals that are within immediate reach*: we're going to be a smart team; we're going to be a well-conditioned team; we're going to be a team that plays hard; we're going to be a team that has pride; we're going to be a team that wants to win collectively; we're going to be a team that doesn't criticize one another.
>
> *When we start acting in ways that fulfill these goals, I make sure everybody knows it.* I accentuate the positive at every possible opportunity, and at the same time I emphasize the next goal that we need to fulfill. If we have a particularly good practice, then I call the team together and say, "We got something done today; we executed real well. I'm very pleased with your work. But here's what I want to do tomorrow: I want to see flawless special teams work. If you accomplish that, we will be ready for the game on Sunday."
>
> *When you set small, visible goals, and people achieve them, they start to get it into* their heads that they can succeed. They break the habit of losing and begin to get into the habit of winning.[3]

We need to consistently celebrate, reward, and encourage faithfulness, obedience, and progress as we seek to embody our organizational principles. This will help create a groundswell of engagement and effort across our organization.

CHANGE YOUR EXPECTATIONS

Back in the Old Testament, God promises Abram (later Abraham) that his offspring will be as numerous as the stars in the sky. Abram believes the Lord, and it's credited to him as righteousness (Gen. 15:4–6).

---

[3] Bill Parcells, "The Tough Work of Turning Around a Team," *Harvard Business Review*, November-December 2000, https://hbr.org/2000/11/the-tough-work-of-turning-around-a-team, emphasis mine.

So far, so good.

But then things start to go off-course.

Abram and his wife, Sarai (later Sarah), begin to realize that this future that God has promised is impossible. Sarai hasn't yet borne Abram any children, and she's getting on in years. So, she decides to take matters into her own hands and comes up with a plan for her and Abram to fulfill the promise themselves: "The Lord has kept me from having children," she tells Abram. "Go, sleep with my slave; perhaps I can build a family through her" (Gen 16:1–2). God had laid out the big dream ahead of them; however, painfully aware of their own inadequacies and the enormity of the dream he has promised, they stop trusting in God and hustle for the counterfeit option in their own strength and on their own timeline.

Abram agrees to Sarai's plan, and Hagar conceives. It all gets very messy, as Sarai begins to despise her slave, mistreats her, and eventually Hagar flees. Yet God in his faithfulness not only provides for Hagar and blesses her son Ishmael, but he also remains faithful to his original promise to Abram and Sarai. Sarai bears a child, and God establishes his covenant with Isaac (Gen. 16–17). The impossible dream is ultimately fulfilled, but much pain could have been avoided if Abram and Sarai had been patient and trusted that God would make good on his promise in *his* way and *his* timing. But being patient is easier said than done.

Throughout the change journey, we need to stay aligned with God so that we move at his pace and in his ways. There's no manual for this. Sometimes the right thing is to be proactive as we discover and experiment; at other times, the right thing is to stop, be patient, and wait for God to reveal our next steps. If we expect that we will always make linear progress along a clearly defined path at a uniform pace, then we will be disappointed and tempted with counterfeits or striving. We need to stay highly attuned to God as we listen and look for his leading.

CHANGE IS THE ONLY CONSTANT

As we explored at the beginning of this book, our world is constantly changing, and as a result, many of us feel like we are living in a world we were not prepared for. If we respond to this reality with generic leadership or cookie-cutter training systems, then what is produced in our venture or organization will become formulaic, brittle, and outdated extremely quickly. What worked previously may contain helpful principles, but it is likely outmoded in its practice before the dust settles on our implementation plan. *Why* we did it might remain valid, but *how* we do it now must adapt to the cultural moment and context. For an organization to embrace and initiate change—whether a start-up, a new church plant, or an age-old church or denomination—the leaders must continually be entrepreneurial, adaptive, and creative. But it also takes discipline, grit, and intentionality to stay the course. You'll need to embrace pruning before experiencing fruitfulness (John 15). You'll need to endure the battles before you enjoy the breakthroughs. You'll need to keep journeying through the process of Dream, Discover, Design, and Deploy ... again and again and again ... because the only constant in life—along with death and taxes—is change!

Proverbs 15:24 says, "The way of life *winds* upward for the wise" (NKJV). Rather than a neat, linear, one-off upward trajectory, the change journey is more of a cyclical, responsive journey that gradually winds upward and forward. Life and leadership are a series of missionary journeys in the same way a book is made up of multiple chapters. God is constantly inviting us to move. We're called to go to the "ends of the earth" (Acts 1:8), and so until the Great Commission is fulfilled or the Lord returns, our ultimate mission continues. In the business world, this concept of continuous growth is represented by the sigmoid curve, where toward the end of the first curve, the next curve of growth begins.[4] As a pioneering leader, often God reveals the next horizon as you come closer to the final stages of the initial change journey. This stimulus brings new life and guards against the plateau that can come as we near the end of our previous journey. The way of the wise winds upward.

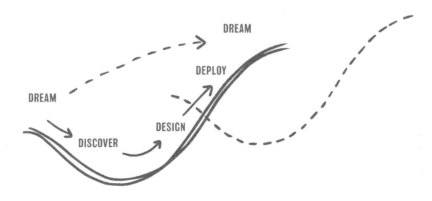

---

[4]   See for example, Rosemary Hipkins and Bronwen Cowie, "The Sigmoid Curve as a Metaphor for Growth and Change," *Teachers and Curriculum*, Volume 16, Issue 2, 2016, https://files.eric.ed.gov/fulltext/EJ1123357.pdf.

ALL CHANGE

As we round off this book, remember "you're the project." This journey is one of continuous internal formation and personal discipleship as much as it is an intentional pathway for organizational change.

Simon Peter didn't return to fishing for long. Through an encounter with Jesus over a second miraculous catch and breakfast (John 21:4–14), he returned to his call as a change agent. Jesus reminded Simon Peter of his identity, renewed his relationship with him, and restated his calling (John 21:15–19). His words to Simon Peter and interactions with him catapulted him into his second change-agent journey with renewed purpose.

The change journey for you and your organization or venture must be kept in the context of the bigger story—the race that Jesus has already run for us and the prize he places before us. We are not initiating and leading change for the sake of change, but rather that heaven may come to earth and the world around us may more beautifully and richly reflect the person of Jesus. We are blessed to be a blessing. Changed by Jesus to be a change agent. Therefore, we need to

> Drop every extra weight, every sin that clings to us and slackens our pace, and let us run with endurance the long race set before us. Now stay focused on Jesus, who designed and perfected our faith.
>
> HEBREWS 12:1–2 VOICE

Our life and leadership are a love response to who Jesus is and what he has done. He is the Pioneer and Perfecter of our faith. We are called to play the long game and run the long race. We run not to compete with others but to serve them and cheer them on as they also run their race.

We run with God to be good news and bring good news to his world. We run in God's power, at the pace he sets, and toward the prize he calls us to.

We run to unlock kingdom potential, catalyze kingdom change, and pursue kingdom transformation.

It's *his* story. But he invites us to join him in this great work.

What part will you play in God's all-change story?

ACKNOWLEDGMENTS

This book is a work of scenius—a true team effort. It would not exist without the collective genius of Anna and my family; the leaders and teams of Movement Leaders Collective, Creo, and Catalyse Change; and the work of 100 Movements Publishing. I will be forever grateful for the investment of each of those teams and individuals.

To start, I would like to thank Anna, whose passion for Jesus and desire to walk faithfully with him is a daily inspiration and challenge. Almost all of what is written on these pages would not have come to pass without her insight, commitment, and partnership. To my kids, whom I love and am so incredibly thankful for: I am energized and stretched by you as you enter your life as teens and young adults. Thank you for who you all are and for the joy of sharing life with each of you.

Special thanks to Alan Hirsch for not only writing the foreword but also for the many years of partnership, friendship, and inspiration. Here's to many more … what would bubble be without squeak or fish without chips!

Life is easier to understand looking backward. As pioneers, we pursue new frontiers and explore new terrain, drawing maps from our adventures for others to follow. What we discover, others are able to benefit from. The teams of Movement Leaders Collective, Creo, and Catalyse Change have shared these pioneering adventures of the last fifteen years that generated the raw material that has produced this book. Anything that is now cohesive and coherent in these pages started out as a new initiative, a test, a prototype, or a misstep as we fumbled our way forward, learning as we went. Thank you to the many leaders who have built the work of these three initiatives over the many years, countries, and contexts. Through your life and leadership, you have contributed to my story and this book. There are too many to name here, but to all of you—thank you.

This book is a gift returned to the many women and men whom I have pioneered alongside and have had the privilege to train and invest in. I hope these pages are a blessing to you as you seek to faithfully unlock the kingdom potential God has placed in you and those you lead and as you create a communal journey toward kingdom transformation. You are my heroes, and this book is for you. The world needs the church to reimagine itself as a Jesus movement, so may you continue to play your part in the all-change story.

AWARENESS AND APPLICATION: THE JOURNEY TO MATURITY

At the end of the Sermon on the Mount (Matt. 7), Jesus tells the parable of the wise and foolish builders, leaving his listeners with a challenge: *Will you put the words that you've heard into practice?*

The question remains today: Will we hear the word God wants to speak to us (*Awareness*) and obey by putting it into practice (*Application*)?

We can map the two responses Jesus encourages onto the following quadrants:

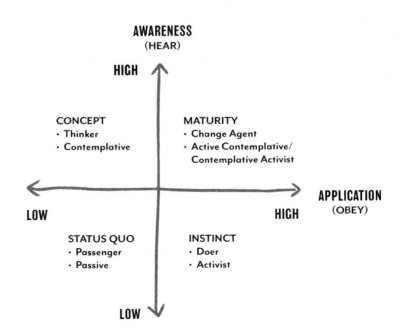

Here is how the dynamics play out according to the four quadrants above:

Status Quo: *low Awareness and low Application.* In this quadrant, nothing changes because a leader is neither open to new ideas nor new initiatives. They are basically passengers. Life passes them by, and circumstances define their reality. Leaders rarely stay in this quadrant for a long time; instead, they are often here as a short-term survival response or because their leadership responsibility outstrips their leadership capacity.

Concept: *high Awareness and low Application.* The currency in the Concept quadrant is ideas and insight. At their best, leaders in this quadrant engage in deep thought, theological reflection, and meaning making. At their worst, they get stuck in endless cycles and death by a thousand conversations or committees. They muse, reflect, think, and muse some more because there is always another angle to be considered, more data to gather, and another exploratory conversation to be had to refine their thinking. They are not driven to put anything into practice, and can continually remain in the reflect, analyze, and discuss phase. Leaders in this quadrant tend to be contemplatives and thinkers. They rarely make the step into embodying change and living differently.

Instinct: *high Application and low Awareness.* In the Instinct quadrant, leaders tend toward an activist response. At their best, they display a catalytic energy and dynamic drive to make things happen. At their worst, they become one-generation leaders, where the work flies when they're present and dies when they leave. Their instincts cannot be scaled or reproduced. Or they become reactionary leaders who jump into activity without stopping to think or listen to what God has said. Like machine gun fire, they initiate plenty of activity, in the hope that something hits the target … if there even is a target. Because they lack Awareness, leaders in this quadrant often don't know what's really happening or ask why. They bounce through life, responding to crisis after crisis or reacting to opportunities that come their way without stopping to reflect, learn, and align with God.

Maturity: *high Application and high Awareness.* This is the quadrant of the mature change agent—a person who is both a contemplative-activist and an active-contemplative. In this quadrant, theological ideas and concepts are wrestled with and earthed in life-changing practices, rhythms, and behaviors. Activity is purposeful and thoughtful and is accompanied by learning and reflection. These leaders focus on regular and repeatable patterns and practices of formation, as well as intentional activity and initiatives to bring transformation.

To fully release potential in ourselves, others, and the environments in which we're called to lead, we must aim for the mature expression of both high Awareness *and* high Application. Like a dominant left or right hand, everyone has a natural leaning toward Awareness or Application, so one or the other will most strongly influence our perception of and interactions with the world. This is why so many leaders and organizations have a vision statement that remains nothing more than a document (Concept) or a hive of frenetic activity that is ineffective (Instinct). If we are naturally more instinctive, we need to become a contemplative-activist; and if we are more conceptual, we need to become an active-contemplative.

This journey toward maturity also applies to organizations or ventures. Some are stronger on Awareness, deeply engaging with reflection, theology, and theory, and tend toward a more conceptual culture. Others are stronger on Application—with an orientation toward effort, activity, and initiatives—and therefore tend toward a more instinctive culture. In every organization or venture, both the conceptual and instinctive will be present, although usually one is dominant. But imagine the synergy that occurs when maturity is expressed through both high Awareness and high Application.

When, as individuals or organizations, we embrace our weaker elements, we can pursue maturity and therefore help others live into positive change. However, if we want to achieve this, we must be prepared to go on a personal journey.

GOING DOWN AND THROUGH

Unfortunately, initiating change is never as simple as moving "upward to the right" from the Instinct quadrant to Maturity or across from Concept to Maturity. Though we would like to believe the "up and over" (one big jump over the valley to the other side) process of change is possible, if we are to become mature change agents, we must embrace our "weaker hand." Change always comes by going "down and through"—unlearning and relearning.

When I'm training leaders, I refer to this process as "the valley of the shadow of death" (Psalm 23). The room usually fills with nervous laughter at this point, as realization dawns on my listeners of both the need for the journey and the challenge ahead. It's an "aha" moment, because people begin to understand that *they* are "the project," and change takes time and won't come without pain, both for themselves and for their organizations. When we move into the quadrant that is unnatural for us, we are taken beyond ourselves and our own resources. We must die to our natural tendencies and instead allow God to form us into more Christlike disciples and leaders. The valley is the place where we discover who God really is, and in light of that, who he has made us and called us to be.

The Journey for a Status Quo Leader

If you currently find yourself in the Status Quo quadrant, you will first need to identify why you are not operating in Awareness and Application. It may be due to a seasonal pressure caused by stretched capacity or a challenging circumstance, but it is important to discern why you are not expressing your natural strength of either Awareness or Application. You may be in survival mode and experiencing extreme stress or burnout. The priority is therefore to seek healing and restoration internally and review your commitments externally. Once you have engaged with this, you will be in a better place to determine whether you lean toward Awareness or Application. Depending on your natural preference, your journey will therefore either begin at the Concept or Instinct quadrant, as outlined below.

The Journey for a Concept Leader

For a Concept leader, going down and through the valley means you will have to break out of your mental constructs and take a step of obedience before everything is all neatly worked out. It's a journey of *Incarnation*—an active and dynamic experience, which is a stretch for the natural contemplative. You must work toward embodied truth rather than simply theological reflection or conceptual thought. *The Message* version of John 1:14 says, "The Word became flesh and blood, and moved into the neighborhood." Jesus was the living Word, who embodied perfect truth in human form. He lived and modeled everything he taught. This typifies the challenge for a Concept leader—the Word has to become flesh. As American philosopher Dallas Willard notes,

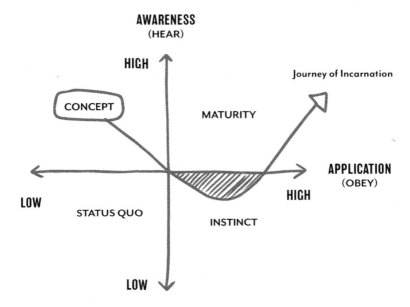

The general human failing is to want what is right and important, but at the same time not to commit to the kind of life that will produce the action we know to be right and the condition we want to enjoy. This is the feature of human character that explains why the road to hell is paved with good intentions. We intend what is right, but we avoid the life that would make it reality.[5]

The Concept leader's journey of *Incarnation* involves active engagement that gets them out of their head and living into the concepts they love to reflect on. Going "down and through" for this leader means increasing their Application (and, by definition, decreasing their Awareness) as they step out into the unknown. They must travel through the Instinct quadrant (high Application/ low Awareness) before moving into maturity. This process strengthens and grounds the faith of the Concept leader as they trust in God and step out into new territory.

---

[5] Dallas Willard, *The Spirit of the Disciplines: Understanding How God Changes Lives* (New York, NY: HarperCollins, 1988), 6.

The Journey for an Instinct Leader

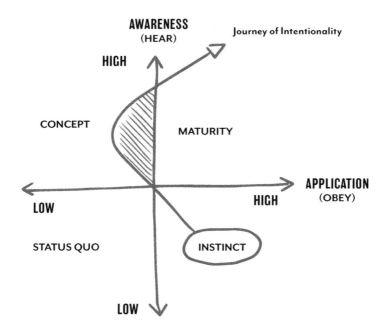

For the Instinct leader, the valley will require taking time to reflect. As Ruth Haley Barton says,

> Many of us are choosing to live lives that do not set us up to pay attention, to notice those places where God is at work, and to ask ourselves what these things mean. We long for a word from the Lord, but somehow we have been suckered into believing that the pace we keep is what leadership requires. We slide inexorably into a way of life that offers little or no opportunity for paying attention and then wonder why we are not hearing from God when we need God most.[6]

Instinct leaders therefore need to slow down, write things down, and take people with them. This is the journey of *Intentionality*—a contemplative and

---

[6]   Haley Barton, *Strengthening the Soul of Your Leadership*, 63.

prayerful experience, which is a stretch for the natural activist. In his three years of earthly ministry, Jesus had much to accomplish; however, we see him regularly retreating to spend time with the Father. His ministry method was to only do what he saw the Father doing (John 5:19). There was constant prayerfulness, reflection, and communion with the Father (Mark 1:35; Luke 5:16). His active response was therefore in perfect partnership with what the Father had said and was doing. Jesus also took time to reflect with his disciples on what he was doing and why he was doing it, so they understood the intentionality and meaning behind his actions (see, for example, John 14 and Matt. 16:5–20).

Instinct leaders need to be much more thoughtful about actions they will take, becoming more aware of the underlying motivations and principles behind what they do and more strategic about whom they apprentice. They need to grow in their prayerfulness and embrace solitude, self-reflection, and communal learning—all of which deepen and strengthen their faith as both a disciple and a leader. Going "down and through" for this leader means increasing their Awareness (and, by definition, decreasing their Application) as they slow down. They must travel through the Concept quadrant (low Application/high Awareness) before moving into maturity.

To pursue maturity, instinct leaders need community and accountability. These guardrails enable them to take a different approach from the one that feels natural to them. It is also essential to work in a team; this process can't be undertaken alone.

APPENDIX TWO

mDNA: THE SIX ESSENTIAL ELEMENTS OF A JESUS MOVEMENT

Jesus movements have historically changed the world because they have transformative energy and a catalytic impact. Movements influence society on every level because they initiate social, spiritual, and systemic change and spark imagination and innovation. The church has gradually become more like an institution than a movement and is rarely the world-changing, transformative movement Jesus intended.

We need to recapture and reimagine the church as a Jesus movement, understanding and applying movement thinking at every level of our leadership and organizations.

Alan Hirsch, author, thought leader, and cofounder of Movement Leaders Collective notes that Jesus movements comprise the following six elements of Movement DNA (mDNA). For more information, see Hirsch, *The Forgotten Ways: Reactivating Apostolic Movements*, 2nd Edition (Baker, 2016) and www.themxplatform.com/startthejourney.

JESUS IS LORD

Paradigm: The recovery of the central role and significance of Jesus for discipleship, spirituality, theology, community, and mission.

Practice: A radical and unwavering commitment to the Way (ethos) of the Founder Jesus at the very center of it all.

All-Change Journey: Rather than maintaining a generic "Jesus is Lord" confessional intent or promotion of badge or brand, leaders cultivate a clear and compelling vocabulary and focus that declares their identity and intent as the radical minimum standard of following Jesus together.

DISCIPLESHIP AND DISCIPLE MAKING:

Paradigm: The pursuit of becoming more like Jesus and enabling others to do so; seeking to do the same things that Jesus did for the same reasons that he did them.

Practice: A clearly articulated vision for discipleship as well as a clear process to ensure that disciple making happens throughout the organization.

All-Change Journey: Rather than aiming for attendance at programmatic offerings and the passing on of information in classes, leaders create practices, processes, language, and models for becoming like Jesus as the irreplaceable core task of the community in all components of ministry design.

MISSIONAL-INCARNATIONAL IMPULSE

Paradigm: Recovering the sentness of God and living incarnationally within the context that we are seeking to be good news to.

Practice: A commitment to extend the movement by going out and going deep into various cultures and contextualizing the gospel in these settings.

All-Change Journey: Rather than attracting new attendees to services through advertising and invitation practices, leaders train every believer to embrace the dynamic outward thrust (being sent) and deepening impulse (to stay with and amongst) to embody the gospel in the different cultures, people groups, and places where they live, work, and play.

APEST CULTURE

Paradigm: APEST as the DNA and latent potential within God's people, realized and expressed to bring fullness, unity, and maturity to the body of Christ.

Practice: A missional ministry (and by extension, leadership) equal to the task of initiating, developing, and maintaining movement.

All-Change Journey: Rather than recruiting volunteers to serve the organizational programming and only a few expressing leadership across the community, leaders help identify and deploy the capabilities of every believer, leader, team, and ministry to develop unity, release a diversity of gifting, and together pursue maturity.

ORGANIC SYSTEMS

Paradigm: The church organizing itself as a living organism, viewed as a movement rather than an institution.

Practice: A system designed around internalized movement DNA, committed to empowering every agent in the system by pushing power and function to the outermost limits, along with a resolute commitment to system-wide reproducibility and scalability.

All-Change Journey: Rather than organizing around the addition of members, groups, services, and campuses with highly centralized control, leaders structure for empowerment at the grassroots level, orientated toward the edge; and, through high accountability and low control, allow for rapid multiplication at every level.

LIMINALITY AND COMMUNITAS

Paradigm: The dynamics of Christian community inspired to shake off their collective securities and form themselves around a common mission that calls them to an adventurous journey to unknown places.

Practice: An inbuilt, culturally embedded willingness to regularly dare and to take risks in the cause of the movement.

All-Change Journey: Rather than allowing an inward focus to reinforce a culture of safety and security, church leaders intentionally design risk-taking practices, environments, and processes to cultivate cause-based community as the normative expression of community.

Returning to the marks of movement in the Deploy phase (chapter twelve), the link to each mDNA element can be seen as follows:

- actively participate (APEST Culture)
- toward a shared kingdom purpose (Jesus is Lord)
- in a relationally bound (Liminality and Communitas)
- DNA-based organism (Discipleship and Disciple Making)
- that has generative energy (Missional-Incarnational Impulse)
- and grows to multiple generations (Organic Systems)

Take Your Next Step in Unlocking Kingdom Potential

If you'd like to learn more about the All Change process, go to

allchangejourney.com

Interested in working with Rich and his team?
Whether you are leading a church, nonprofit, faith-driven venture, network, or denomination, Rich and his team offer training, consultancy, and coaching to unlock kingdom potential and catalyze kingdom transformation.

Get in touch at

hello@allchangejourney.com

Words Create Worlds

Want to buy bulk copies of
All Change?

By purchasing bulk copies from us, you are not only getting a better price per book, but you are also helping us to:

- ✔ Invest in training and equipping the church through insightful resources
- ✔ Support and publish authors from the global church
- ✔ Give voice and platform to emerging authors

To order bulk copies, go to
www.themxplatform.com/ onlineshop

100 MOVEMENTS
PUBLISHING

Unlock Imagination. Release Potential.